Iraq

Other books in the Current Controversies series:

Iraq

Andrea C. Nakaya, *Book Editor*

Bruce Glassman, *Vice President*
Bonnie Szumski, *Publisher*
Helen Cothran, *Managing Editor*

GREENHAVEN
PRESS®

San Diego • Detroit • New York • San Francisco • Cleveland
New Haven, Conn. • Waterville, Maine • London • Munich

THOMSON
★
™
GALE

For my father

For more information, contact
Greenhaven Press
27500 Drake Rd.
Farmington Hills, MI 48331-3535
Or you can visit our Internet site at http://www.gale.com

Cover credit: © Bob Daemmrich/CORBIS

LIBRARY OF CONGRESS CATALOGING-IN-PUBLICATION DATA
Iraq / Andrea C. Nakaya, book editor.
p. cm. — (Current controversies)
Includes bibliographical references and index.
ISBN 0-7377-2210-X (lib. : alk. paper) — ISBN 0-7377-2211-8 (pbk. : alk. paper)
1. Iraq War, 2003. 2. Iraq War, 2003—Causes. 3. Iraq War, 2003—
Reconstruction. I. Nakaya, Andrea C., 1976– . II. Series.
DS79.76.I7245 2004
956.7044'3—dc22   2004042522

Printed in the United States of America

Contents

Chapter 2: Should the United States Play an Active Role in Iraq?

Yes: The United States Should Play an Active Role in Iraq

No: The United States Should Not Play an Active Role in Iraq

Chapter 3: Do the Iraqis Have a Good Quality of Life?

Yes: The Quality of Life in Iraq Is Good

No: The Quality of Life in Iraq Is Poor

Chapter 4: How Should Iraq Be Reconstructed?

Foreword

By definition, controversies are "discussions of questions in which opposing opinions clash" (Webster's Twentieth Century Dictionary Unabridged). Few would deny that controversies are a pervasive part of the human condition and exist on virtually every level of human enterprise. Controversies transpire between individuals and among groups, within nations and between nations. Controversies supply the grist necessary for progress by providing challenges and challengers to the status quo. They also create atmospheres where strife and warfare can flourish. A world without controversies would be a peaceful world; but it also would be, by and large, static and prosaic.

The Series' Purpose

The purpose of the Current Controversies series is to explore many of the social, political, and economic controversies dominating the national and international scenes today. Titles selected for inclusion in the series are highly focused and specific. For example, from the larger category of criminal justice, Current Controversies deals with specific topics such as police brutality, gun control, white collar crime, and others. The debates in Current Controversies also are presented in a useful, timeless fashion. Articles and book excerpts included in each title are selected if they contribute valuable, long-range ideas to the overall debate. And wherever possible, current information is enhanced with historical documents and other relevant materials. Thus, while individual titles are current in focus, every effort is made to ensure that they will not become quickly outdated. Books in the Current Controversies series will remain important resources for librarians, teachers, and students for many years.

In addition to keeping the titles focused and specific, great care is taken in the editorial format of each book in the series. Book introductions and chapter prefaces are offered to provide background material for readers. Chapters are organized around several key questions that are answered with diverse opinions representing all points on the political spectrum. Materials in each chapter include opinions in which authors clearly disagree as well as alternative opinions in which authors may agree on a broader issue but disagree on the possible solutions. In this way, the content of each volume in Current Controversies mirrors the mosaic of opinions encountered in society. Readers will quickly realize that there are many viable answers to these complex issues. By questioning each author's conclusions, students and casual readers can begin to develop the critical thinking skills so important to evaluating opinionated material.

Current Controversies is also ideal for controlled research. Each anthology in the series is composed of primary sources taken from a wide gamut of informational categories including periodicals, newspapers, books, United States and foreign government documents, and the publications of private and public organizations. Readers will find factual support for reports, debates, and research papers covering all areas of important issues. In addition, an annotated table of contents, an index, a book and periodical bibliography, and a list of organizations to contact are included in each book to expedite further research.

Perhaps more than ever before in history, people are confronted with diverse and contradictory information. During the Persian Gulf War, for example, the public was not only treated to minute-to-minute coverage of the war, it was also inundated with critiques of the coverage and countless analyses of the factors motivating U.S. involvement. Being able to sort through the plethora of opinions accompanying today's major issues, and to draw one's own conclusions, can be a complicated and frustrating struggle. It is the editors' hope that Current Controversies will help readers with this struggle.

Greenhaven Press anthologies primarily consist of previously published material taken from a variety of sources, including periodicals, books, scholarly journals, newspapers, government documents, and position papers from private and public organizations. These original sources are often edited for length and to ensure their accessibility for a young adult audience. The anthology editors also change the original titles of these works in order to clearly present the main thesis of each viewpoint and to explicitly indicate the opinion presented in the viewpoint. These alterations are made in consideration of both the reading and comprehension levels of a young adult audience. Every effort is made to ensure that Greenhaven Press accurately reflects the original intent of the authors included in this anthology.

Introduction

In 1927 a team of British geologists was drilling near Kirkuk, 150 miles north of Baghdad, when black crude oil and gas gushed violently to the surface with a thunderous sound, carrying rocks fifty feet above the derrick. In what oil hands call a "blowout"—losing control of a live oil well—the countryside was drenched with oil, and poisonous gas filled the air. Two drillers lost their lives, and whole villages in the area were threatened. Approximately seven hundred tribesmen were recruited to build dikes and walls to try to contain the flood of oil. In the end it took nine days to bring the well under control.

While the 1927 blowout caused destruction, there was also widespread celebration at the first discovery of a major oil reserve in Iraq. This event foreshadowed a future for Iraq in which oil would bring both ruin and prosperity. Oil has played a central role in events that have occurred in Iraq, including ongoing conflict there, and by the end of the twentieth century, the United States became enmeshed in many of those conflicts.

Iraq is an important part of the global oil industry. It is located atop a proven oil reserve of 112 billion barrels, the second-largest reserve in the world after Saudi Arabia's. Up until now, Iraq's oil potential has been largely unexplored and undeveloped, meaning that additional oil is likely to be discovered there. In addition, Iraqi oil can be easily extracted and thus produced at a very low cost, giving Iraq the potential to take a large share in worldwide oil production. According to journalist Anthony Sampson, "The new oilfields, when developed, could produce up to eight million barrels a day within a few years—thus rivaling Saudi Arabia, the present kingpin of oil."

What happens to that oil is of great interest and importance to the rest of the world. Almost every country needs a constant supply of oil; however, few possess enough to meet their needs, forcing them to import it from countries like Iraq that have excess. Moreover, the demand for imported oil increases every year. The U.S. Department of Energy predicts that by 2025, global demand will have risen by more than half. Journalist John Cassidy reports:

> It is far from clear where the oil to meet this additional demand will come from. Fields in the United States and the North Sea are running down. Many of the biggest producers, such as Iraq and Kuwait, are operating at or close to maximum capacity. New production areas, such as those in northern Russia, Kazakhstan, and West Africa, are often remote and inhospitable, which makes

them difficult and expensive to exploit. Iraq remains one of the few countries with large supplies of readily accessible oil, and what happens there will have an enormous impact on the global economy.

Iraq will thus become increasingly important to nations around the world.

Interest in this country's oil reserves is far from new, however. Beginning in 1918, when the British government rushed troops to northern Iraq in an attempt to gain control of the oil fields there, many nations have struggled for a share of this valuable resource. In 1927 the Turkish Petroleum Company (TPC) struck oil near Kirkuk, and while Iraq became an independent state five years later, foreign oil companies such as TPC remained in control of the country's oil reserves for decades. Finally, in 1973 all foreign oil companies in Iraq were taken over by the government. However, foreign interest in Iraq's oil continued. "Iraq's oil is a huge prize," says James Paul, executive director for Global Policy Forum. He adds, "There's a tremendous interest from foreign oil companies to lay their hands on it." Prior to the toppling of Saddam Hussein's regime in 2003, Iraq was reportedly in the process of making several multi–billion dollar development deals with foreign oil companies mainly from China, France, and Russia.

Conflict over control of Iraq's oil continues today, and the United States, a country that depends heavily on imported oil and takes a keen interest in the worldwide oil supply, is playing an increasingly central role in this battle for oil. While in 1940 the United States was producing two-thirds of the entire world's oil supply, in 2003 it could not produce enough oil to meet its own demand. U.S. consumption of oil is approximately a quarter of the world total. More than half of this is imported—much from the Persian Gulf, including from Iraq—and this dependence on imported oil is expected to increase, making the United States vulnerable to the policies of oil-producing nations. In a 2001 study commissioned by the U.S. government, "Strategic Energy Policy Challenges for the 21st Century," a task force found that "it is clear that energy disruptions could have a potentially enormous impact on the U.S. and the world economy, and would affect U.S. national security and foreign policy in dramatic ways." One conclusion of the study was that the U.S. must pursue strategies to ensure a steady oil supply. The report states:

> It is vital for the United States to assure stable and transparent international energy markets that provide prices which foster economic growth. It is also in the strategic interest of the United States to assure that appropriate national and international mechanisms are in place to prevent disruptions in energy supplies where possible, and to manage efficiently and equitably any disruption that might occur. . . . The United States should promote a global network of arrangements that protects against disruption, while securing equitable mechanisms for burden-sharing if required.

The report goes on to explain how the Iraqi government may prove an impediment to the implementation of such strategies. It says, "Iraq remains a destabilizing influence to U.S. allies in the Middle East, as well as to regional and global order, and to the flow of oil to international markets from the Middle East."

Not only does the United States need a steady supply of oil to keep its economy running, it also needs that oil at low prices in order to maintain its current standard of living. Many people argue that the U.S.-led war against Iraq in 2003 was a result of this need and was primarily a war for control of Iraq's oil fields. Journalist Arthur Macewan questions the motives behind the invasion, which officials of the George W. Bush administration claim was necessary to rid Iraq of weapons of mass destruction. "While weapons of mass destruction are hard to find in Iraq," he says, "there is one thing that is relatively easy to find: oil. . . . This combination—lots of oil and no weapons of mass destruction—begs the question: *Is it oil . . .* that motivates the U.S. government's aggressive policy towards Iraq?"

Before the United States, Iraq, or any other country can benefit from that plentiful oil supply, however, the Iraqi oil industry must be reconstructed. Iraq's oil fields, while extremely valuable and a significant source of revenue in the past, are currently in need of heavy investment before they will yield large profits. Between 1972 and 1980, Iraqi citizens benefited greatly from their country's oil as the Iraqi National Oil Company doubled Iraq's daily production, and annual oil revenues rose from 575 million dollars to 26 billion. During that time, the Iraqi government used the money to finance a nationwide development program, including the building of irrigation projects and dams, the creation of iron and steel factories, and the construction of schools and hospitals— resulting in a brief period of prosperity. However, Iraq then experienced two major wars—the Iran-Iraq War from 1980 to 1988 and the 1990 Persian Gulf War—plus more than a decade of economic sanctions. As a result, the condition of the country's economy and infrastructure, including its oil fields, has deteriorated sharply. In December 2002 the U.S. Council on Foreign Relations and the Baker Institute released a report on Iraq's oil sector. The report concluded that Iraq's oil sector infrastructure is in bad shape, being held together by "band-aids." It reported that increasing Iraqi oil production will require "massive repairs and reconstruction . . . costing several billions of dollars."

While Iraq needs an infusion of dollars to aid reconstruction, many Iraqis are worried that as a result of foreign investment they will lose control of their oil. They fear that foreign corporations will instead reap the profits. Although U.S. secretary of state Colin Powell promised prior to the 2003 war that "if we are the occupying power, [Iraq's oil] will be held for the benefit of the Iraqi people and it will be operated for the benefit of the Iraqi people," there are fears that this may not be the case. According to journalist Robert Fisk, immediately following the war there was little effort by the United States to stop the looting and destruction of many public buildings, including hospitals and universities, while in contrast, the Iraqi Ministry of Oil was heavily guarded by U.S. troops. "Why?" asks Fisk. According to him, "The archives and files of Iraq's most valuable asset—its oilfields and, even more important, its massive reserves—

are safe and sound, sealed off from the mobs and looters, and safe to be shared, as Washington almost certainly intends, with American oil companies." After the war, Kellogg Brown & Root, a subsidiary of the giant U.S. oil company Halliburton, received a $2,261,200,000 contract to repair damage to Iraq's oil industry, further increasing fears that oil profits would be flowing out of the country.

Following years of war, sanctions, and oppression under Saddam Hussein's regime, Iraq is a country plagued by many problems, only one of which is conflict over oil. The authors in *Current Controversies: Iraq* offer various perspectives on some of the problems facing the nation as well as possible solutions. This anthology examines justifications for the 2003 war, whether the United States should remain actively involved in Iraq, what the quality of life is like for Iraqis, and how reconstruction efforts should proceed. The viewpoints give readers a better understanding of the challenges Iraq faces and its hopes for the future.

Chapter 1

Was the 2003 War Against Iraq Justified?

Chapter Preface

More than fifty thousand Americans gathered at the National Mall in the center of Washington, D.C., on January 18, 2003, to protest the looming possibility of a U.S.-led war against Iraq. With chants such as "No War for Oil," and placards stating "Regime Change Starts at Home," the protesters were part of a massive barrage of antiwar demonstrations taking place around the United States and the world.

On the same day thousands of protesters marched in Paris, shouting in English, "Stop Bush! Stop War!" In Moscow, Russians chanted "U.S., Hands Off Iraq!" and "Yankee, Go Home!" at a march outside the U.S. embassy. One Russian banner read "U.S.A. Is International Terrorist No. 1." More than four thousand people attended a peace concert in Tokyo—the largest of about ten demonstrations in Japan—and in the Pakistani capital of Islamabad, hundreds of schoolchildren joined protesters to try to form a human chain to the town of Rawalpindi, six miles away. As these events illustrate, there was great opposition to the 2003 war against Iraq before it began, and even today, with Saddam Hussein's regime toppled and the war over, arguments continue over whether war was justified.

Despite fervent opposition from millions of people around the world, and without the backing of the United Nations, American and British troops invaded Iraq on March 19, 2003. In justification of the preemptive attack, coalition forces cited Iraq's failure to cooperate with its UN-mandated disarmament obligations and the imminent threat it posed to international security. In a March 17, 2003, speech, U.S. president George W. Bush stated:

> The United States and other nations did nothing to deserve or invite this threat. But we will do everything to defeat it. Instead of drifting along toward tragedy, we will set a course toward safety. Before the day of horror can come, before it is too late to act, this danger will be removed.

Despite these assurances, on the eve of the war, there was widespread opposition. A Gallup poll showed that half of the American population opposed the war. UN secretary-general Kofi Annan criticized the coalition's disregard of UN authority, stating, "This logic represents a fundamental challenge to the principles on which, however imperfectly, world peace and stability have rested for the last 58 years."

The 2003 war ended less than two months later on May 1, with Hussein deposed, and the U.S.-led coalition overseeing reconstruction of the country. However, debate continues over the decision by the United States and Great Britain to attack Iraq. Intensifying the dispute is the fact that there has been no validation of prewar claims that Iraq possessed weapons of mass destruction, thereby posing an immediate threat to world security. In a September 2003 interview, former UN chief weapons inspector Hans Blix argued that the war "was not justified" because Saddam Hussein's regime did not pose an imminent threat. "The threat was not what it was made out to be," according to Blix. However, others such as U.S. senator Tom Daschle argue that the toppling of Hussein's regime was enough justification for the war. Daschle states: "Regime change was a legitimate goal, it was accomplished and I think that's laudable in and of its own right." The authors of the following viewpoints offer various opinions on this much-debated topic.

War Against Iraq Was Necessary to Protect the World from Terrorism

by George W. Bush

About the author: *George W. Bush was elected as the forty-third president of the United States in November 2000. Prior to that he was governor of Texas.*

Editor's Note: The following viewpoint was originally given as an address to the nation on September 7, 2003.

Nearly two years ago [on September 11, 2001], following deadly attacks on our country, we began a systematic campaign against terrorism. These months have been a time of new responsibilities, and sacrifice, and national resolve and great progress.

America and a broad coalition acted first in Afghanistan, by destroying the training camps of terror, and removing the regime that harbored al Qaeda [the terrorist group responsible for the September 11 attacks]. In a series of raids and actions around the world, nearly two-thirds of al Qaeda's known leaders have been captured or killed, and we continue on al Qaeda's trail. We have exposed terrorist front groups, seized terrorist accounts, taken new measures to protect our homeland, and uncovered sleeper cells inside the United States. And we acted in Iraq, where the former regime sponsored terror, possessed and used weapons of mass destruction, and for 12 years defied the clear demands of the United Nations Security Council. Our coalition enforced these international demands in one of the swiftest and most humane military campaigns in history.

Striking at the Heart of Terrorism

For a generation leading up to September the 11th, 2001, terrorists and their radical allies attacked innocent people in the Middle East and beyond, without facing a sustained and serious response. The terrorists became convinced that

George W. Bush, address to the nation, Washington, DC, September 7, 2003.

free nations were decadent and weak. And they grew bolder, believing that history was on their side. Since America put out the fires of September the 11th, and mourned our dead, and went to war, history has taken a different turn. We have carried the fight to the enemy. We are rolling back the terrorist threat to civilization, not on the fringes of its influence, but at the heart of its power.

This work continues. In Iraq, we are helping the long suffering people of that country to build a decent and democratic society at the center of the Middle East. Together we are transforming a place of torture chambers and mass graves into a nation of laws and free institutions. This undertaking is difficult and costly—yet worthy of our country, and critical to our security.

The Middle East will either become a place of progress and peace, or it will be an exporter of violence and terror that takes more lives in America and in other free nations. The triumph of democracy and tolerance in Iraq, in Afghanistan and beyond would be a grave setback for international terrorism. The terrorists thrive on the support of tyrants and the resentments of oppressed peoples. When tyrants fall, and resentment gives way to hope, men and women in every culture reject the ideologies of terror, and turn to the pursuits of peace. Everywhere that freedom takes hold, terror will retreat.

Our enemies understand this. They know that a free Iraq will be free of them—free of assassins, and torturers, and secret police. They know that as democracy rises in Iraq, all of their hateful ambitions will fall like the statues of the former dictator. And that is why, five months after we liberated Iraq, a collection of killers is desperately trying to undermine Iraq's progress and throw the country into chaos.

Some of the attackers are members of the old Saddam [Hussein] regime, who fled the battlefield and now fight in the shadows. Some of the attackers are foreign terrorists, who have come to Iraq to pursue their war on America and other free nations. We cannot be certain to what extent these groups work together. We do know they have a common goal—reclaiming Iraq for tyranny.

Most, but not all, of these killers operate in one area of the country. The attacks you have heard and read about in [August and September 2003] have occurred predominantly in the central region of Iraq, between Baghdad and Tikrit—Saddam Hussein's former stronghold. The north of Iraq is generally stable and is moving forward with reconstruction and self-government. The same trends are evident in the south, despite recent attacks by terrorist groups.

Though their attacks are localized, the terrorists and Saddam loyalists

"We are rolling back the terrorist threat to civilization, not on the fringes of its influence, but at the heart of its power."

have done great harm. They have ambushed American and British service members—who stand for freedom and order. They have killed civilian aid workers of the United Nations—who represent the compassion and generosity of the world. They have bombed the Jordanian embassy—the symbol of a peaceful Arab country. And last week they murdered a respected cleric and over a hundred Muslims at prayer—bombing a holy shrine and a symbol of Islam's peaceful teachings.

This violence is directed not only against our coalition, but against anyone in Iraq who stands for decency, and freedom and progress.

More Work Ahead

There is more at work in these attacks than blind rage. The terrorists have a strategic goal. They want us to leave Iraq before our work is done. They want to shake the will of the civilized world. In the past, the terrorists have cited the examples of Beirut and Somalia, claiming that if you inflict harm on Americans, we will run from a challenge. In this, they are mistaken.

Two years ago, I told the Congress and the country that the war on terror would be a lengthy war, a different kind of war, fought on many fronts in many places. Iraq is now the central front. Enemies of freedom are making a desperate stand there—and there they must be defeated. This will take time and require sacrifice. Yet we will do what is necessary, we will spend what is necessary, to achieve this essential victory in the war on terror, to promote freedom and to make our own nation more secure.

> *"Terrorists in Iraq have attacked representatives of the civilized world, and opposing them must be the cause of the civilized world."*

America has done this kind of work before. Following World War II, we lifted up the defeated nations of Japan and Germany, and stood with them as they built representative governments. We committed years and resources to this cause. And that effort has been repaid many times over in three generations of friendship and peace. America today accepts the challenge of helping Iraq in the same spirit—for their sake, and our own.

Our strategy in Iraq has three objectives: destroying the terrorists, enlisting the support of other nations for a free Iraq and helping Iraqis assume responsibility for their own defense and their own future.

First, we are taking direct action against the terrorists in the Iraqi theater, which is the surest way to prevent future attacks on coalition forces and the Iraqi people. We are staying on the offensive, with a series of precise strikes against enemy targets increasingly guided by intelligence given to us by Iraqi citizens.

Since the end of major combat operations, we have conducted raids seizing many caches of enemy weapons and massive amounts of ammunition, and we have captured or killed hundreds of Saddam loyalists and terrorists. So far [in September 2003] of the 55 most wanted former Iraqi leaders, 42 are dead or in custody. We are sending a clear message: anyone who seeks to harm our soldiers can know that our soldiers are hunting for them.

Second, we are committed to expanding international cooperation in the re-construction and security of Iraq, just as we are in Afghanistan. Our military commanders in Iraq advise me that the current number of American troops—nearly 130,000—is appropriate to their mission. They are joined by over 20,000 service members from 29 other countries. Two multinational divisions, led by the British and the Poles, are serving alongside our forces—and in order to share the burden more broadly, our commanders have requested a third multina-tional division to serve in Iraq.

Some countries have requested an explicit authorization of the United Nations Security Council before committing troops to Iraq. I have directed Secretary of State Colin Powell to introduce a new Security Council resolution, which would authorize the creation of a multinational force in Iraq, to be led by America.

Self-Government for Iraq

I recognize that not all of our friends agreed with our decision to enforce the Security Council resolutions and remove Saddam Hussein from power. Yet we cannot let past differences interfere with present duties. Terrorists in Iraq have attacked representatives of the civilized world, and opposing them must be the cause of the civilized world. Members of the United Nations now have an op-portunity—and the responsibility—to assume a broader role in assuring that Iraq becomes a free and democratic nation.

Third, we are encouraging the orderly transfer of sovereignty and authority to the Iraqi people. Our coalition came to Iraq as liberators and we will depart as liberators. [In September 2003] Iraq has its own Governing Council, comprised of 25 leaders representing Iraq's diverse people. The Governing Council re-cently appointed cabinet ministers to run government departments. Already more than 90 percent of towns and cities have functioning local governments, which are restoring basic services. We're helping to train civil defense forces to keep order, and an Iraqi police service to enforce the law, a facilities protection service, Iraqi border guards to help secure the borders, and a new Iraqi army. In all these roles, there are now some 60,000 Iraqi citizens under arms, defending the security of their own country, and we are accelerating the training of more.

Iraq is ready to take the next steps toward self-government. The Security Council resolution we introduce will encourage Iraq's Governing Council to submit a plan and a timetable for the drafting of a constitution and for free elec-tions. From the outset, I have expressed confidence in the ability of the Iraqi people to govern themselves. Now they must rise to the responsibilities of a free people and secure the blessings of their own liberty.

Reconstructing Iraq

Our strategy in Iraq will require new resources. We have conducted a thor-ough assessment of our military and reconstruction needs in Iraq, and also in

Afghanistan. I will soon submit to Congress a request for $87 billion.[1] The request will cover ongoing military and intelligence operations in Iraq, Afghanistan and elsewhere, which we expect will cost $66 billion over the next year. This budget request will also support our commitment to helping the Iraqi and Afghan people rebuild their own nations, after decades of oppression and mismanagement. We will provide funds to help them improve security. And we will help them to restore basic services, such as electricity and water, and to build new schools, roads, and medical clinics. This effort is essential to the stability of those nations, and therefore, to our own security. Now and in the future, we will support our troops and we will keep our word to the more than 50 million people of Afghanistan and Iraq.

Later [in September 2003], U.S. secretary of state Secretary Powell will meet with representatives of many nations to discuss their financial contributions to the reconstruction of Afghanistan. [In October], he will hold a similar funding conference for the reconstruction of Iraq. Europe, Japan and states in the Middle East all will benefit from the success of freedom in these two countries, and they should contribute to that success.

The people of Iraq are emerging from a long trial. For them, there will be no going back to the days of the dictator, to the miseries and humiliation he inflicted on that good country. For the Middle East and the world, there will be no going back to the days of fear, when a brutal and aggressive tyrant possessed terrible weapons. And for America, there will be no going back to the era before September the 11th, 2001—to false comfort in a dangerous world. We have learned that terrorist attacks are not caused by the use of strength; they are invited by the perception of weakness. And the surest way to avoid attacks on our own people is to engage the enemy where he lives and plans. We are fighting that enemy in Iraq and Afghanistan today so that we do not meet him again on our own streets, in our own cities.

> "We have learned that terrorist attacks are not caused by the use of strength; they are invited by the perception of weakness."

The heaviest burdens in our war on terror fall, as always, on the men and women of our Armed Forces and our intelligence services. They have removed gathering threats to America and our friends, and this nation takes great pride in their incredible achievements. We are grateful for their skill and courage, and for their acts of decency, which have shown America's character to the world. We honor the sacrifice of their families. And we mourn every American who has died so bravely, so far from home.

The Americans who assume great risk overseas understand the great cause they are in. Not long ago I received a letter from a captain in the 3rd Infantry

1. The request for $87 billion was submitted to Congress in September 2003, and it was later approved.

Division in Baghdad. He wrote about his pride in serving a just cause, and about the deep desire of Iraqis for liberty. "I see it," he said, "in the eyes of a hungry people every day here. They are starved for freedom and opportunity." And he concluded, "I just thought you'd like a note from the 'front lines of freedom.'" That Army captain, and all of our men and women serving in the war on terror, are on the front lines of freedom. And I want each of them to know, your country thanks you, and your country supports you.

Fellow citizens: We've been tested these past 24 months, and the dangers have not passed. Yet Americans are responding with courage and confidence. We accept the duties of our generation. We are active and resolute in our own defense. We are serving in freedom's cause—and that is the cause of all mankind.

The Threat from Iraq's Weapons of Mass Destruction Justified War

by Colin L. Powell

About the author: *Colin L. Powell was appointed U.S. secretary of state on January 20, 2001.*

Editor's Note: On February 5, 2003, Colin L. Powell gave the following speech to the UN Security Council to support the U.S. position that the use of military force might be necessary because of Iraq's failure to disarm as required by UN Resolution 1441.

Last November 8 [2002], this Council [the UN Security Council] passed Resolution 1441 by a unanimous vote. The purpose of that resolution was to disarm Iraq of its weapons of mass destruction. Iraq had already been found guilty of material breach of its obligations stretching back over 16 previous resolutions and 12 years.

Resolution 1441 was not dealing with an innocent party, but a regime this Council has repeatedly convicted over the years.

Resolution 1441 gave Iraq one last chance, one last chance to come into compliance or to face serious consequences. No Council member present and voting on that day had any illusions about the nature and intent of the resolution or what serious consequences meant if Iraq did not comply.

And to assist in its disarmament, we called on Iraq to cooperate with returning inspectors from UNMOVIC [United Nations Monitoring, Verification and Inspection Commission] and IAEA [International Atomic Energy Agency]. We laid down tough standards for Iraq to meet to allow the inspectors to do their job.

This Council placed the burden on Iraq to comply and disarm, and not on the inspectors to find that which Iraq has gone out of its way to conceal for so long. Inspectors are inspectors; they are not detectives.

Colin L. Powell, address before the UN Security Council, New York, February 5, 2003.

I asked for this session today for two purposes. First, to support the core assessments made by [weapons inspectors] Dr. [Hans] Blix and Dr. [Mohammed] ElBaradei. As Dr. Blix reported to this Council on January 27, "Iraq appears not to have come to a genuine acceptance, not even today, of the disarmament which was demanded of it."

And as Dr. ElBaradei reported, Iraq's declaration of December 7 [2002] "did not provide any new information relevant to certain questions that have been outstanding since 1998."

My second purpose today is to provide you with additional information, to share with you what the United States knows about Iraq's weapons of mass destruction, as well as Iraq's involvement in terrorism, which is also the subject of Resolution 1441 and other earlier resolutions.

"Saddam Hussein and his regime have made no effort, no effort, to disarm, as required by the international community."

I might add at this point that we are providing all relevant information we can to the inspection teams for them to do their work.

The material I will present to you comes from a variety of sources. Some are U.S. sources and some are those of other countries. Some of the sources are technical, such as intercepted telephone conversations and photos taken by satellites. Other sources are people who have risked their lives to let the world know what Saddam Hussein is really up to.

I cannot tell you everything that we know, but what I can share with you, when combined with what all of us have learned over the years, is deeply troubling. What you will see is an accumulation of facts and disturbing patterns of behavior. The facts and Iraqis' behavior, Iraq's behavior, demonstrate that Saddam Hussein and his regime have made no effort, no effort, to disarm, as required by the international community.

Indeed, the facts and Iraq's behavior show that Saddam Hussein and his regime are concealing their efforts to produce more weapons of mass destruction.

Evidence of Concealment

Let me begin by playing a tape for you. What you're about to hear is a conversation that my government monitored. It takes place on November 26th of [2002], on the day before United Nations teams resumed inspections in Iraq. The conversation involves two senior officers, a colonel and a brigadier general from Iraq's elite military unit, the Republican Guard.

[The tape is played.]

Let me pause and review some of the key elements of this conversation that you just heard between these two officers.

First, they acknowledge that our colleague, Mohammed ElBaradei is coming, and they know what he's coming for and they know he's coming the next day. He's coming to look for things that are prohibited. He is expecting these gentlemen to cooperate with him and not hide things.

But they're worried. We have this modified vehicle. What do we say if one of them sees it? What is their concern? Their concern is that it's something they should not have, something that should not be seen.

The general was incredulous: "You didn't get it modified. You don't have one of those, do you?"

Colonel: "I have one."

General: "Which? From where?"

Col: "From the workshop. From the Al-Kindi Company."

Gen: "What?"

Col: "From Al-Kindi."

Gen: "I'll come to see you in the morning. I'm worried you all have something left."

Col: "We evacuated everything. We don't have anything left."

Note what he says: "We evacuated everything." We didn't destroy it. We didn't line it up for inspection. We didn't turn it into the inspectors. We evacuated it to make sure it was not around when the inspectors showed up. "I will come to you tomorrow."

The Al-Kindi Company. This is a company that is well known to have been involved in prohibited weapons systems activity.

> *"Saddam Hussein and his regime are busy doing all they possibly can to ensure that inspectors succeed in finding absolutely nothing."*

Let me play another tape for you. As you will recall, the inspectors found 12 empty chemical warheads on January 16th [2003]. January 20th, four days later, Iraq promised the inspectors it would search for more. You will now hear an officer from Republican Guard headquarters issuing an instruction to an officer in the field. Their conversation took place just last week, on January 30 [2003].

[The tape was played.]

Let me pause again and review the elements of this message.

Republican Guard: "They are inspecting the ammunition you have, yes?"

Field Officer: "Yes. For the possibility there are forbidden ammo."

RG: "For the possibility there is, by chance, forbidden ammo?"

FO: "Yes."

RG: "And we sent you a message yesterday to clean out all the areas, the scrap areas, the abandoned areas. Make sure there is nothing there. Remember the first message: evacuate it."

This is all part of a system of hiding things and moving things out of the way and making sure they have left nothing behind.

You go a little further into this message and you see the specific instructions from headquarters: "After you have carried out what is contained in this message, destroy the message because I don't want anyone to see this message."...

Why? Why? This message would have verified to the inspectors that they have been trying to turn over things. They were looking for things, but they don't want that message seen because they were trying to clean up the area, to leave no evidence behind of the presence of weapons of mass destruction. And they can claim that nothing was there and the inspectors can look all they want and they will find nothing.

History of Evasion and Deception

This effort to hide things from the inspectors is not one or two isolated events. Quite the contrary, this is part and parcel of a policy of evasion and deception that goes back 12 years, a policy set at the highest levels of the Iraqi regime.

We know that Saddam Hussein has what is called "a Higher Committee for Monitoring the Inspection Teams." Think about that. Iraq has a high-level committee to monitor the inspectors who were sent in to monitor Iraq's disarmament—not to cooperate with them, not to assist them, but to spy on them and keep them from doing their jobs.

The committee reports directly to Saddam Hussein. It is headed by Iraq's Vice President, Taha Yasin Ramadan. Its members include Saddam Hussein's son, Qusay.

This committee also includes Lieutenant General Amir al-Sa'di, an advisor to Saddam. In case that name isn't immediately familiar to you, General Sa'di has been the Iraqi regime's primary point of contact for Dr. Blix and Dr. ElBaradei. It was General Sa'di who last fall publicly pledged that Iraq was prepared to cooperate unconditionally with inspectors. Quite the contrary, Sa'di's job is not to cooperate; it is to deceive, not to disarm, but to undermine the inspectors; not to support them, but to frustrate them and to make sure they learn nothing.

We have learned a lot about the work of this special committee. We learned that just prior to the return of inspectors last November, the regime had decided to resume what we heard called "the old game of cat-and-mouse."

For example, let me focus on the now famous declaration that Iraq submitted to this Council on December 7th [2002]. Iraq never had any intention of complying with this Council's mandate. Instead, Iraq planned to use the declaration to overwhelm us and to overwhelm the inspectors with useless information about Iraq's permitted weapons so that we would not

> *"The Iraqis have never accounted for all of the biological weapons they admitted they had and we know they had."*

have time to pursue Iraq's prohibited weapons. Iraq's goal was to give us in this room, to give those of us on this Council, the false impression that the inspection process was working.

You saw the result. Dr. Blix pronounced the 12,200-page declaration "rich in volume" but "poor in information and practically devoid of new evidence." Could any member of this Council honestly rise in defense of this false declaration?

Everything we have seen and heard indicates that instead of cooperating actively with the inspectors to ensure the success of their mission, Saddam Hussein and his regime are busy doing all they possibly can to ensure that inspectors succeed in finding absolutely nothing.

Examples of Deception

My colleagues, every statement I make today is backed up by sources, solid sources. These are not assertions. What we are giving you are facts and conclusions based on solid intelligence. I will cite some examples, and these are from human sources.

Orders were issued to Iraq's security organizations, as well as to Saddam Hussein's own office, to hide all correspondence with the Organization of Military Industrialization [OMI]. This is the organization that oversees Iraq's weapons of mass destruction activities. Make sure there are no documents left which would connect you to the OMI.

"There can be no doubt that Saddam Hussein has biological weapons and the capability to rapidly produce more, many more."

We know that Saddam's son, Qusay, ordered the removal of all prohibited weapons from Saddam's numerous palace complexes. We know that Iraqi government officials, members of the ruling Ba'ath Party and scientists have hidden prohibited items in their homes. Other key files from military and scientific establishments have been placed in cars that are being driven around the countryside by Iraqi intelligence agents to avoid detection.

Thanks to intelligence they were provided, the inspectors recently found dramatic confirmation of these reports. When they searched the homes of an Iraqi nuclear scientist, they uncovered roughly 2,000 pages of documents. You see them here being brought out of the home and placed in UN hands. Some of the material is classified and related to Iraq's nuclear program.

Tell me, answer me: Are the inspectors to search the house of every government official, every Ba'ath Party member and every scientist in the country to find the truth, to get the information they need to satisfy the demands of our Council?

Our sources tell us that in some cases the hard drives of computers at Iraqi weapons facilities were replaced. Who took the hard drives? Where did they go? What is being hidden? Why?

There is only one answer to the why: to deceive, to hide, to keep from the inspectors.

Numerous human sources tell us that the Iraqis are moving not just documents and hard drives, but weapons of mass destruction, to keep them from being found by inspectors. While we were here in this Council chamber debating Resolution 1441 last fall [2002], we know, we know from sources that a missile brigade outside Baghdad was dispersing rocket launchers and warheads containing biological warfare agent to various locations, distributing them to various locations in western Iraq.

Most of the launchers and warheads had been hidden in large groves of palm trees and were to be moved every one to four weeks to escape detection.

We also have satellite photos that indicate that banned materials have recently been moved from a number of Iraqi weapons of mass destruction facilities. . . .

Hiding Scientists

Saddam Hussein and his regime are not just trying to conceal weapons; they are also trying to hide people. You know the basic facts. Iraq has not complied with its obligation to allow immediate, unimpeded, unrestricted and private access to all officials and other persons, as required by Resolution 1441. The regime only allows interviews with inspectors in the presence of an Iraqi official, a minder. The official Iraqi organization charged with facilitating inspections announced publicly and announced ominously, that, "Nobody is ready" to leave Iraq to be interviewed.

[Former] Iraqi Vice President [Taha Yasin] Ramadan accused the inspectors of conducting espionage, a veiled threat that anyone cooperating with UN inspectors was committing treason.

Iraq did not meet its obligations under 1441 to provide a comprehensive list of scientists associated with its weapons of mass destruction programs. Iraq's list was out of date and contained only about 500 names despite the fact that UNSCOM [UN Special Commission] had earlier put together a list of about 3,500 names.

Let me just tell you what a number of human sources have told us. Saddam Hussein has directly participated in the effort to prevent interviews. In early December, Saddam Hussein had all Iraqi scientists warned of the serious consequences that they and their families would face if they revealed any sensitive information to the inspectors. They were forced to sign documents acknowledging that divulging information is punishable by death.

> *"We have no indication that Saddam Hussein has ever abandoned his nuclear weapons program. On the contrary . . . he remains determined to acquire nuclear weapons."*

Saddam Hussein also said that scientists should be told not to agree to leave Iraq; anyone who agreed to be interviewed outside Iraq would be treated as a spy. This violates 1441.

In mid-November [2002], just before the inspectors returned, Iraqi experts were ordered to report to the headquarters of the Special Security Organization to receive counter-intelligence training. The training focused on evasion methods, interrogation resistance techniques, and how to mislead inspectors.

Ladies and gentlemen, these are not assertions. These are facts corroborated by many sources, some of them sources of the intelligence services of other countries.

For example, in mid-December [2002], weapons experts at one facility were replaced by Iraqi intelligence agents who were to deceive inspectors about the work that was being done there. On orders from Saddam Hussein, Iraqi officials issued a false death certificate for one scientist and he was sent into hiding.

In the middle of January [2003], experts at one facility that was related to weapons of mass destruction, those experts had been ordered to stay home from work to avoid the inspectors. Workers from other Iraqi military facilities not engaged in illicit weapons projects were to replace the workers who had been sent home. A dozen experts have been placed under house arrest—not in their own houses, but as a group at one of Saddam Hussein's guest houses.

It goes on and on and on. As the examples I have just presented show, the information and intelligence we have gathered point to an active and systematic effort on the part of the Iraqi regime to keep key materials and people from the inspectors, in direct violation of Resolution 1441. . . .

This issue before us is not how much time we are willing to give the inspectors to be frustrated by Iraqi obstruction. But how much longer are we willing to put up with Iraq's non-compliance before we, as a Council, we as the United Nations say, "Enough. Enough."

The gravity of this moment is matched by the gravity of the threat that Iraq's weapons of mass destruction pose to the world. Let me now turn to those deadly weapons programs and describe why they are real and present dangers to the region and to the world.

Biological Weapons

First, biological weapons. We have talked frequently here about biological weapons. By way of introduction and history, I think there are just three quick points I need to make. First, you will recall that it took UNSCOM four long and frustrating years to pry, to pry an admission out of Iraq that it had biological weapons. Second, when Iraq finally admitted having these weapons in 1995, the quantities were vast. Less than a teaspoon of dry anthrax, a little bit—about this amount. This is just about the amount of a teaspoon. Less than a teaspoonful of dry anthrax in an envelope shut down the United States Senate in the fall of 2001.

This forced several hundred people to undergo emergency medical treatment and killed two postal workers just from an amount, just about this quantity that was inside of an envelope.

Iraq declared 8500 liters of anthrax. But UNSCOM estimates that Saddam Hussein could have produced 25,000 liters. If concentrated into this dry form, this amount would be enough to fill tens upon tens upon tens of thousands of teaspoons. And Saddam Hussein has not verifiably accounted for even one teaspoonful of this deadly material. And that is my third point. And it is key. The Iraqis have never accounted for all of the biological weapons they admitted they had and we know they had.

They have never accounted for all the organic material used to make them. And they have not accounted for many of the weapons filled with these agents such as their R-400 bombs. This is evidence, not conjecture. This is true. This is all well documented.

Dr. Blix told this Council that Iraq has provided little evidence to verify anthrax production and no convincing evidence of its destruction. It should come as no shock then that since Saddam Hussein forced out the last inspectors in 1998, we have amassed much intelligence indicating that Iraq is continuing to make these weapons.

One of the most worrisome things that emerges from the thick intelligence file we have on Iraq's biological weapons is the existence of mobile production facilities used to make biological agents.

Let me take you inside that intelligence file and share with you what we know from eyewitness accounts. We have first-hand descriptions of biological weapons factories on wheels and on rails.

The trucks and train cars are easily moved and are designed to evade detection by inspectors. In a matter of months, they can produce a quantity of biological poison equal to the entire amount that Iraq claimed to have produced in the years prior to the Gulf War.

> *"We know that Saddam Hussein is determined to keep his weapons of mass destruction, is determined to make more."*

Although Iraq's mobile production program began in the mid-1990s, UN inspectors at the time only had vague hints of such programs. Confirmation came later, in the year 2000. The source was an eyewitness, an Iraqi chemical engineer who supervised one of these facilities. He actually was present during biological agent production runs. He was also at the site when an accident occurred in 1998. 12 technicians died from exposure to biological agents.

He reported that when UNSCOM was in country and inspecting, the biological weapons agent production always began on Thursdays at midnight, because Iraq thought UNSCOM would not inspect on the Muslim holy day, Thursday night through Friday.

He added that this was important because the units could not be broken down in the middle of a production run, which had to be completed by Friday evening before the inspectors might arrive again. This defector is currently hiding in another country with the certain knowledge that Saddam Hussein will kill him if he finds him. His eyewitness account of these mobile production facilities has been corroborated by other sources.

A second source. An Iraqi civil engineer in a position to know the details of the program confirmed the existence of transportable facilities moving on trailers.

A third source, also in a position to know, reported in summer, 2002, that Iraq had manufactured mobile production systems mounted on road-trailer units and on rail cars.

Finally, a fourth source. An Iraqi major who defected confirmed that Iraq has mobile biological research laboratories in addition to the production facilities I mentioned earlier. . . .

There can be no doubt that Saddam Hussein has biological weapons and the capability to rapidly produce more, many more. And he has the ability to dispense these lethal poisons and diseases in ways that can cause massive death and destruction.

Chemical Weapons

If biological weapons seem too terrible to contemplate, chemical weapons are equally chilling. UNMOVIC already laid out much of this and it is documented for all of us to read in UNSCOM's 1999 report on the subject. Let me set the stage with three key points that all of us need to keep in mind. First, Saddam Hussein has used these horrific weapons on another country and on his own people. In fact, in the history of chemical warfare, no country has had more battlefield experience with chemical weapons since World War I than Saddam Hussein's Iraq.

Second, as with biological weapons, Saddam Hussein has never accounted for vast amounts of chemical weaponry: 550 artillery shells with mustard, 30,000 empty munitions and enough precursors to increase his stockpile to as much as 500 tons of chemical agents.

If we consider just one category of missing weaponry, 6500 bombs from the Iran-Iraq War UNMOVIC says the amount of chemical agent in them would be on the order of a thousand tons.

These quantities of chemical weapons are now unaccounted for. Dr. Blix has quipped that, "Mustard gas is not marmalade. You are supposed to know what you did with it." We believe Saddam Hussein knows what he did with it and he has not come clean with the international community.

We have evidence these weapons existed. What we don't have is evidence from Iraq that they have been destroyed or where they are. That is what we are still waiting for. . . .

Nuclear Weapons

Let me turn now to nuclear weapons. We have no indication that Saddam Hussein has ever abandoned his nuclear weapons program. On the contrary, we have more than a decade of proof that he remains determined to acquire nuclear weapons.

To fully appreciate the challenge that we face today, remember that in 1991 the inspectors searched Iraq's primary nuclear weapons facilities for the first time, and they found nothing to conclude that Iraq had a nuclear weapons program. But, based on defector information in May of 1991, Saddam Hussein's lie was exposed. In truth, Saddam Hussein had a massive clandestine nuclear weapons program that covered several different techniques to enrich uranium, including electromagnetic isotope separation, gas centrifuge and gas diffusion.

> *"Leaving Saddam Hussein in possession of weapons of mass destruction for a few more months or years is not an option."*

We estimate that this illicit program cost the Iraqis several billion dollars. Nonetheless, Iraq continued to tell the IAEA that it had no nuclear weapons program. If Saddam had not been stopped, Iraq could have produced a nuclear bomb by 1993, years earlier than most worst case assessments that had been made before the war.

In 1995, as a result of another defector, we find out that, after his invasion of Kuwait, Saddam Hussein had initiated a crash program to build a crude nuclear weapon, in violation of Iraq's UN obligations. Saddam Hussein already possesses two out of the three key components needed to build a nuclear bomb. He has a cadre of nuclear scientists with the expertise and he has a bomb design.

The Final Component

Since 1998, his efforts to reconstitute his nuclear program have been focused on acquiring the third and last component: sufficient fissile material to produce a nuclear explosion. To make the fissile material, he needs to develop an ability to enrich uranium. Saddam Hussein is determined to get his hands on a nuclear bomb.

He is so determined that he has made repeated covert attempts to acquire high-specification aluminum tubes from 11 different countries, even after inspections resumed. These tubes are controlled by the Nuclear Suppliers Group precisely because they can be used as centrifuges for enriching uranium.

By now, just about everyone has heard of these tubes and we all know that there are differences of opinion. There is controversy about what these tubes are for. Most U.S. experts think they are intended to serve as rotors in centrifuges used to enrich uranium. Other experts, and the Iraqis themselves, argue that they are really to produce the rocket bodies for a conventional weapon, a multiple rocket launcher.

Let me tell you what is not controversial about these tubes. First, all the experts who have analyzed the tubes in our possession agree that they can be adapted for centrifuge use.

Second, Iraq had no business buying them for any purpose. They are banned for Iraq.

I am no expert on centrifuge tubes, but this is an old army trooper. I can tell you a couple things. First, it strikes me as quite odd that these tubes are manufactured to a tolerance that far exceeds U.S. requirements for comparable rockets. Maybe Iraqis just manufacture their conventional weapons to a higher standard than we do, but I don't think so.

Second, we actually have examined tubes from several different batches that were seized clandestinely before they reached Baghdad. What we notice in these different batches is a progression to higher and higher levels of specification, including in the latest batch an anodized coating on extremely smooth inner and outer surfaces.

Why would they continue refining the specifications? Why would they continuing refining the specification, go to all that trouble for something that, if it was a rocket, would soon be blown into shrapnel when it went off?

The high-tolerance aluminum tubes are only part of the story. We also have intelligence from multiple sources that Iraq is attempting to acquire magnets and high-speed balancing machines. Both items can be used in a gas centrifuge program to enrich uranium.

In 1999 and 2000, Iraqi officials negotiated with firms in Romania, India, Russia and Slovenia for the purchase of a magnet production plant. Iraq wanted the plant to produce magnets weighing 20 to 30 grams. That's the same weight as the magnets used in Iraq's gas centrifuge program before the Gulf War.

This incident, linked with the tubes, is another indicator of Iraq's attempt to reconstitute its nuclear weapons program. . . .

Iraq Must Be Disarmed

For more than 20 years, by word and by deed, Saddam Hussein has pursued his ambition to dominate Iraq and the broader Middle East using the only means he knows: intimidation, coercion and annihilation of all those who might stand in his way. For Saddam Hussein, possession of the world's most deadly weapons is the ultimate trump card, the one he must hold to fulfill his ambition.

We know that Saddam Hussein is determined to keep his weapons of mass destruction, is determined to make more. Given Saddam Hussein's history of aggression, given what we know of his grandiose plans, given what we know of his terrorist associations, and given his determination to exact revenge on those who oppose him, should we take the risk that he will not someday use these weapons at a time and a place and in a manner of his choosing, at a time when the world is in a much weaker position to respond?

The United States will not and cannot run that risk for the American people. Leaving Saddam Hussein in possession of weapons of mass destruction for a few more months or years is not an option, not in a post–September 11th world.[1]

---

1. The United States went to war against Iraq in 2003.

War Against Iraq Was Justified to Protect the World from a Dangerous Regime

by John McCain

About the author: *John McCain was first elected to the U.S. Senate in 1986. He is the ranking Republican on the Commerce, Science, and Transportation Committee, and he also serves on the Armed Services Committee and the Committee on Indian Affairs.*

Editor's Note: The following speech was given on October 10, 2002, as part of a Senate floor debate on H.J. Resolution 114 to authorize the use of U.S. armed forces against Iraq. The Senate subsequently approved the resolution, and on March 19, 2003, the United States began offensive operations against Iraq.

America's leaders today have a choice. It will determine whether our people live in fear behind walls that have already been breached, as our enemies plan our defeat in time we have given them to do it. It will answer the fundamental question about America's purpose in the world—whether we perceive our beliefs to be uniquely American principles or universal values, for if they are so dear to us that we believe all people have the right to enjoy them, we should be willing to stand up for them, wherever they are threatened.

It will reveal whether we are brave and wise, or reluctant, self-doubting, and in retreat from a world that still, in its cruelest corners, possesses a merciless hostility to our values and interests. It will test us, as did [the September 11, 2001, terrorist attacks]—except that we can choose to engage the enemy on our terms rather than wait for the battle to be brought to us.

Our choice is whether to assume history's burden to make the world safe

John McCain, address to the U.S. Senate, Washington, DC, October 10, 2002.

from a megalomaniacal tyrant whose cruelty and offense to the norms of civilization are infamous, or whether to wait for this man, armed with the world's worst weapons and willing and able to use them, to make history for us.

It is a question of whether preemptive action to defeat an adversary whose designs would imperil our vital interests is not only appropriate but moral—and whether our morality and security give us cause to fire the first shot in this battle. It will help determine whether the greater Middle East will progress toward possession of the values Americans hold to be universal, or whether the Arab and Islamic worlds will be further influenced by a tyrant whose intent is to breed his own virulent anti-Americanism in all who fall under his influence, and use that influence to hurt us gravely.

A Clear and Present Danger

The government of Saddam Hussein is a clear and present danger to the United States of America. Would that he were just another Arab dictator, pumping oil and repressing his people but satisfied with his personal circumstances within the confines of his country's borders. That situation alone would offend our sense of justice and compel us to militate for a regime change, but by means short of preemptive military action. But Saddam Hussein has shown he has greater ambitions.

His ambitions lie not in Baghdad, or Tikrit, or Basra, but in the deserts of Kuwait and Saudi Arabia. They lie in Jerusalem and Tel Aviv, where he sponsors suicide bombings by Palestinians he calls "martyrs" and the civ-

> *"The government of Saddam Hussein is a clear and present danger to the United States of America."*

ilized world calls terrorists, using murder by proxy to advance his aspirations to lead the Arab world and fan hatred of Israel, America, and the universal ideal of freedom. These ambitions have led him to attack his sovereign neighbors— Kuwait, Saudi Arabia, Israel, Iran, and Bahrain. His will to power has so affected his judgment that he has started two major wars and lost them, each time imperiling his own grip on power.

His moral code is so spare that he has gassed his own people. . . . We are told that he enjoys watching video of his opponents being tortured, for fun. He kills not just his political opponents but their families, cruelly.

Weapons of Mass Destruction

He has developed stocks of germs and toxins in sufficient quantities to kill the entire population of the Earth multiple times. He has placed weapons laden with these poisons on alert to fire at his neighbors within minutes, not hours, and has devolved authority to fire them to subordinates. He develops nuclear weapons with which he would hold his neighbors and us hostage.

He has unrepentantly violated United Nations Security Council resolutions, defying the will of the international community so consistently, so compulsively, so completely that no leader who professes allegiance to the values the United Nations was formed to uphold can sanction his audacity. His defiance, if not ended, is a threat to every nation that claims membership in the civilized world by virtue of its respect for law and fundamental human values.

Because Saddam Hussein respects neither law nor values, advocating inspections of his weapons facilities as an alternative to war posits a false choice between ending the threat he poses peaceably or by force of arms. His character, his ambition, and his record make clear that he will never accept the intrusive inspections that, by depriving him of his arsenal of dangerous weapons, would deprive him of

> *"[Saddam Hussein's] moral code is so spare that he has gassed his own people. . . . He kills not just his political opponents but their families, cruelly."*

his power. This power gives him international stature, feeds his fantasy of being a Saladin[1] for our time, and sustains his ability to repress his people and thus remain the ruler of Iraq.

Saddam Hussein is on a crash course to construct a nuclear weapon—as he was in 1981 when Israel preemptively destroyed his reactor at Osirak, enabling U.S. forces to go into Iraq a decade later without the threat of nuclear attack, and as he was in 1990, when he thought development of such a weapon, if completed in time, would have deterred American military action against him, allowing him to secure his control over his neighbors and dominate the region.

Saddam has masterfully manipulated the international weapons inspections regime over the course of a decade, enabling him to remain in power with his weapons of mass destruction intact, and growing in lethality. He knows how to play for time, and how to exploit divisions within the international community, greased by the prospect of oil contracts for friendly foreign powers.

His calculated ambiguity about his willingness to accept a new inspections regime is intended to stave off military attack until such time as he is able to deter it through deployment of an Iraqi nuclear weapon. He is using opponents of war in America, including well-intentioned individuals who honestly believe inspections represent an alternative to war, to advance his own ends, sowing divisions within our ranks that encourage reasonable people to believe he may be sincere.

He is not. He has had 10 years to prove otherwise, and he has transparently failed. His regime would be secure if he would only acquiesce to the international community's demands to disarm, but he has not. It is Saddam Hussein who puts his own regime at risk by developing these weapons. The burden is not on America to justify going to war. The burden is Saddam Hussein's, to jus-

---

1. Muslim warrior famous for recapturing Jerusalem from the Christian Crusaders in the 1100s

tify why his regime should continue to exist as long as its continuing existence threatens the world.

War Is the Only Option

Giving peace a chance only gives Saddam Hussein more time to prepare for war—on his terms, at a time of his choosing, in pursuit of ambitions that will only grow as his power to achieve them grows. American credibility, American security and the future of the United Nations Security Council rest on the will of the United States to enforce the legitimate demands of the international community for Iraq's disarmament, by means that match the menace posed by his ambitions.[2]

Saddam Hussein's regime cannot be contained, deterred, or accommodated. Containment has failed. It failed to halt Saddam's attacks on five sovereign nations. The sanctions regime has collapsed. As long as Saddam remains in power, he will be able to deceive, bribe, intimidate, and attack his way out of any containment scheme.

Some say we can deter Saddam Hussein—even though deterrence has failed utterly in the past. I fail to see how waiting for some unspecified period of time, allowing Saddam's nuclear ambitions to grow unchecked, will ever result in a stable deterrence regime. Not only would deterrence condemn the Iraqi people to more unspeakable tyranny, it would condemn Saddam's neighbors to perpetual instability.

Our regional allies who oppose using force against Saddam Hussein warn of uncontrollable popular hostility to an American attack on Iraq. But what would really be the effect on Arab populations of seeing other Arabs liberated from oppression? Most Iraqi soldiers will not willingly die for Saddam Hussein. Far from fighting to the last Iraqi, the people of that tortured society will surely dance on the regime's grave.

At the end of the day, we will not wage this war alone. Many nations are threatened by Saddam Hussein's rule, and many nations have a stake in the new order that will be built atop the ruins of Saddam Hussein's fascist state.

America Must Act Now

Failure now to make the choice to remove Saddam Hussein from power will leave us with few choices later, when Saddam's inevitable acquisition of nuclear weapons will make it much more dangerous to defend our friends and interests in the region. It will permit Saddam to control much of the region, and to wield its resources in ways that can only weaken America's position. It will put Israel's very survival at risk, with moral consequences no American can welcome.

Failure to end the danger posed by Saddam Hussein's Iraq makes it more likely that the interaction we believe to have occurred between members of

---

2. The United States went to war against Iraq in the spring of 2003.

al Qaeda and Saddam's regime may increasingly take the form of active cooperation to target the United States.

We live in a world in which international terrorists continue to this day to plot mass murder in America, Saddam Hussein unquestionably has strong incentives to cooperate with al Qaeda. Whatever they may or may not have in common, their overwhelming hostility to America and rejection of any moral code suggest that collaboration against us would be natural. The odds favor it—and they are not odds the United States can accept.

Standing by while an odious regime with a history of support for terrorism develops weapons whose use by terrorists could literally kill millions of Americans is not a choice. It is an abdication. In this new era, preventive action to target rogue regimes is not only imaginable but necessary.

What ensures our success in this long struggle against terrorism and rogue leaders who conspire against us is that our military strength is surpassed only by the strength of our ideals. Our enemies are weaker than we are in men and arms, but weaker still in causes. They fight to express an irrational hatred for all that is good in humanity, a hatred that has fallen time and again to the armies and ideals of the righteous. We fight for love of freedom and justice, a love that is invincible. We will never surrender. They will.

The Terrorist Threat Posed by Iraq Did Not Justify the War

by Nicholas Lemann

About the author: *Nicholas Lemann is an award-winning writer and dean of the Columbia University School of Journalism.*

The war in Iraq was a long time coming—so long that it was obvious in Washington that war was certain even before the diplomatic drama that preceded it began to unfold. President [George W.] Bush and Secretary of State [Colin] Powell went to the United Nations, made their charges against Saddam Hussein, forced the weapons inspectors to return, presented evidence of their own when the inspectors found none, and, finally, concluded that Iraq would not disarm and war could not be postponed, no matter what the Security Council thought—and all that, evidently, came after the decision was made to invade. Disarmament may have been a sincere (if, it now appears, unwarranted) reason for war, but it wasn't dispositive. It was the plot device that powered a preordained procession.

The President's television speech about Iraq last week [on September 7, 2003] had the feeling of something real being revealed after a thick, obscuring outer layer has been stripped away. Called upon to justify the war anew (because things haven't been going well in Iraq), and deprived of his main prewar argument (because no forbidden weapons have been found), Bush gave us something that seemed much closer to what his true thinking was when he made the decision for war. The news in his speech was the request for eighty-seven billion dollars and the decision to ask for international troops, but the greater significance lay in what Bush told us about his own beliefs and, therefore, about what the country is committed to while he is President.

Chapter 1

Fighting Terrorism

Bush's speech was not limited to Iraq; he gave us a general argument about the Middle East, terrorism, and democracy. The first link in his chain of logic was the idea that, as he put it, "for a generation leading up to [the terrorist attacks of] September 11th, 2001, terrorists and their radical allies attacked innocent people in the Middle East and beyond, without facing a sustained and serious response." (This formulation is notable for its implicit indictment of the first President Bush for pusillanimity, and for putting the son in the position of correcting the father's mistake.) So just about any forceful response to terrorism, or to the "radical allies" of terrorism (a group that included Saddam, evidently), would cause terrorism to decrease. As Bush said, "We have learned that terrorist attacks are not caused by the use of strength. They are invited by the perception of weakness."

> *"As we are finding out in Iraq, military boldness does not always decrease terrorism. It can, in fact, inspire it."*

This doesn't quite parse—it doesn't allow for the terrorist attacks that have followed the use of force in Iraq, or for the evident immunity of most of the world's weaklings to terrorist attacks. Terrorists, unfortunately, appear to target qualities more specific than mere meekness. But Bush's statement does claim that reducing terrorism justifies virtually any use of American force. If you believe this, as Bush seems to do with every fibre of his being, how could you in good conscience not go to war in the region from which the worst terrorism emanates? Back in June [2003], Thomas Friedman, of the *Times*, wrote breezily, "The 'real reason' for this war, which was never stated, was that after 9/11 America needed to hit someone in the Arab-Muslim world." Well, now Bush has as much as stated it. Friedman went on, "Smashing Saudi Arabia or Syria would have been fine. But we hit Saddam for one simple reason: because we could, and because he deserved it, and because he was right in the heart of that world."

Questionable Logic

Bush's second point was that, like the use of strength, freedom and democracy inevitably reduce terrorism, too. The choice is simple: "The Middle East will either become a place of progress and peace, or it will be an exporter of violence and terror that takes more lives in America and in other free nations." This, again, is impressive in its clarity and certainty, but counter-examples fairly leap to mind. What about Pakistan—a quasi-democracy, but also one of the world's leading terrorist sanctuaries? What about Saddam's Iraq—the Middle East's most oppressive regime, but one that left little maneuvering room for terrorists? What about the supranational Al Qaeda, the most dangerous of the terrorist organizations, whose survival apparently requires less the help of "tyrants" than of chaotic conditions in weak states—such as Iraq and Afghanistan now [after America's wars on their soil]? As Bush makes the case, all such troublesome particulars must yield to an ironclad general rule: "Everywhere that freedom takes hold, terror will retreat." Therefore, every American military attack on a Middle Eastern tyrant—a term that plausibly encompasses most of the region's heads of state, reduces the risk of terrorist attacks on the United States. It's hard to imagine a broader charter than the one Bush grants himself through this set of assumptions.

Goals as morally grand as defeating terrorism and ending tyranny make any objection to the program for reasons of logic or practicality look puny, niggling, and cynical. The President's rhetoric divides the world into those who have passion and courage and those who believe in nothing except a self-defeating caution. The willingness to make the gesture overwhelms whatever difficulties there are on the ground. This is not just a habit of thought that Bush conveniently seized upon after the war. The understaffing of the reconstruction and the lack of post-combat planning wasn't the result merely of [U.S. defense secretary] Donald Rumsfeld's bullheadedness. It stemmed from the President's soaring conviction that courageous intentions must inevitably produce pleasing results.

Intentions Versus Reality

As we are finding out in Iraq, military boldness does not always decrease terrorism. It can, in fact, inspire it—witness the terrorists swarming into Iraq, including members of Al Qaeda, who weren't there before. Toppling tyrants does not automatically decrease terrorism, either, and in the short run it isn't even guaranteed to make life better for people in the countries the tyrants ruled. Even the most powerful nation in history does not have an infinitely large army or infinite funds, and must live in the realm of calculations about what is possible and what will be effective. Consequences are not, alas, inevitably the product of intentions; they are determined by the collision of intentions and reality. It isn't cowardly to be (dread word) realistic. It isn't amoral to think through what will follow from particular actions. Quite the opposite. Bush's desire to end terrorism and spread democracy can't be gainsaid. But if, using the almost unlimited license he has given himself, he winds up making brave-seeming lunges at those goals without actually attaining them, then confronting evil, his proudest purpose, will soon become a luxury he can no longer afford. That is about the worst outcome imaginable, and not just for Bush personally.

The Threat from Iraq's Weapons of Mass Destruction Was Exaggerated

by the *Economist*

About the author: *The* Economist *is a weekly newspaper that provides analysis of world business and current affairs.*

Patience is a special virtue if you are searching for weapons of mass destruction (WMD) in Iraq. For months, [British prime minister] Tony Blair and George [W.] Bush have urged the world to wait for the findings of their weapons sleuths before accusing them of making a dishonest case for ousting Saddam Hussein. That team, it now seems, has found, well, not much.[1] No matter, some British and American officials imply: the war is won, and there are bigger things to worry about. They are wrong: on the vindication of the pre-war claims about Iraq's illegal arsenal hangs public trust in government; the practicality of the doctrine of pre-emptive war; and much besides.

Since Baghdad fell, both leaders have faced vitriolic but limited skirmishes over Iraq's WMD. George Bush was harangued over the line, in his state-of-the-union address, about Iraq trying to buy uranium from Africa, after it emerged that some of the documents that purportedly substantiated this claim were fake. Similar uranium charges were levelled by Colin Powell, Donald Rumsfeld, Paul Wolfowitz and Condoleezza Rice, all members of the president's national-security inner circle. Mr Bush attributed the allegation to Britain's intelligence service, which still stands by it; but it turned out that the CIA had asked the White House to excise it from another presidential speech in

---

1. Prior to the 2003 invasion of Iraq, Blair and Bush claimed that Iraq possessed weapons of mass destruction; however, as of press time, these weapons had not been found in Iraq.

October 2002. The affair blew over, but it left an impression of (at best) officials failing to communicate properly with each other and with allies.

Mr Blair's troubles have seemed more acute—partly because the war was less popular in Britain than in America, and partly because of the suicide of David Kelly, a government weapons expert. He was a source for a controversial story on BBC [British Broadcasting Corporation] radio that alleged the British government had "sexed-up" a dossier it published last September [2002], detailing Iraq's weapons capabilities. In particular, Alastair Campbell, then Mr Blair's top spin-doctor, stood accused of inserting into the dossier the notion that Iraq's "military planning allows for some of the WMD to be ready within 45 minutes of an order to use them". The government set up an inquiry, ostensibly to look into the circumstances surrounding Mr Kelly's death.

The 45-minute claim has been Mr Blair's equivalent of Mr Bush's uranium trauma, only more so. It is an odd sticking-point, since if Iraq possessed WMD—actual weapons, and not just the means to make them—it ought to have been able to deploy them swiftly, as it did in the 1980s. Mr Blair, testifying to the inquiry, said that, if he thought the government had lied to the public, he would have resigned. No evidence of outright lying has come to light, and the spy chief nominally in charge of compiling the dossier insisted that the buck had stopped with him. But the inquiry has revealed some fishy goings-on.

Killer Facts

For instance, one of Mr Blair's most senior aides observed in an e-mail that "The dossier does nothing to demonstrate a threat, let alone an imminent threat." Yet in his foreword to the published version, Mr Blair described the threat as "serious and current", arguably equally alarming adjectives. Just before publication, the same aide successfully requested that a sentence predicting Mr Hussein would use his WMD if threatened be changed to reflect a vaguer danger. The weapons that were allegedly good-to-go within 45 minutes, it turns out, were battlefield munitions—nasty, but much less worrisome than the longer-range missiles that were conjured up by the ensuing newspaper headlines, such as "Brits 45 minutes from Doom" (the *Sun*). The government did nothing to correct such misreadings.

And the inquiry confirmed that the 45-minute factlet—also deployed by Mr Bush—derived from a single, uncorroborated source, who had himself picked it up from an Iraqi officer. A committee of British MPs [members of Parliament] concluded that, given this provenance, the government ought not to have given the claim such prominence in the dossier. Mr Campbell urged that some of the document's language be tightened—for instance, successfully arguing that the word "may" be jettisoned in a passage about the 45-

> *"If Iraq possessed WMD . . . it ought to have been able to deploy them swiftly, as it did in the 1980s."*

minute capability. Some experts, it emerged, were concerned over the certainty the dossier evinced, particularly the notion that Iraq had continued to produce chemical weapons. Their political and spy masters seem to have tried to cover up those concerns. The inquiry's report will be published later this year [2003].

Other participants in and supporters of the invasion have been under pressure too. In Spain, where the war was even more unpopular than it was in Britain, Jose Maria Aznar's government has been accused of exaggerating the Iraqi threat, and of telling senior military officers what to say about it. In Australia, an intelligence analyst has accused the government

> *"There appears to have been little fresh evidence to justify the apocalyptic talk with which American officials attempted to daunt and galvanise the public."*

of dishonesty—strenuously denied by John Howard, the prime minister.

So not only Mr Blair and Mr Bush will have had hopes pinned on the interim findings due to be presented to Congress by David Kay, leader of their inspection team, as *The Economist* went to press.[2] Alas, he seemed unlikely to pacify the sceptics. He is said to have uncovered some details of the Iraqi concealment effort, and some documentary proof that Mr Hussein was thinking about resuming WMD manufacture, especially biological weapons. There may also be news about Iraq's efforts to extend, illegally, the range of its missiles.

But Mr Blair and Mr Bush did not just claim that Mr Hussein intended to make illegal weapons, nor just that he had the kit to do it, but that he had retained stocks of the things themselves. They clearly believed this, as did their spies. The fact that British and American soldiers went into battle encumbered by those sweaty chemical-protection suits is proof of that. Independent think-tanks, such as the International Institute for Strategic Studies, which produced an influential assessment of the Iraqi threat before the war, also believed that the WMD threat was real.

Mr Kay may yet find such weapons, and extricate the two leaders from the Scud-shaped hole in which their pre-war warnings have landed them: London and Washington are both stressing that he has many more months, and possibly years, of sleuthing still to do. But his findings (or lack of them) suggest that the uranium farrago and the messy genesis of the 45-minute claim were part of a broader sloppiness in making the case for war.

Lest We Forget

Critics of the war ought to remember that, quite apart from the guesstimates of spies, there was ample evidence that Mr Hussein was up to no good. Some of it came from UNSCOM [United Nations Special Commission] the UN inspec-

---

2. David Kay's report in October 2003 stated that while there was evidence of intent to produce WMD, no weapons had been found.

tion team during the 1990s, which, thanks in part to high-level defections, uncovered among other things a biological-weapons programme that Iraq had concealed. Discrepancies in Iraqi record-keeping, lies and Mr Hussein's determination to thwart them made it impossible for UNMOVIC [United Nations Monitoring, Verification and Inspection Commission], the latter-day inspection body led by Hans Blix, to be sure how much illegal ordnance Iraq possessed, and what deadly agents—if any—it had retained to put in them. But on the eve of the war, UNMOVIC reported a "strong presumption" that around 10,000 litres of Iraqi anthrax might still exist.

Then there was Mr Hussein's indisputable record of making and using WMD. The idea that he voluntarily disposed of all his illegal gear between 1998 (when UNSCOM left Iraq), and 2002 (when UNMOVIC arrived), having gone to such lengths, and submitted his country to such hardship, in order to retain them, seemed incredible. It still does.

The trouble—from Mr Bush's and Mr Blair's point of view—was that the UN inspectors' findings, though alarming for anyone with the stamina to digest them, were complicated and circumstantial. So they added some less nuanced and more blood-curdling accusations of their own.

In February [2003], Colin Powell, Mr Bush's secretary of state, told the UN

> *"The simplest explanation is, of course, that Iraq had destroyed its WMD, and that the British and American intelligence services . . . got it badly wrong."*

that biological warheads had been distributed across western Iraq. He also talked at length about a putative connection between Iraq and [the terrorist group] al-Qaeda, and estimated that Iraq still had a few dozen Scud missiles. In the October speech from which the uranium allegation was dropped, Mr Bush said that "Iraq has a growing fleet of manned and unmanned aerial vehicles that could be used to disperse chemical or biological weapons. . . . We're concerned that Iraq is exploring ways of using these UAVS for missions targeting the United States." In his state-of-the-union address, he said that Iraq had "upwards of 30,000 munitions capable of delivering chemical agents". Announcing the start of the war, Mr Bush said America would "not live at the mercy of an outlaw regime that threatens the peace with weapons of mass murder."

Pull the Other One

The al-Qaeda link always looked thin, and has received little corroboration in Iraq or from captured terrorists. Ansar al-Islam, an Islamist group fingered by Mr Powell as proof of the link, operated in a part of Iraq that was outside Mr Hussein's control. British intelligence, it has emerged, gave warning that the threat from al-Qaeda could be heightened by an attack on Iraq, as could the risk that Iraqi WMD would fall into terrorist hands. The CIA once held a similar view. Mr Bush recently conceded that, contrary to many Americans' beliefs, there was no evidence to link Mr Hussein to September 11th.

In retrospect, the next weakest part of the case concerned Iraq's nuclear efforts. Here the Americans were especially cavalier. Mr Bush argued that Mr Hussein was actively pursuing nuclear weapons. Along with the uranium accusation, an important plank in this theory was Iraq's efforts to import aluminium tubes: Mr Bush and Mr Powell alleged that these were intended for use in the production of bomb-grade uranium. Yet the IAEA (the international nuclear inspectorate) disagreed—as, it has since emerged, did some agencies within the American government, including Mr Powell's own intelligence unit. Mr Powell confessed that there were two opinions on this, but plumped for the more sinister one.

> *"Did the [British and American] governments 'cherry-pick' the most gloomy assessments and prognoses?"*

Mr Hussein certainly had a well-hidden and scarily advanced nuclear programme before the 1991 war. He retained a cadre of nuclear scientists, and was acquiring other kit that might have had nuclear applications. But there appears to have been little fresh evidence to justify the apocalyptic talk with which American officials attempted to daunt and galvanise the public. "We don't want the smoking gun to be a mushroom cloud," said Ms Rice, the president's national security adviser, and the image was also used by her boss. The best guess of American spies was that Mr Hussein would not have a nuclear bomb until 2007 or 2009. Both the Americans and the Brits predicted that he could get one sooner if he obtained fissile material from abroad—a big if.

All this was not merely the icing on the UNMOVIC cake: these allegations helped to make the threat seem imminent—or, if you prefer, "serious and current". None of them has been substantiated. Some chemical-protection gear was seized in Iraq during the war, and some very old nuclear documents and parts were dug up in an Iraqi scientist's garden. But inspectors who visited the sites mentioned in the British dossier and Mr Powell's presentation as WMD facilities found nothing incriminating. America once seemed confident that it had seized two mobile biological-weapons facilities, like the ones Mr Powell described at the UN. But outside (and some inside) experts disputed this analysis, and they are no longer much talked about.

Fools or Knaves?

So: no stocks of chemical shells, no Scuds, no illegal UAVS. This has astonished even doveish doubters. At the very least, the weapons that were thought to have been deployed to the battlefield should have turned up. But they haven't. Mr Bush and others have conjectured that Mr Hussein may have destroyed his illegal munitions on the eve of war, or sunk them in the Tigris and Euphrates (an odd move, if true). But if this had happened on a large scale, and the ISG

[Iraq Survey Group] knew where, they might well have found some traces. They haven't.

Why? A number of excuses have been advanced. Iraq is a big country, and Mr Hussein was very good at hiding things. Valuable paper trails have been erased by looting. Some of the weapons kit can be used to make other, innocent things, and, once scrubbed-up, can be hard to identify for certain. Iraqi WMD experts are still too scared of the Saddamites to spill the beans—though many of them have now been in custody for months. The weapons programmes were dismantled and dispersed to hide them from the inspectors—though that would suggest a containment strategy might not have been quite so untenable after all. Some still suspect that illicit material may have been smuggled out of the country, perhaps to Syria.

The line in Washington is that the team first assigned to the WMD hunt spent its time vainly searching suspect sites rather than interrogating scientists and henchmen—though, at the time, they were said to be doing a fine job. An incentive scheme to encourage bean-spilling is now in place (though the imprisonment of some Iraqi scientists may have discouraged others from coming forward). Others may co-operate if Mr Hussein is nabbed or killed.

The simplest explanation is, of course, that Iraq had destroyed its WMD, and that the British and American intelligence services—and, it must be said, others who largely agreed with them, even if their governments did not advertise the fact—got it badly wrong. Even if more compelling discoveries are made in Iraq, it is too late for the spooks to be wholly vindicated. But their political bosses also have questions to answer about the way they used or abused the intelligence.

For instance: why did Mr Bush and Mr Blair often omit the caveats and subjunctives with which the spies hedged their judgments, as is clear from the little intelligence material that has been declassified? And how much fresh data did Britain and America really get from inside Iraq after the UNSCOM inspectors left in 1998? If it wasn't much, why did the politicians give the impression that it was? The datedness of the Iraq intelligence was one of the main anxieties expressed in a letter reportedly sent by the heads of a congressional intelligence committee to the CIA last week. "Lack of specific intelligence", they reportedly wrote, "appears to have hampered the [intelligence community's] ability to provide a better assessment to policymakers from 1998 through 2003."

Contradictory answers to this question have been given by Mr Rumsfeld, Mr Bush's defence secretary, who said that old data came to look different after September 11th, and by George Tenet, the CIA chief, who says that there were indeed newer sources. If there weren't any or many, did analysts and their masters extrapolate from what they knew, or thought they knew, and present the outcome as fact? Did the two governments "cherry-pick" the most gloomy assessments and prognoses? The underestimation of Iraq's nuclear progress before 1991 would have encouraged such an approach, and the aluminium-tube affair suggests that it was adopted. As late as February of 2001, Mr Powell believed that Mr Hussein "had not developed any significant capability with respect to weapons of mass destruction." Something happened to change his mind.

And how much weight was given to the testimony of defectors, often eager to please, and (still less reliably) to exiles, who are often out of touch with their native lands, and busily grinding private axes? Their influence seems to explain, in part, why some Americans expected ordinary Iraqis to be throwing flowers at their occupiers. A leak from the Pentagon's Defence Intelligence Agency reportedly suggests that information from defectors furnished by the Iraqi National Congress turns out to have been distinctly suspect. Was there a kind of un-virtuous competition among the various American agencies, with some trying to outdo others by furnishing the administration with evidence that most suited its prejudices?

Mr Bush and Mr Blair could have erected a strong case purely on the UN reports and Mr Hussein's atrocious record. But they didn't. They probably expected the sceptics to be quietened and chastened by the use of WMD during the war. But such weapons were never unleashed. Now they face a variety of congressional and other probes into their case for toppling Mr Hussein. One British committee has already complained that too much "intelligence" has been withheld for it to reach properly informed conclusions. If that continues, it will be impossible to tell whether Mr Bush and Mr Blair or their publics were the more deceived.

The United States Invaded Iraq to Ensure Its Global Dominance

by Rahul Mahajan

About the author: *Rahul Mahajan is a founding member of the Nowar Collective, an organization that is opposed to the 2003 war against Iraq.*

The United States is now a formal colonial power in Iraq, and the combination of the [George W. Bush] Administration's deceptions and the mounting American casualties has dimmed the shine on the colonialists' boots. In March and April [2003], public support for the war was in the neighborhood of 75 percent; by the end of July, it had fallen below 60 percent.

It might have fallen further but for the notion—peddled by Bush, as well as by Thomas Friedman of *The New York Times*—that the reason for the war didn't matter because the United States liberated the Iraqi people and is now building democracy in Iraq.

It is certainly true that the Iraqis are free from the extreme authoritarian brutality of Saddam Hussein's regime; unfortunately, it doesn't exactly follow that the Administration intends to create democracy in Iraq. An Administration that will play fast and loose with the truth on Iraq's putative weapons of mass destruction is entirely capable of doing the same regarding its true intentions for the future Iraqi government.

The question of what sort of society the United States is building in Iraq takes on tremendous significance, since Iraq may be just one of many. "We're going to get better over time," Lawrence Di Rita, a special assistant to Defense Secretary Donald Rumsfeld, told the *Los Angeles Times*. "We'll get better as we do it more often."

To get a hint of what the Bush Administration has in mind, it's instructive to take a quick look at its previous effort in democracy building: Afghanistan. Since routing the Taliban [regime in fall 2001], Washington has been propping up some of the most undemocratic forces in Afghanistan, including the various regional warlords, like Ismail Khan of Herat and Abdul Rashid Dostum of Mazar-i-Sharif. A study by the Center for Economic and Social Rights found that one of the most common complaints from ordinary Afghans was about U.S. support for the warlords. Many Afghans, the report noted, "named U.S. policy as the prime obstacle to disarming warlords."

A recent report from Human Rights Watch charges that U.S. support for these warlords could jeopardize attempts to adopt a new constitution and to hold elections in 2004. "Gunmen and warlords who were propelled into power by the United States and its coalition partners" have "essentially hijacked the country outside of Kabul," says Brad Adams, executive director of the Asia division of Human Rights Watch.

To convey the appearance of democracy, the United States called together a loya jirga, or grand council. Washington essentially deputized the warlords to manipulate it in order to attain U.S. aims. "We delegates were denied anything more than a symbolic role in the selection process," wrote loya jirga delegates Omar Zakhilwal and Adeena Niazi in *The New York Times*. "A small group of Northern Alliance chieftains decided everything behind closed doors." Early on, more than 800 of the 1,500 delegates had called for the election of Zahir Shah as interim president, but he was unsuitable to U.S. interests. "The entire loya jirga was postponed for almost two days while the former king was strong-armed into renouncing any meaningful role in the government," the delegates wrote.

After Zahir Shah stepped down, the delegates were presented with a fait accompli. Hamid Karzai, handpicked by the United States, was the only viable candidate (there were two "protest" candidates who were largely unknown). There was no meaningful decision for them to make. In the end, the whole thing was scarcely more democratic than the loya jirga conducted by the Soviet Union in 1987 in order to legitimize its client government.

In Afghanistan, the United States had no particular desire to run the country. Its primary objective, a permanent or semi-permanent military presence throughout Central Asia, was easily achieved. The creation of a pro-American central government helped give a veneer of international legitimacy to its continuing military operations there. But, aside from some economically minor plans for oil and gas pipelines, there are no compelling interests for the United States in Afghanistan—at least none so compelling that it wishes to risk a significant commitment.

The Importance of Iraq's Oil

Iraq is a different matter, for several reasons. Its oil reserves, second in the world behind Saudi Arabia, will be increasingly important to the world market. According to the [Vice President Richard B.] Cheney energy plan, by 2020 Middle East oil may have to supply up to two-thirds of world demand. With virtually no spare production capacity in the Middle East outside Saudi Arabia, this indicates that Iraq's production must be not only restored to prewar levels but dramatically increased. Even before the war, the State Department had convened the Oil and Energy Working Group of the Future of Iraq project. It was peopled with the appropriate Iraqi exile figures, like Fadhil Chalabi ([leader of the Iraqi National Congress] Ahmad Chalabi's cousin), who called early on for "privatization or partial privatization" of Iraq's state-owned oil companies. Later, *The Wall Street Journal* reported on the existence of a USAID document entitled "Moving the Iraqi Economy from Recovery to Sustainable Growth" that called for "private sector involvement in strategic sectors, including privatization, asset sales, concessions, leases, and management contracts, especially in the oil and supporting industries." Not only will the Iraqi economy be sold off to foreigners, but, according to the *Journal*, private American contractors will actually play a leading role in the process of selling it off. In June [2003], at a meeting of the World Economic Forum, L. Paul Bremer III, the head of the Coalition Provisional Authority, the nice term for the occupying forces, issued a call to privatize not only the oil companies but a total of forty state-owned companies.

> *"The question of what sort of society the United States is building in Iraq takes on tremendous significance, since Iraq may be just one of many."*

The Bush Administration has actually gone far beyond the basic goals of controlling the military and taking over the oil industry to implement full-scale "economic shock therapy." As in the case of Russia, it is likely to be all shock and very little therapy. Already, the holiday on import tariffs (except for basic items like those that go into the food ration) has meant that Iraqi industry, crippled by twelve years of sanctions, is forced to compete on equal terms with the entire world market. Outside of the oil sector, massive deindustrialization is a likely result. And those companies that can compete will likely be sold off to foreigners.

Military Dominance

Iraq is also the ideal staging area for military "force projection" in the rest of the Middle East. In fact, within weeks of the fall of Saddam's statue, *The New York Times* reported tentative plans for the establishment of four permanent military bases in Iraq. And the *Los Angeles Times* quoted unnamed government sources talking about U.S. plans to use the "unspoken but obvious leverage of its new regional dominance." The Israeli ambassador to the United States, Daniel Ayalon, speculated that regime change in Syria and Iran might not require direct military intervention but could be achieved by diplomatic isolation, economic sanctions, and "psychological pressure" with the U.S. military next door.

In essence, the United States went into Iraq with clear, if unstated, goals: controlling Iraq's oil, privatizing the economy, establishing a permanent military presence, and dominating Iraq's foreign and defense policies. The Bush Administration set the policies of the Iraqi government first and then went about creating a government that would implement them. It hoped such a government could quickly control Iraq internally, at which point all would hail the triumph of democracy.

"Democratization" of Iraq

But creating such a government is a tortuous process, largely because Iraq came along with the baggage of numerous political groupings, not all of them independent (many of the standard "Iraqi opposition" groups, for example, were taking CIA money after passage of the 1998 Iraq Liberation Act), but many of them too independent for U.S. wishes. At every stage, Washington artfully combined the threat of exclusion from the political process with inducements to enter it.

The first round of the "democratization" process began while major combat operations were still proceeding. The U.S. military convened a series of meetings in Nasiriyah, where carefully selected Iraqi political figures were supposed to start the ball rolling on creating an interim government. There was no meaningful international participation—not even a fig leaf, as there was with the Bonn conference for Afghanistan.[1]

The Supreme Council for the Islamic Revolution in Iraq, one of the main "Iraqi opposition" groups, initially boycotted the meetings, calling for immediate withdrawal of the troops. According to *The Washington Post*, the Americans deliberately excluded the Iraqi Communist Party. Across the political spectrum, from Adnan Pachachi, former foreign minister of the pre-Ba'ath 1968 Iraqi government, to the Communist Party, there were calls for the United Nations to sponsor the conference instead of the United States, because many participants felt that U.S. control of the process deprived it of legitimacy.

Popular opinion echoed that feeling. In April [2003], there were mass protests in Baghdad, Mosul, and across the country, including 20,000 in Nasiriyah at the site of the talks, saying, "No to Saddam, No to America, Yes to Islam, Yes to Democracy."

> *"The Bush Administration set the policies of the Iraqi government first and then went about creating a government that would implement them."*

In May [2003], Bremer briefly postponed talks on creating an interim government. Then he announced that instead of allowing Iraqis to form the government, Bremer himself would appoint a political council of twenty-five to thirty Iraqis, who would then oversee further steps toward creating a government. He

1. held in November 2001 to establish an interim government for Afghanistan after the fall of the Taliban

also stressed that this council would be strictly advisory and that he would veto decisions that "are fundamentally against coalition interests" or against the "better interests of Iraq." John Sawers, British Prime Minister Tony Blair's special envoy for Iraq, justified the plan on the basis that Iraq's political culture was "too weak" for democracy. Shortly thereafter, Bremer canceled all local elections.

Major Iraqi political groups denounced Bremer's plans, and many signed a letter of protest against them. Amir al-Basri, the spokesman for the Islamist al-Dawa Party, said they "create the impression that the Americans are not very serious about getting out of [an] interim period and arriving at an Iraqi sovereign government."

> *"Democracy was never Bush's goal in Iraq. The goal was establishing U.S. dominance, not only militarily but also economically."*

And yet, when the council came together on July 13 [2003], all the major parties had signed on to it. Bremer formed the twenty-five-member council with careful attention to ethnic and religious balance: It has thirteen Shia Arabs, five Kurds, one Turkoman, and one Assyrian. Three members are women. Ahmad Chalabi, the Pentagon's favorite for future leader of Iraq, is a member, as is Adnan Pachachi, who has emerged as the State Department's favorite. The council also has a member from the Iraqi Communist Party, a member from the Supreme Council for the Islamic Revolution, and a member from al-Dawa.

But the council's first action gave a taste of the degree of political servility it is likely to show. It not only declared April 9, the day of the fall of Baghdad, a new national holiday, but it canceled the holiday of July 14, the anniversary of the anti-monarchist, anti-colonialist uprising in 1958 that ushered in the most progressive government that Iraq ever had. There is a widespread understanding that it has a limited mandate, and that, in particular, the big three of military policy, foreign affairs, and oil are essentially out of its hands. Bremer did throw participants a bone: The council is not explicitly an advisory one, and members have rejected the idea that Bremer has a veto over decisions. In practice, however, it seems clear that participants know how far they can go and what lines not to cross.

Censorship of the Press

Manipulation of the press has followed the same general trajectory. There is more openness in the Iraqi media than in the past thirty-five years, but Washington controls the spectrum of discussion. In May [2003], Major General David Petraeus, the military governor of northern Iraq, seized control of Mosul's only TV station because of its "predominantly nonfactual/unbalanced news coverage." While admitting this was a blatant act of censorship, he justified it because of the need to keep from "inflaming passions." Washington has also prevented the U.S.-sponsored Iraqi Media Network—one of many new "democratic infrastructure" projects—from airing programs that are critical of U.S. policies.

In early June [2003], Bremer issued an order against "inimical media activity." He listed nine different possible reasons for shutting down a media outlet. For example, putting out news that is "patently false and calculated to promote opposition" to the occupation authority is verboten. Promoting "civil disorder, riot, or damage to property" is also a no-no. Punishment for such an offense can include a prison term of one year.

So far, Bremer has shut down two newspapers and one radio outlet. Reporters Without Borders has called for immediate action to replace "restrictive media regulations" in Iraq.

No Real Democracy

Democracy was never Bush's goal in Iraq. The goal was establishing U.S. dominance, not only militarily but also economically. The council Bremer has set up is designed to ratify that dominance, not usher in genuine democracy.

Many Iraqis understand this. Their recognition of Bush's cynical motives—along with the brutality and ineptness of the occupation—is spurring the protests in the streets and helping recruit the guerrilla army that even the U.S. military now recognizes it faces.

Chapter 2

Should the United States Play an Active Role in Iraq?

Chapter Preface

On January 9, 2003, thirty-one U.S. soldiers were wounded by a bomb blast at the 101 Airborne Division base at Tall'Afar in northern Iraq. The blast was set off by a suspected suicide bomber who drove to the gates of the base. U.S. troops opened fire on the vehicle after it failed to stop at an entry point, and the vehicle then detonated. In a second attack that same day, a suicide bomber approached a gate at Forward Operating Base Thunder in Ba'qubah—about thirty miles northeast of Baghdad—pretending to be ill. When troops did not come to his aid, the man detonated himself, wounding two American soldiers. These incidents are just two examples of the prevalence of Iraqi resistance to the presence of American forces in their country, and illustrate the ongoing conflict over U.S. involvement in Iraq.

As of mid-January 2004, there had been more than five hundred American casualties in Iraq, most of them occurring after major combat operations were declared over on May 1, 2003. According to the Pentagon, the number of Americans wounded during and after the war was more than twenty-eight hundred. A large number of these injuries and casualties are the result of opposition to the U.S. presence in Iraq.

As active U.S. involvement in Iraq continues, so does Iraqi resistance to that involvement. In a November 2003 interview, residents of Fallujah, a town thirty-five miles west of Baghdad, expressed their hostility to the American occupation. Osam Fahdawi, owner of a construction company, said, "We don't like Saddam; he was a dictator. But the Americans, they handcuff us, they put us on the floor in front of our wives and children. It's shameful for us." Brigadier General Riyad Abbas al Karbuli, Fallujah's police chief echoed this objection, stating, "At first, Americans were very helpful. Now Americans are committing a crime."

Yet many people believe that the United States cannot withdraw from Iraq immediately. Journalist John O'Sullivan argues in the *National Review* that America must maintain its presence in Iraq until a stable democratic government is established. He states, "The U.S. can withstand the death of one soldier a day—or fewer than 4,000 soldiers a decade—indefinitely" for this cause. According to the Middle East Media Research Institute, a July 2003 poll found that while they did not like being under American occupation, the majority of Iraqis were willing to give occupation forces one to two years to initiate political and economic reforms.

As casualties continue to rise among both Americans and Iraqis in Iraq, there is heated debate over whether the United States should be actively involved in Iraq, and what the extent of that involvement should be. The authors in the following chapter offer various views on this controversial issue.

The United States Should Send More Troops to Iraq

by William Kristol and Robert Kagan

About the authors: *William Kristol is editor of the* Weekly Standard, *a weekly political journal. Robert Kagan is a contributing editor to the* Weekly Standard.

National security adviser Condoleezza Rice gave an important speech a couple of weeks ago [in August 2003], in which she called on the United States to make a "generational commitment" to bringing political and economic reform to the long-neglected Middle East—a commitment not unlike that which we made to rebuild Europe after the Second World War. It was a stirring speech, made all the more potent by the knowledge that it reflects the president's own vision. President [George W.] Bush recognizes that, as is so often the case, American ideals and American interests converge in such a project, that a more democratic Middle East will both improve the lives of long-suffering peoples and enhance America's national security.

Reason to Worry

For all our admiration for this bold, long-term vision, however, there is reason to be worried about the execution of that policy in the first and probably most important test of our "generational commitment." Make no mistake: The president's vision will, in the coming months [late 2003], either be launched successfully in Iraq, or it will die in Iraq. Indeed, there is more at stake in Iraq than even this vision of a better, safer Middle East. The future course of American foreign policy, American world leadership, and American security is at stake. Failure in Iraq would be a devastating blow to everything the United States hopes to accomplish, and must accomplish, in the decades ahead.

We believe the president and his top advisers understand the magnitude of the task. That is why it is so baffling that, up until now, the Bush administration has failed to commit resources to the rebuilding of Iraq commensurate with these very high stakes. Certainly, American efforts in Iraq since the end of the war

William Kristol and Robert Kagan, "Do What It Takes in Iraq," *Weekly Standard*, vol. 8, September 1, 2003. Copyright © 2003 by News Corporation, *Weekly Standard*. All rights reserved. Reproduced by permission.

have not been a failure. And considering what might have gone wrong—and which so many critics predicted would go wrong—the results have been in many ways admirable. Iraq has not descended into inter-religious and inter-ethnic violence. There is food and water. Hospitals are up and running. The Arab and Muslim worlds have not erupted in chaos or anger, as so many of our European friends confidently predicted.

But the absence of catastrophic failure is not, unfortunately, evidence of impending success. As any number of respected analysts visiting Iraq have reported, and as recent horrific

> *"It is painfully obvious that there are too few American troops operating in Iraq."*

events have demonstrated, there is much to worry about. Basic security, both for Iraqis and for coalition and other international workers in Iraq, is lacking. Continuing power shortages throughout much of the country have damaged the reputation of the United States as a responsible occupying power and have led many Iraqis to question American intentions. Ongoing assassinations and sabotage of public utilities by pro-Saddam [Hussein] forces and, possibly, by terrorists entering the country from neighboring Syria and Iran threaten to destabilize the tenuous peace that has held in Iraq since the end of the [2003] war.

In short, while it is indeed possible that, with a little luck, the United States can muddle through to success in Iraq over the coming months, the danger is that the resources the administration is devoting to Iraq right now are insufficient, and the speed with which they are being deployed is insufficiently urgent. These failings, if not corrected soon, could over time lead to disaster. Three big issues stand out.

Where Are the Troops?

It is painfully obvious that there are too few American troops operating in Iraq. Senior military officials privately suggest that we need two more divisions. The simple fact is, right now there are too few good guys chasing the bad guys—hence the continuing sabotage. There are too few forces to patrol the Syrian and Iranian borders to prevent the infiltration of international terrorists trying to open a new front against the United States in Iraq. There are too few forces to protect vital infrastructure and public buildings. And contrary to what some say, more troops don't mean more casualties. More troops mean fewer casualties—both American and Iraqi.

The really bad news is that the Pentagon plans to draw down U.S. forces even further in coming months. Their hope is that U.S. forces will be replaced by new Iraqi forces and by an influx of allied troops from around the world. We fear this is wishful thinking. It seems unlikely that any Iraqi force capable of providing security will be in place by the spring. And as for the international community—never mind whether we could ever convince France and other countries to make a serious contribution. In truth, our European allies do not have that many troops to spare. And consider the possibly unfortunate effects of turning over the security of Iraqis to a patchwork of ill-prepared forces from elsewhere in the world.

That's why calls from members of Congress to "internationalize" the force and give the U.N. a preeminent role are unhelpful, and really beside the point, at this critical juncture. Senator [Joseph] Biden is correct to say that "we have a hell of a team over there, but they don't have enough of anything." But he's wrong to suggest that a meaningful part of the solution would be "to internationalize" this. And when Rep. Mark Kirk says that "every international peacekeeper brought in is a chance to replace an American," he's raising false hopes among the American people. Such calls for "internationalization" also signal to Iraqi Baathists and Islamic radicals an inclination on the part of the United States to cut and run.

It's true that, unfortunately, we don't have many troops to spare, either: We should have begun rebuilding our military two years ago. And it is true that increasing the size of our forces, both in Iraq and overall, is unattractive to administration officials. But this is the time to bite the bullet and pay the price. Next spring, if disaster looms, it will be harder. And it may be too late.

Where Is the Money?

The same goes for the financial resources the administration has sought for Iraqi reconstruction. It is simply unconscionable that debilitating power shortages persist in Iraq, turning Iraqi public opinion against the United States. This is one of those problems that can be solved with enough money. And yet the money has not been made available. This is just the most disturbing example of a general pattern. The Iraqi economy needs an infusion of assistance, to build up infrastructure, to improve the daily lives of the Iraqi people, to put a little money in Iraqi pockets so that pessimism can turn to optimism. There has also been a stunning shortage of democracy assistance, at a time when, according to surveys taken by the National Democratic Institute for International Affairs, Iraq is undergoing an explosion of political activity.

"Getting the job done in Iraq is our highest priority, and our government needs to treat it as such."

We understand the administration's fear of asking Congress for the necessary funds for Iraq. The price tag, which may be close to $60 billion, will provide fodder for opportunistic Democratic presidential hopefuls who are already complaining that money spent in Iraq would be better spent in the United States. But, again, the time to bite the bullet is now, not six months from now when Iraq turns to crisis and the American campaign season is fully underway. If Rice and others are serious about making a "generational commitment" equivalent to that which followed the Second World War, then this is the necessary down payment.

Where Are the Personnel?

The American military is not alone in facing a shortage of people in Iraq. Everyone returning from Iraq comments on the astonishing lack of American civilians as well. Until recently, only a handful of State Department employees have been at work in Iraq. The State Department, we gather, has had a difficult time attracting volunteers to work in Iraq. This is understandable. But it is unacceptable. If the administration is serious about drawing an analogy with the early Cold War years, it should remember that the entire U.S. government oriented itself then to the new challenge. We need to do the same now. The administration must insist that the State Department pull its weight. Indeed, we need to deploy diplomats and civil servants, hire contract workers, and mobilize people and resources in an urgent and serious way. Business as usual is not acceptable. Getting the job done in Iraq is our highest priority, and our government needs to treat it as such.

These are the core problems the Bush administration needs to address. Success in Iraq is within our reach. But there are grounds to fear that on the current trajectory, we won't get there. The president knows that failure in Iraq is intolerable. Now is the time to act decisively to prevent it.

America Must Make a Long-Term, Costly Commitment to Iraq

by the *Economist*

About the author: *The* Economist *is a weekly newspaper that provides analysis of world business and current affairs.*

There are many good arguments against war, but high among them is its ability to bring surprises, many of them unpleasant. The second Iraq war was no exception to that, though it may have been unusual in bringing surprises both to those who were in favour of it and to those against.

Many advocates of the war were surprised by how rapidly it was won, by how few casualties were caused among both soldiers and civilians, by the fact that no biological or chemical weapons were used by Saddam Hussein and, most controversially, by the fact that no stockpiles of such weapons have yet been found in Iraq. Advocates were also surprised and dismayed, though, to find that America appeared to have no coherent plan for what to do in Iraq once the war was won. Many of those who were against the war were also taken by surprise, however, by its speed, by the lack of a deadly street battle for Baghdad, of a flood of refugees or an epidemic of cholera, and by the lack of uprisings or instability in other Arab countries and of terrorist attacks during the war. Most were further surprised, though presumably not dismayed, by the serious commitment to Arab-Israeli peace shown by President George [W.] Bush soon after the invasion.

More of those surprises have been [more] pleasant than unpleasant, though it is too soon to make a definitive reckoning of that sort. In Iraq, many civilians feel insecure and poorly served with such basics as electricity and clean water, and American soldiers are being killed almost daily. . . . Nevertheless, three months after the war was won [in July 2003], one question demands to be answered, mainly because no weapons of mass destruction have yet been found: was the war really justified?

Chapter 2

The Threat Posed by Saddam

The *Economist* certainly said it was. We did so most strongly and clearly in a survey ("Present at the creation", June 29th 2002) on America's world role; and in leaders on August 3rd that year ("The case for war"), February 22nd 2003 ("Why war would be justified") and March 15th 2003 ("Saddam's last victory"). Readers who want to check what we said and argued can find all those articles on our website, Economist.com.

People who favoured war on the ground that Saddam Hussein posed a threat by virtue of his weapons must, if they are honest, admit to feeling undermined and even slightly unnerved by the fact that none have yet been found. They could well still be found: Iraq is a big country, chemical and biological weapons are often small, and Mr Hussein was shown during the 1990s to be a past master at concealment. Three months is not long for a search, especially amid the chaos and other tasks of the immediate post-war period. Still, the fact that no stocks have been found does at least imply that weapons were not widely deployed for use during the war, as otherwise some would surely have been captured during the allies' rapid advance. The British government's much-derided claim that weapons were capable of being launched within 45 minutes therefore does look to have been wrong.[1]

However, the question of whether the war was, in retrospect, justified does not rest on that claim, or on the issue of whether Mr Bush or [British prime minister] Tony Blair may at times have gone too far in turning possibilities raised by their spies into apparent certainties. Rather, the justification for the war is best addressed by dividing it into three questions: 1) Were there good grounds to threaten Mr Hussein with an imminent military attack if he did not comply with United Nations resolutions [requiring Iraq to let weapons inspectors into his country]? 2) When he did not comply, were there good grounds for carrying out that threat? 3) After the military victory, have the allies acted in such a way as to make things better both in Iraq and in the region as a whole?

Mr Hussein himself provided the answer to the first question. He had signed an agreement in 1991, after the first Iraq war, under which he promised to get rid of his nuclear,

> *"The case for [going to war] ... depended on the notion that America and its allies were determined to make the country and its troubled region more peaceful."*

chemical and biological weapons and programmes, to scrap long-range ballistic missiles, and to stop brutalising his people, among other things, all within a year. He did not comply, and UN weapons inspectors established that he had concealed his weapons, thanks to tip-offs from defectors. For example, having at

---

1. As this book went to press, weapons of mass destruction had not been found in Iraq.

first denied that he had ever produced a deadly nerve agent called VX, he then responded to a discovery by claiming to have made only 200 litres, but then the UN inspectors showed that at least 3,900 litres had been made. Having established that he could not be trusted, inspectors were barred from Iraq after withdrawing in 1998. Given that, by 2002, he had flouted 16 binding UN resolutions, how best to persuade him to allow inspectors to return? By making a credible threat that the measure promised by such resolutions, the use of force, would be carried out if he didn't. That required the stationing of troops on his border and the passing of a further UN resolution in November [2002], stating what he had to do to comply.

> *"America . . . must simultaneously prove that it is committed to staying in order to rebuild Iraq . . . and that it is preparing to hand over power."*

None of that has been called into doubt by the lack of discoveries since the war. Mr Hussein had a clear record of developing these weapons, using them and concealing them. There can also be no doubt both that he was a brutal, ruthless dictator who murdered hundreds of thousands of his own citizens and that he harboured ambitions to dominate his region: he had fought Iran during the 1980s, had invaded Kuwait in 1990, and threatened Israel, Saudi Arabia and (in 1994) Kuwait again. He was thus plainly a dangerous man, in whose hands such dangerous weapons could pose a real threat, both to regional peace and, through the power that dominance of the world's oil reserves would bring, to the whole world.

The Case for Impatience

What, then, of the second question? Was it right to carry out the threat, making the war both punitive and preemptive? Of one thing there can be no doubt: he did not comply with November's resolution. The weapons inspectors appointed by the UN said that he did not, either in his formal (vast) declaration in December or in the inspections process itself. For a man with a proven record of concealment, to choose not to comply, even as American and British troops were massing on his border, was remarkable. There was also then, however, a debate: might he be persuaded to comply by further UN inspections, during which (for instance) he might at last agree to allow Iraqi scientists to be flown out of the country for questioning, with their families? Those who opposed war in March, but had voted for the November resolution (including France), thought he could be, since he seemed to have become more co-operative. Those in favour of carrying out the threat, including *The Economist*, thought that to wait was too risky. He had successfully wriggled away in the past when offered the chance of delay, and could well do so again.

Reasonable people could disagree about that decision, and about whether it might have been better first to get a unanimous vote on a new Security Council resolution. But neither the non-discovery of weapons nor the recent evidence of exaggeration by the British and American governments of elements of their claims alters the argument for or against permitting further delay. Mr Hussein was believed, on good grounds, to be both dangerous and a liar. On previous occasions the UN process had fallen apart after delays led to divisions. The attempt to use containment, sanctions and inspections had lasted 12 years: hardly a sign of impatience. The prospect that he could emerge from it able, after a year or two, say, to revamp his weapons programmes and threaten his region was real. Both at the time, and in retrospect, the decision to go to war rather than to wait was justified.

What then, it is reasonable to ask, might change *The Economist*'s mind? If Messrs Bush and Blair are shown not just to have exaggerated but actually to have lied, knowingly putting false information before their voters, it would be a huge scandal and would destroy their governments' credibility for future interventions overseas. But to make the Iraq war look unjustified in retrospect, such a scandal would have to amount to clear evidence that it had not, in fact, been reasonable to believe that Mr Hussein was a dangerous liar and concealer— which would require the distortions or deceits to have been astonishingly widespread and conducted over a long period of time. Given that spying agencies currently look incompetent rather than capable of such a broad, effective campaign, this looks unlikely. But there is another mind-changing possibility. It lies in the answer to the third question: After the military victory, have the allies acted in such a way as to make things better both in Iraq and in the region as a whole? If they hadn't, or didn't in the future, that could indeed make us decide that the war had not, after all, been justified.

They Have to Be Serious

Ultimately, even if the grounds for going to war in March 2003 were strong, the case for it also depended on the notion that America and its allies were determined to make the country and its troubled region more peaceful, more prosperous and less threatening in the future than might have been the case had Mr Hussein been left in place. Many of the opponents of the war thought they were not: that Iraq might be left to collapse in civil war or else might be repressed and exploited as an American colony; that countless fresh grievances would be created, causing more terrorism; and that there would be no serious American effort to bring about peace between Israel and the Palestinians.

It is, of course, far too soon to come to a judgment about this. What can be said, though, is that so far the picture is mixed but on balance moderately encouraging. President Bush has certainly begun a serious effort to persuade Israel and Palestine to make peace, and that process has inched edgily forwards. The future question will be whether he maintains that effort in the face of inevitable setbacks, and of the fact that both Yasser Arafat, still the Palestinian figurehead, and Ariel Sharon, the Israeli prime minister, are reluctant either to compromise or to help build trust. There is also the distraction of the 2004 presidential election in America. The grounds for cautious optimism are that President Bush really cannot afford to shrink back now that he has made his commitment; and that the opportunity for change provided by the victory in Iraq will not last forever. That must be the hope, and must be what Mr Bush's allies should urge.

> *"A long-term, costly commitment is going to be needed [in Iraq]."*

In Iraq itself the Americans made an appallingly bad start. Their reasons for having had no post-war plan are almost as incomprehensible as Saddam's reasons for having neither complied with the UN resolution nor deployed any banned weapons. They have also failed, so far, to beat back or deter the guerrilla tactics being used against them. There are, though, some encouraging signs too. Chief among them is the establishment during the past week [July 2003] of the new 25-member Iraqi Governing Council, the first big step the Americans have taken towards devolving power to Iraqis themselves and towards establishing some sort of representative democracy.

The new council is far from democratic—its members were picked by Paul Bremer, America's chief administrator, albeit after consultation—but it is fairly representative. It is hardly surprising that it took three months before such a council was set up, given that Iraq has only just emerged from a long and repressive dictatorship. But the delay still sowed doubts about America's intentions. So too has the slowness, in the face of sabotage, to restore electricity supplies. America's predicament is that it must simultaneously prove that it is committed to staying in order to rebuild Iraq as a secure, stable and peaceful country, and that it is preparing to hand over power to democratic institutions and to leave.

Making the council a success will be an important part of that. So too will be the commencement of real work to prepare for elections, first at a local level and later at national level. Alongside that, however, there can be no substitute for the deployment of people and money: more troops, to pacify the areas of Iraq in which guerrilla campaigns are being fostered and to show that America is not going to allow the Baathists to claw their way back; more money, to restore utilities faster and as a further show of commitment, particularly given that oil exports have been much slower to resume than was expected.

But will America really remain committed, especially in the face of daily casualties? Again, the answer is that it cannot afford not to be. Afghanistan has been left, both by America and by other rich countries, in far too vulnerable and disorderly a state [after the 2001 war]. That is tragic and shameful, but if the same were to happen in Iraq the result could be catastrophic: a deadly civil war in which neighbouring countries felt they had no option but to become involved, and a huge stain on America's reputation, not only for justice but also for effectiveness.

In America's history there are too many examples of a short attention span. But there are also bigger examples of the country's ability to pick itself up after initial stumbles and to sustain a long-term commitment: the troops that have sat in danger by North Korea's border with the South for 50 years; the Marshall Plan that boosted Europe's economic recovery a full two years after victory in the second world war. Again, a long-term, costly commitment is going to be needed.

The United States Should Help Iraqis Build a Democracy

by Mark N. Katz

About the author: *Mark N. Katz is a professor of government and politics at George Mason University in Fairfax, Virginia.*

Plenty of warnings have been issued about what might go wrong in Iraq: the Shiite clergy might set up an Islamic republic, as in neighboring Iran; the Sunni minority—with help from neighboring Arab states—might reassert some form of dictatorial rule; or a Kurdish attempt at secession might trigger Turkish and Iranian intervention. It is also possible, however, that things might actually go right in Iraq, and that a liberal democracy will come into being there.

This possibility must be taken seriously. The American (or American-led) oc-cupations of West Germany, Italy, and Japan after World War II helped incubate democracy successfully in those countries. The American and British occupa-tion of Iraq now could serve a similar function. Democracy, of course, is not something that can be imposed from outside: there has to be fertile soil if it is to grow and prosper. Many see Iraq as a country where the obstacles to democrati-zation are simply too great for it to take root. West Germany and Japan, though, also seemed to be unlikely candidates for democratization in late 1945.

Serious obstacles to the democratization of Iraq, of course, do exist and can-not be ignored. These include (1) fractious relations between the Sunni Arab minority favored by Saddam [Hussein] and the Shiite Arab majority whom he suppressed; (2) Kurdish-Arab tensions in northern Iraq (involving the possibil-ity of Kurdish secession); (3) the rise of Islamic fundamentalism within both the Shiite Arab and Sunni Arab communities; (4) the state of economic collapse pervading Iraq; and (5) the widespread belief in Iraq that any political leader or group supported by Washington is an American puppet and hence illegitimate.

Even greater obstacles may be the lack of experience with democratization in

Iraq and the fact that most of the emerging political groups there advocate different types of authoritarianism instead of liberal democracy. Yet despite all these obstacles, the American-led occupation of Iraq may still be able to foster democracy in this seemingly impossible situation. Here's how.

Bringing Democracy to Iraq

Each of Iraq's major groups would prefer an authoritarian regime that it would dominate. None, however, wishes to live under an authoritarian regime that it does not dominate. If these major groups could be persuaded that they will be unable to dominate Iraq, then each might reasonably be expected to prefer a democracy in which it would at least have some say, rather than an authoritarian regime dominated by others in which it would have none. If, for example, the Sunni Arabs became convinced that they could not reassert the predominant position they enjoyed under Saddam Hussein, they would clearly be better off living in a democracy that they could participate in than under a dictatorship that they could not.

Similarly, while many Kurds would prefer to secede from Iraq and establish an independent state, the Turkish government has threatened to intervene to suppress any such effort. Not wanting to face a situation in which it is forced to choose between the Turks and Kurds, Washington is doing everything it can to dissuade the Kurds from attempting secession. If the Kurds come to understand that present circumstances simply will not allow them to become independent and that they will remain in Iraq, they too should see that they would be better off living in a democracy than under a dictatorship.

It is easy to see why the Sunni Arab and Kurdish minorities would be better off in a democracy than in a dictatorship dominated by the Arab Shiite majority. What, then, would be the incentive for the Shiites to forgo a dictatorship they dominated and accept democracy instead? Indeed, it is clear that clerical rule, as in Iran, is the form of government that many Iraqi Shiite religious leaders prefer, since this would put power into their hands.

Even this group, though, might come to accept democracy. For the fact of the matter is that the Iraqi Shiites—including their religious leaders—are divided among themselves. All too many wish to be leaders, while all too few are willing to be followers. Thus, even those within the Iraqi Shiite community who would prefer an Islamic republic they dominated

> *"Despite all these obstacles [to democracy], the American-led occupation of Iraq may still be able to foster democracy in this seemingly impossible situation."*

might prefer a Western-style one that they could play a role in to an Islamic republic dominated by their rivals.

Finally, while Iraqis are now voicing their opposition to a continued American and British military "occupation," each group might come to realize that it would be better off if this presence were prolonged. For example, if American and British forces departed right around the time of the first national elections, there would be real danger that whatever party won the elections would do away with democracy and rule dictatorially. If American and British forces remained in Iraq, however, they could prevent this from happening. Similarly, a continued American and British presence could prevent the electoral losers from rebelling—something they might well do if they feared the winners were about to impose a dictatorship.

A London-based newspaper, *Al-Quds al-Arabi*, editorialized that "if this U.S. Administration says that it will not accept an Islamic Government in Iraq like the one in Iran and goes on to uproot the Ba'ath party altogether, then the democracy it is proposing is more like a dictatorship than the true democracy for which the Iraqis are hoping."

> *"Without a successful Iraqi example, it is doubtful that democratization will occur elsewhere in the Middle East anytime soon."*

Iraqis are the ones who must build their own democracy. A continued American and British presence, though, may be what is needed to allow them to do so. This presence could guard against what some of America's founders feared: the tyranny of the majority. As successive elections occur, different Iraqi groups will gain experience as governing parties and opposition parties. Above all, they will learn to cooperate across ethnic and religions lines. Just as American-led occupation helped West Germany, Italy, and Japan make the transition from totalitarianism to liberal democracy, so might it help Iraq make a similar transition.

Democratic Ramifications

The successful democratization of Iraq would have ramifications for the entire region. Just as the rise of [Gamal Abdel] Nasser in Egypt [in 1954] boosted the Arab nationalist cause in many Arab countries and the rise of the Ayatollah [Ruhollah] Khomeini in Iran [in 1979] boosted the Islamic fundamentalist cause in several Muslim countries, the rise of democracy in Iraq would boost the democratic cause throughout the Middle East.

The rise of a liberal democracy in Iraq, where the majority of the population is Shiite, could have a major impact on the political evolution of Iran. The reformers have been winning Iran's recent elections, but the government there is controlled by hard-line Shiite clerics. A democratic Iraq would strengthen the reformers in Iran and would provide a model for the separation of mosque and state that could benefit Iran.

Ayatollah Seyyed Musavi Tabrizi, secretary of the Association of Researchers and Lecturers at Qom Seminary in Iran, has said: "If those officials who are involved in the management of the country implement the constitution properly, and refrain from imposed and shallow interpretations of the constitution, this very constitution with its existing capacities will be sufficient to guarantee democracy in Iran."

The position of the Kurds in Turkey is extremely difficult, since the Turkish government is fearful that this minority will attempt to secede. A democratic Iraq in which there are peaceful, cooperative relations between Kurds and Arabs might serve as a model for Kurdish-Turkish relations. A policy of tolerance toward its Kurds would strengthen the rule of law and civil society generally in Turkey.

The biggest impact of a democratic Iraq, though, would be felt in the Arab world. Some note the absence of a strong democratic movement there as an indication that Arab political culture is inhospitable to democracy. The lack of such a movement may actually be due, however, not just to the ease with which it could be suppressed but to the lack of a successful role model within the Arab world. While many Arab governments claim to be democratic, none of them actually are. If Iraq becomes a role model, democratic movements might arise quickly throughout the rest of the Arab world.

Nor would this necessarily portend conflict. Seeing that democratization was inevitable, royal families might be able to preserve an honored role for themselves by presiding over transitions from absolute to constitutional monarchies. "Republics" ruled by the armed forces leadership would not have this possibility, but as transitions in Latin America and elsewhere have shown, armed forces that cease ruling still have an important role to play in society. The type of regime most unwilling to democratize might be those ruled by an authoritarian political party, as in Syria. But as the democratic transitions in eastern Europe and Russia have shown, even erstwhile ruling parties can adapt to the democratic process.

It is not clear how widely or rapidly a democratic movement would spread from Iraq to other Arab countries. It seems likely, though, that as more democratic transitions take place in the Arab world, autocratic governments there will find it more difficult to cling to power.

If a democratic movement spread from Iraq to the rest of the Arab world, it would also spread to the Palestinians. If it gained ascendancy among them, this would have a profound impact on the Arab-Israeli conflict. What the Palestinians have not won by suicide bombings and other forms of violence they might well win by nonviolent, democratic means.

If instead of [Palestinian leader] Yasser Arafat or Islamic militants, the Palestinians were led by the equivalent of a [Polish antigovernment union activist] Lech Walesa or [South African activist] Nelson Mandela, there would be far more sympathy for them everywhere, including the United States and Israel itself. If a democratic Palestinian leadership reassured the Israelis that the two peoples could coexist peacefully, Israel's fear of granting independence to a Palestinian state would be greatly reduced.

There are opposing views in the Arab world. Dr. Mustafa Kamil al-Sayyid, a professor at Cairo University and human rights activist, remarks: "It is for this reason that I think that the United States will use the veto on those the Iraqis will choose. We have the experience of Yasser Arafat, who was elected by the Palestinian people, but the U.S. administration has said that it would not deal with him. If elections were held and Arafat won, the U.S. administration would not deal with him even then. This shows us the limits that the United States lays down for democracy."

Stepping Toward Arab Unity

The democratization of the Arab world might also help the Arabs better achieve their long-sought goal of unity. Previous attempts at seeking to "unite" authoritarian Arab regimes attempted or proposed by Nasser, the Ba'ath Party, [Libyan president Muammar] Qaddafi, and others would have meant that one authoritarian leadership would have supplanted another. This is why the 1958 merger of Egypt and Syria into the United Arab Republic ended in divorce when Syria withdrew from the union in 1961. The leadership of democratic Arab states that united with each other, by contrast, could share power.

Or if actual unity seemed undesirable, democratic Arab states might be able to create something akin to the European Union. An Arab Union consisting of democratic states would have far more credibility and legitimacy than the current Arab League, which consists solely of authoritarian regimes.

If the American-led occupation of Iraq leads to the democratization of the Middle East in general, then this occupation will have been the most positive event in the modern history of the region. Even if it leads just to the democratization of Iraq, this will be the most positive development since that country was created after World War I.

But will the American-led occupation of Iraq bring about democratization even there? The obstacles are formidable; there is no guarantee that any such effort will succeed. One thing seems certain: if Iraq is not democratized with the help of America now, it is not likely to democratize on its own in the near future. Without a successful Iraqi example, it is doubtful that democratization will occur elsewhere in the Middle East anytime soon, either.

The American-led occupation of Iraq presents a precious opportunity to democratize that country and perhaps others in the Middle East. Such an opportunity might not arise again for many years or even decades. Even if the effort ultimately fails, it is still worth making. For until it experiences democratization, the Middle East will remain mired in violence, dictatorship, and the false hopes promised by nondemocratic ideologies. If the United States and its true allies have just the possibility of helping the people of the Middle East avoid this fate, then surely it must try to do so.

The United States Should Maintain a Nonmilitary Influence in Iraq

by Christopher Preble

About the author: *Christopher Preble is director of foreign policy studies at the Cato Institute, a nonprofit public policy research foundation.*

The American military's swift victory over the Baathist regime in Iraq seems in retrospect to have been a nearly textbook case of the vaunted "shock and awe" strategy made famous in the weeks leading up to the war. On the morning of March 20, 2003, the U.S. military launched a lightning "decapitation strike" against Saddam Hussein's government. A mere 21 days later, Americans were treated to televised images of Iraqis celebrating in the streets of Baghdad, tearing down statues of Hussein, and banging the soles of their shoes (an especially insulting gesture in Arab culture) on his nearly ubiquitous image.

The overwhelming military victory set the stage for a shift in U.S. military deployments in the region. On April 29, less than three weeks after the fall of Baghdad, Defense Secretary Donald Rumsfeld announced that U.S. troops would be removed from Saudi Arabia, where they had been stationed since late 1990. "It is now a safer region because of the change of regime in Iraq," the secretary said. Drawing on the early lessons learned from the just-concluded war, Rumsfeld's announcement represented a significant change in U.S. policy in the Persian Gulf, and it was entirely appropriate given the nature of the threats in the region. Indeed, it was long overdue.

Although withdrawal from Saudi Arabia is both appropriate and welcome, that action should be only the first of several steps leading to a wholesale reduction in the American military's "footprint" in the entire region. Rather than tinkering on the margins, the collapse of Saddam Hussein's decrepit regime provides a golden opportunity for a fundamental change in U.S. policy in the Persian Gulf. In addition to the removal of troops from Saudi Arabia, U.S.

Christopher Preble, "After Victory: Towards a New Military Posture in the Persian Gulf," *Policy Analysis*, no. 477, June 10, 2003. Copyright © 2003 by the Cato Institute. All rights reserved. Reproduced by permission.

forces should be withdrawn from the other Gulf states, including Qatar, Kuwait, and Iraq, and the U.S. Navy should terminate its longstanding policy of deploying a carrier battle group in the Persian Gulf. The troops are unnecessary. They are costly. And their presence makes us less, not more, secure because they have become a lightning rod, used by the most extremist, anti-American individuals and groups to mobilize a disheartened population frustrated by a lack of political freedom and economic opportunity.

The United States will retain an enormous influence in the region by virtue of our extensive economic ties, but we need not station our troops in foreign lands in order to remain engaged. Absent the threat allegedly posed by Saddam Hussein, the United States can return to its rightful role as a balancer of last resort, intervening only in the highly unlikely event that a crisis in the region threatens to harm vital American interests.

The More Things Change, the More They Stay the Same

Some observers have asserted that U.S. troops must remain in the region, even after Saddam's fall. Tom Donnelly of the American Enterprise Institute [AEI] argued that the American interest in Iraq had actually increased following Hussein's ouster. "The liberation of Iraq adds to the substantial list of U.S. interests in the region," wrote Donnelly in the *Weekly Standard*, and he called for a "quasi-permanent American garrison in Iraq" to protect those interests. Donnelly elaborated in an interview with the *Washington Post*, saying "we're now not just interested in the gas and oil from the region but we have a political commitment and a huge amount of chips bet on whether political reconstruction in Iraq is going to work." Anthony Cordesman of the Center for Strategic and International Studies agreed, arguing the United States needs "to have strong regional allies, good basing options and some degree of pre-positioning" of U.S. forces for years to come. When Rumsfeld asserted that the Pentagon was not planning to keep permanent bases in Iraq, avowed imperialist Max Boot of the Council on Foreign Relations exclaimed, "If they're not, they should be." Indeed, Boot called on *USA Today* readers to "get used to U.S. troops being deployed [in Iraq] for years, possibly decades, to come."

> *"The collapse of Saddam Hussein's decrepit regime provides a golden opportunity for a fundamental change in U.S. policy in the Persian Gulf."*

In truth, policymakers and analysts were planning for the eventuality of a long-term U.S. presence even before Saddam Hussein disappeared. Writing in early 2003, before the outbreak of the war with Iraq, Richard D. Sokolsky of the Institute for National Strategic Studies at the National Defense University predicted: "Regardless of the outcome of the Iraqi scenario, the United States will need to maintain forces in the region."

These assertions largely ignore the costs and risks associated with leaving a large U.S. force in the region. They similarly ignore some of the most important lessons from the last war. Even casual observers have noted that the Saudi bases were completely superfluous. The Saudis, sensitive to domestic opinion, officially barred U.S. aircraft based in the kingdom from conducting strikes on Iraq. No matter. Hundreds of sorties were flown by aircraft launched from bases located thousands of miles away from the target area. We know of aircraft launching from the United Kingdom and tiny Diego Garcia in the Indian Ocean. Even more incredible: a number of bombing missions were conducted by aircraft flying round-trip from the United States. Clearly, the American military's capacity for projecting power knows few limits.

> *"Our troops need not sit for months or years in the midst of a hostile landscape preparing for offensive operations against presumed threats yet to materialize."*

Meanwhile, the U.S. Army, which risked being rendered nearly irrelevant in the 1990s, borrowed a page from the Marines, becoming lighter and more capable of conducting operations from temporary bases. NATO [North Atlantic Treaty Organization] ally Turkey's decision to block an invasion launched from Turkish soil into Northern Iraq certainly complicated war planning, and the U.S. Fourth Infantry Division spent much of the war in ships, first waiting to debark into Turkey, and then transiting the Suez Canal, the Red Sea, and the Straits of Hormuz into the Persian Gulf. But, in the end, the 4th I.D. wasn't needed. Many of the most successful infantry operations combined vertical envelopment—inserting troops into combat zones from the air—with ground assault by tanks and armored vehicles. While a handful of talking heads and media pundits wrung their hands over the alleged inadequacy of the American invasion forces, the Pentagon deployed more than enough troops to cover hundreds of miles in less than three weeks, and to efficiently defeat Iraqi forces.

A change away from forward deployment toward an expeditionary force, based largely in the United States, is made possible because the Pentagon has now twice demonstrated its ability to conduct expeditionary military operations, first in Afghanistan [in 2001] and then in Iraq. Those campaigns were launched from temporary bases, constructed over the course of just a few months. In the future, our troops need not sit for months or years in the midst of a hostile landscape preparing for offensive operations against presumed threats yet to materialize. With the removal of Saddam's regime, no sensible person is contemplating another ground invasion of any country in the region.

The Specious Oil Argument

Many of those who called for an end to the American presence in Saudi Arabia argue that the United States military must remain in the region indefinitely for one reason: oil. To those who are focused on the Gulf's energy resources and who argue that U.S. troops must remain in the region, the euphemism most frequently used is "engagement," as in, the presence of U.S. troops ensures that the United States is "engaged." By this logic, engagement comes only at the barrel of a gun. But why can we not assume that individual initiative, private enterprise, and cultural exchange are also forms of engagement? Do people only travel to places where U.S. troops are stationed? Can commerce only take place in the presence of American troops? Of course not.

The American military presence is not essential to ensure access to Persian Gulf oil. Nonetheless, oil seems to govern much of what the United States does in Iraq, as it has done throughout the region for decades. For example, critics note that U.S. troops protected the files at the Iraqi Oil Ministry while looters ransacked hospitals and made off with priceless treasures from Iraq's National Museum of Antiquities.

The strategic and economic significance of Persian Gulf oil should not be overstated. Saudi Arabia is the leading source of foreign crude oil imported into the United States, but the Persian Gulf region as a whole accounts for less than 15 percent of U.S. oil needs. Meanwhile, the United States buys the vast majority of its oil from the Western Hemisphere. In addition to domestic production, which provides over 50 percent of our energy needs, an additional 20 percent comes from Mexico, Canada, and Venezuela. If one includes both crude and refined petroleum, the share is slightly larger.

> *"The American military presence is not essential to ensure access to Persian Gulf oil."*

Those favoring a continued American troop presence in the Middle East presume that this military pressure will prevent hostile governments from refusing to sell oil to the United States. Many Americans still shudder at the memories of the Arab oil embargoes of the 1970s. But research shows that the economic effects of these embargoes were extremely limited. Embargoes increase transaction and transportation costs—adding one or more middlemen willing to sell to the embargoed end-user and forcing embargoed products to take a roundabout route to their final destination—but short of a naval blockade of an enemy's ports, governments cannot prevent products from eventually making their way into particular countries.

Others may contend that the presence of the United States military in all corners of the globe ensures "stability" in various regions, and that this stability is a precondition for the proper functioning of economic markets. Stability in the Middle East is particularly crucial given the history of volatility in the region and given that military conflict can—and has—disrupted oil flows, with detrimental consequences for the United States.

Of course, markets respond negatively to inefficiencies, and the greatest of these are conflict and lawlessness. But just as embargoes can cause temporary disruptions that affect the price of oil in the United States, world markets likewise adjust to disruptions caused by violence. If a military conflict threatens to slow or halt the flow of oil, the market draws on an increased supply of products from other regions.

To be sure, political leaders try to minimize these economic effects. Governments assume responsibility for enforcing the rule of law in order to protect citizens from harm; from a strictly economic standpoint, these same enforcement mechanisms provide security for market actors—consumers willing to travel to their local store to buy products, and merchants willing to open their doors, freed from the fear that their goods will be stolen rather than sold.

But while this analogy makes sense on the local level, and the U.S. government does have a responsibility for protecting American citizens in the United States, the U.S. government does not have a responsibility to protect merchants and consumers of other countries. That obligation falls to the countries themselves. Collectively, all Gulf states have an incentive to ensure that regional conflicts do not threaten the flow of oil; over the past two decades, however, policymakers in Washington have effectively absolved those regional players of the responsibility for policing their own markets by providing a military force for the Gulf. In this sense, the U.S. military serves as a sort of insurance policy, with the Gulf states—and their autocratic governments—as the beneficiaries, and the U.S. taxpayers paying the premiums.

U.S. policy in the Persian Gulf should not be based on the assumption that the region's energy resources will not make it to market without the presence of U.S. troops. Iraqi oil will begin to flow in earnest now that punitive economic sanctions have been lifted, and will accelerate as Iraq's oil damaged and decrepit equipment and infrastructure are returned to operability. Oil revenue will be the key to Iraq's rebuilding effort. It is in the interest of Iraq's government, even a government not necessarily committed to principles of western-style democracy, to ensure that its oil reaches global markets. Likewise, all Gulf states, including those countries governed by nondemocratic regimes, will continue to sell oil on the world market because it is in their economic interest to do so.

On a broader level, the Middle East need not be stabilized by an overwhelming American military presence. U.S. troops provide a greater level of security than what regional actors might choose to provide. To the extent that American troops have become a lightning rod for anti-American extremists, however, U.S. troops have been a notably destabilizing influence. In short, there is a middle ground between U.S. hegemony and total chaos wherein stability can exist without the presence of thousands of American troops and without generating an anti-American, anti-democratic backlash.

Other Objections to a Swift Withdrawal

Some observers have argued that the United States must remain in Iraq long enough to ensure that a pro-Western, multi-ethnic, liberal democratic government is elected and remains in power. AEI's Donnelly declared "the protection of the embryonic Iraqi democracy" to be a "duty that will likely extend for decades" similar to the defense of "Western Europe from the Soviet Union after World War II." But there is no global hegemon threatening to seize control of the entire Middle East, as the Soviets were poised to do to Europe in the early days of the Cold War. The collapse of Europe to Communist rule would have posed a direct threat to U.S. vital security interests, but no comparable situation exists in the Middle East (or anywhere else in the world, for that matter). The presumption that the American military must defend other countries from imagined future threats is a reflection of the persistence of Cold War–era thinking, 12 years after the end of the Cold War.

The argument that the U.S. military must protect and defend Iraqi democracy forgets or ignores that the primary justification for taking action was the removal of Saddam Hussein from power and the elimination of Iraq's weapons of mass destruction. Our servicemen and women fulfilled their mission by separating Saddam Hussein from the instruments of power. Hussein may have been the primary impediment to effective governance in Iraq, but the removal of this impediment is merely a useful byproduct of the American military victory. The United States cannot ensure that the Iraqis will elect liberal democrats to represent them. The tasks of governing must be left to the Iraqi people.

President [George W.] Bush argued before a group of Iraqi-Americans in Dearborn, Michigan, in April [2003] that freedom "is the universal hope of human beings in every culture." People with fresh memories of political and economic repression are unlikely to willingly choose anti-democratic rulers who would replace a secular autocracy under Hussein with a religious autocracy under the mullahs. However, it is possible, that the Iraqi people would choose to be governed by religious leaders who systematically trample individual rights. A slightly more plausible scenario involves voters unwittingly electing leaders who then transformed the government into an undemocratic regime through the process of one man, one vote, one time.

> *"The Middle East need not be stabilized by an overwhelming American military presence."*

Faced with either scenario, there appear to be two strands of thinking with respect to democracy in Iraq. Before the start of the war, President Bush declared, "The form and leadership of that government is for the Iraqi people to choose. Anything they choose will be better than the misery and torture and murder they have known under Saddam Hussein." He repeated that argument in Ohio, less than three weeks after the war's end: "One thing is certain," the president declared at the Lima Army Tank Plant: "We will not impose a government on Iraq. We will help that nation build a government of, by, and for the Iraqi people." On the other hand, Secretary of Defense Rumsfeld declared that the United States would not tolerate the creation of an Islamic regime in Iraq. When asked how the United States would respond if an Iranian-style theocracy were elected to power,

Rumsfeld replied "That isn't going to happen." Based on those and other comments, many observers expect that the United States will play an active role in promoting a certain type of government in Iraq. Those comments also suggest that the United States will prohibit certain individuals from holding office and overrule election results deemed unfavorable to U.S. interests.

> *"The United States should follow up its military victory and the establishment of a new Iraqi government with swift troop withdrawal from Iraq."*

But U.S. policymakers should not be unduly fearful that a democratically elected government—even a government not committed to principles of liberal democracy—would be hostile to Americans and American interests. It is appropriate and natural that we should "hope," as Rumsfeld said . . . that the Iraqis will choose "a system that will be democratic and have free speech and free press and freedom of religion," but the Bush administration should require only that the new government not pose a threat to the United States. Rumsfeld delineated some of those conditions as well, including the removal of the Baath Party from power and a prohibition on the possession of weapons of mass destruction. One should add to that list the requirement that the new government have no ties to Al Qaeda or other anti-U.S. terrorist organizations.

Beyond those prudent demands on the new Iraqi government, the United States can best encourage the emergence of a democratic government in Iraq by fostering an environment of economic engagement among private enterprises. The president's recent proposal to encourage trade in the region is a helpful measure in this regard. On the other hand, a heavy-handed attempt to engineer results of Iraqi elections will only engender further hostility and suspicion. As a recent study by the Washington Institute for Near East Peace warned, "America's endeavor in Iraq will ultimately fail if the United States attempts to remake Iraq in its own image." . . .

Policy Recommendations

The Bush administration opted for a policy of preventive war against Iraq, arguing that the risks of inaction outweighed the risks of action. That policy was based on a presumption of a swift victory and inherently dismissed warnings, raised prior to the war, that the removal of Hussein's regime might ultimately prove contrary to U.S. interests by destabilizing the region, fomenting ethnic conflict, and fanning the flames of Muslim resentment. Now that the United States has won a sweeping military victory, the following measures should be taken to ensure that we do not remain needlessly entangled in the region in the pursuit of dubious foreign policy objectives.

Allow the Iraqi People to Create Their Own System of Governance

As discussed above, members of the Bush administration seem to be trapped by their own rhetoric. On the one hand, the president has repeatedly declared his commitment to democracy and to allowing the Iraqi people to govern themselves. On the other hand, others in the administration have said that they will not allow an Islamic government similar to that in Iran to come to power. Florida senator and Democratic presidential hopeful Bob Graham noted the contradictions of the Bush administration's statements. Graham told viewers on ABC's *This Week*, "If you talk about democracy, which means that people vote and select the political leadership that they desire, then you can't say, 'But there are certain segments of the population that are off-limits.'"

Every day that the United States remains in Iraq in the pursuit of a particular system of government, the moderates will grow weaker and the extremists will become emboldened. This is the classic Catch-22 of nation-building efforts. The harder an occupying government tries to build a nation, the higher the likelihood that the citizens of the nation being "built" will grow to resent the efforts of well-meaning foreigners.

To ensure that American troops are not viewed as an occupying force imposing an unpopular government on a resentful populace, the United States must provide an environment for democratization. Having removed

> *"The United States can foster an atmosphere for reform in the Middle East . . . by adopting a largely hands-off approach."*

Saddam Hussein from power, the United States may rightly demand that the new government in Iraq not adopt a foreign policy that is hostile to the United States. In this vein, Washington may require that Iraqis disavow the possession of weapons of mass destruction and refuse to provide aid and comfort to Al Qaeda and other terrorist groups intent on harming Americans. But beyond deterring clear and direct threats to Americans and American vital interests, American policymakers in Washington and Iraq should direct all military and diplomatic efforts toward turning Iraq over to the Iraqi people promptly and should studiously avoid placing preconditions on the Iraqis that will slow progress toward self-government. . . .

Follow the Creation of a New Government with a Swift Exit from Iraq

The United States should follow up its military victory and the establishment of a new Iraqi government with swift troop withdrawal from Iraq. President Bush declared before the commencement of hostilities that American forces would remain in the country "as long as is necessary, and not a day more." A permanent American military presence in Iraq is simply unnecessary. The Iraqi people are exceptionally skilled as administrators, and they are therefore eminently capable of governing themselves. Iraq is blessed with enormous oil and natural gas resources that will provide a solid financial foundation for a new government.

The surest way to snatch defeat from the jaws of an overwhelming military victory would be to overstay our welcome in Iraq. Pockets of open resistance to the American and British forces have been quashed, but resentment lingers below the surface. American policy must be directed toward ensuring that this resentment does not spread. A sizable portion of the Iraqi citizenry will allow the coalition forces to carry forward an interim plan for stabilizing the Iraqi government and turning that government over to the Iraqi people. But this group is competing with fanatical elements opposed to an American occupation at all costs, who demand the immediate withdrawal of U.S. troops.

Follow the Withdrawal from Iraq with a Military Withdrawal from the Region

The Bush administration's wise decision to shift U.S. forces out of the kingdom of Saudi Arabia should be only the first of several steps to substantially reduce the U.S. presence throughout the region.

Americans rightly marvel at the proficiency of our armed forces, and American taxpayers have funded the military's transformation. The Pentagon should reorient policy in a way that takes advantage of our technological superiority and capitalizes on our ability to project power from a distance, by eliminating our expensive and unnecessary policy of forward deployment throughout the region. The troops are unnecessary. They are costly. And they do little to make the United States safer and more secure.

The Bush administration should clearly articulate its plans for removing troops from the region. It should follow up the Saudi announcement with changes to U.S. Navy deployment cycles, which have included a regular presence in the Persian Gulf since before the first Gulf War. It should make a clear statement about planned troop withdrawals from Iraq. The United States should also reconsider pre-positioning of forces and material in Turkey. The forces in Turkey were used primarily to police the northern no-fly zone over Iraq, protecting especially the ethnic Kurds living in the region. The no-fly zone operations, also known as Northern Watch, successfully protected the Kurds from Hussein's brutal repression, but are no longer needed now that Hussein is gone.

Fostering an Atmosphere for Reform

Before launching the military operation that ultimately resulted in the removal of Saddam Hussein from power, the Bush administration argued that this would set in motion a chain of events that would eventually democratize the entire region. That may happen, but U.S. policy should not be directed toward that end. Our overriding goal should be the protection of vital U.S. interests, and the mitigation or elimination of threats to the United States and its citizens. Given the United States' low standing in the region, skeptics are likely to question U.S. motives, inherently weakening would-be reformers. Rather than take a direct, active role in the creation of new governments in the region, the United States can foster an atmosphere for reform in the Middle East, including the expansion of liberal democratic principles, and free market economics and entrepreneurship, by adopting a largely hands-off approach.

U.S. policymakers should do so with a clear eye on the lessons of recent history. Many scholars warned of the dangers long before the [terrorist attacks] of

September 11 [2001]. There were alternatives to a lengthy U.S. presence in the region throughout the 1990s, a presence that most people realized posed grave risks for American military personnel, and American interests. There are even more alternatives today. A decision by the Bush administration to substantially reduce the number of U.S. military personnel stationed in the region will be welcomed by the troops, and by the U.S. taxpayers, and could set the stage for a stable and sustainable relationship between Americans and the men and women living in the Middle East for many years to come.

The United States Should Transfer the Administration of Iraq to the United Nations

by Stephen Zunes

About the author: *Stephen Zunes is Middle East editor for* Foreign Policy in Focus *and serves as an associate professor of politics and chair of the Peace & Justice Studies Program at the University of San Francisco.*

The invasion and occupation of Iraq posed new challenges to peace and justice activists. The growing credibility crisis of the Bush administration with respect to Iraq, as well as the ongoing crisis on the ground in Iraq, provides us with new opportunities. Below I present four theses on one campaign that could use these opportunities in a creative way: a campaign to turn the administration of Iraq over to the United Nations.

The Campaign

1. A United Nations administration would be more likely to bring peace and stability to Iraq.

The United States government is widely perceived by most Iraqis and other Middle Easterners as being less interested in the well-being of the Iraqi people than it is in the advancement of American political, military, and economic interests in the region. The apparent eagerness of the United States to invade Iraq, the gross exaggeration by U.S. officials of Iraq's military capabilities and its ties to terrorism, and many of the policies pursued by U.S. military authorities since the collapse of the Iraqi government have led many to see the U.S. invasion and occupation of Iraq not as an act of liberation but an act of imperialism.

As a result, there is a growing opposition in Iraq to the U.S. occupation, including a low-level armed insurgency against U.S. occupation forces, which has resulted in the deaths of scores of American servicemen. Most evidence suggests that these anti-American demonstrations and guerrilla attacks come not as much from supporters of the old regime but from ordinary Iraqis who resent a foreign military occupation of their country. Counter-insurgency operations by U.S. forces in response have resulted in the deaths of scores of Iraqi civilians, which has in turn led to an escalating spiral of violence.

> *"The Iraqi government that would emerge under UN trusteeship would be far more credible, both inside and outside Iraq, than one set up by U.S. occupation authorities."*

By contrast, administration by the United Nations—which represents the entire international community, including eighteen Arab states—is less likely to be seen as a foreign military occupation but rather as a transitional administration, and is therefore less likely to encourage armed opposition. Without the disruption of a growing armed insurgency, efforts at restoring basic services, maintaining stability, and setting up a democratic and representative Iraqi government would be far easier.

The Iraqi government that would emerge under UN trusteeship would be far more credible, both inside and outside Iraq, than one set up by U.S. occupation authorities, which—rightly or wrongly—would more likely be seen as nothing more than a puppet regime installed by a foreign army. Should such a U.S.-backed regime indeed not be seen as legitimate, popular resistance and instability—which would likely encourage the rise of radical nationalist and radical Islamist elements—would probably continue, requiring the continued presence of U.S. occupation forces for many years.

Supporting U.S. Interests

2. Turning over control of Iraq to the UN would be in the best interests of Americans.

American soldiers continue to die every week in Iraq. American deaths since the end of formal hostilities will likely soon surpass those killed during the war itself. The consultative council appointed by U.S. occupation forces appears to have little power or credibility among the population and Iraq appears to be a long way from genuine self-governance. It is unlikely that the Bush administration will be able to bring to power a new Iraqi regime that has the support of the majority of the Iraqi people.

The ongoing U.S. occupation of Iraq, particularly the killings of Iraqi civilians by American soldiers, is resulting in the growth of anti-American sentiment throughout the Arab and Islamic world. This could increase the ranks of extremist groups like the terrorist al Qaeda network, whose leaders are now more easily able to portray the United States as an imperialist power committed to the conquest and subjugation of Muslim peoples and the exploitation of the region's natural resources. This would be far more difficult to do, however, if Iraq were instead provisionally governed by an international regime under UN auspices.

The 150,000 American troops currently [in July 2003] deployed in Iraq are causing a shortage of available personnel for other potential U.S. military operations, ranging from peacekeeping operations in Liberia (which could help save that country from a humanitarian disaster) to challenging real threats to regional security (such as North Korea, which—unlike Iraq—really is developing a weapons of mass destruction program). In addition, the need for a large number of reservists to fill the ranks of U.S. occupation forces is having a detrimental impact on many thousands of families and businesses back home that depend on them.

In addition, the U.S. occupation is expensive. Currently, the American taxpayer is paying for more than 85% of the costs of the post-war occupation, peacekeeping, and administration in Iraq. Under UN leadership, U.S. contributions would be no more than 20%, a major savings for the American taxpayer that would make available funding for badly needed social services at home, as well as tax relief and deficit reduction.

A Greater Chance for Success

3. The United Nations could succeed in such an effort.

The United Nations, like other intergovernmental bodies, is an imperfect organization made up of a large number of governments with their own distinct national interests. However, because the UN represents virtually the entire international community and would be under a clear mandate to help bring stability and democracy to Iraq, it is less likely to allow narrow political and economic interests to shape its decisions.

There have been both successes and failures in major UN peacekeeping operations in the past. Most of the failures have been a result of inadequate funding and limits placed upon UN peacekeepers' authority, not anything innately lacking in the United Nations' ability to carry out its mission.

Rarely has the UN been called upon to govern an entire nation. The most clear-cut precedent for a direct UN administration of a country for a period of time until it was ready for self-rule involved East Timor. This former Portuguese colony was under

> *"Because the UN represents virtually the entire international community . . . it is less likely to allow narrow political and economic interests to shape its decisions."*

a UN trusteeship for two years between the withdrawal of Indonesian occupation forces and the establishment of an independent, democratically elected government last year [2002]. While much smaller than Iraq, East Timor in many ways presented an even more formidable challenge than Iraq: It is one of the poorest countries in the world, one-third of its population lost their lives in the initial Indonesian invasion and occupation in the late 1970s, and much of the country's infrastructure was destroyed in a scorched-earth policy by Indonesian occupation forces and their East Timorese collaborators as they withdrew in September 2000. Despite some logistical problems, the UN operation in East Timor has widely been hailed as a major success and the new East Timorese government has emerged as a strong and democratic U.S. ally.

Should the Bush administration decide it does not want any Americans to stay in Iraq under UN command, it could simply withdraw U.S. forces and not contribute to the peacekeeping operations. While the United States is indispensable in certain kinds of military operations, such as those requiring rapid power projection, there are more than adequate forces available for deployment in Iraq from other UN member states for the peacekeeping and administrative operations necessary to maintain order and oversee the transition to a democratic government. There are quite a few countries, including major Western European allies, which are currently unwilling to contribute troops under what they see as an illegal U.S. occupation that would be quite ready to submit forces under a legitimate UN operation.

Growing Support for UN Intervention

4. Such a campaign is winnable.

Public opinion polls published during the first week of July [2003] indicate that 60% of the American public believes that the United Nations should take leadership in post-war Iraq. Not surprisingly, there is strong support from liberals who have traditionally been skeptical of U.S. unilateralism and have supported a stronger role for the United Nations. However, there is also strong support from some moderates and conservatives who believe that there should be greater burden-sharing in the cause of nation-building and that it should not primarily be Americans who sacrifice lives and resources to bring greater freedom and stability to Iraq.

This could finally lead Democratic members of Congress and presidential aspirants, who have largely supported the U.S. invasion and occupation of Iraq, to distance themselves from the policies of the Bush administration and join the majority of Americans who support giving the United Nations the leading role in Iraq. The Bush administration has been able to get away with its policies toward Iraq up to this point because only smaller parties, like the Greens and Libertarians, have been willing to voice their opposition. With the Democrats joining the call for turning over administration and peacekeeping to the United Nations, the Bush administration would find itself far more isolated politically than it has been up until now.

The Bush administration is already finding that popular support for its policies in post-invasion Iraq is significantly less than during the actual invasion itself, particularly given the growing realization by the American public that they were misled regarding the threat Saddam Hussein's regime posed to the United

States and the world. There are already concerns among Republican leaders about facing an election year with American soldiers coming home from Iraq in body bags week after week with no clear end in sight.

Bush administration officials may decide that fighting off reasonable proposals for a UN administration may call into question their last remaining credible rationalization for the invasion: the desire to bring stability and democracy to Iraq. In insisting that the United States, not the international community, has the right to determine the future of Iraq, it would only increase uncharitable speculation regarding the actual U.S. motivation for controlling that oil-rich country. The result could be that the administration may find that it would be in its favor to cut its losses and acquiesce to domestic and international pressure.

A U.S. Occupation of Iraq Will Not Be Successful

by the *Progressive*

About the author: *The* Progressive *is a monthly magazine that supports peace, social and economic justice, and civil rights.*

> We ought to be beating our chests every day. We ought to look in a mirror and get proud and stick out our chests and suck in our bellies and say, "Damn, we're Americans." —General Jay Garner

No one wants to be occupied; no one wants to be colonized; no one wants to see foreign troops patrolling their streets. What most people want, around the world, is to rule themselves and to have enough food and water for their families.

For more than twelve years, the United States helped to decimate Iraq's food supply and pollute its water by insisting that the U.N. impose economic sanctions. (In a sadistic irony, [news commentator] George Will and others used the brutality of these sanctions as a justification for the war: Essentially, we need to invade your country so we can stop starving your kids.) As the United States rolled in, President [George W.] Bush and Defense Secretary Donald Rumsfeld assured the Iraqi people that the American conquerors would take care of them. But that care was not immediately forthcoming.

Protesting American Occupation

"With no law and no government, the people of Baghdad feel alone, afraid, and angry," Reuters reported on April 30 [2003]. "Three weeks after Saddam Hussein's overthrow, many parts of the capital still have no water or electricity, there are floods of sewage, and only a trickle of convoys have made it through with urgently needed food and medical supplies."

Reuters quoted a woman in Baghdad named Nada Ali: "It has never been this bad before," she said. "It just seems to get worse every day. I used to have hope, but I can no longer believe we will be saved. No one cares for us. I have four people at home and my husband was killed during fighting in Basra. I have no money, and I no longer know what to do."

One retired civil servant, Nizar Sarhan, told Reuters: "We did not defend Saddam because we did not want him. But if this situation continues, all the Iraqi people will fight the Americans."

It may be that General Jay Garner's colonial administration will start delivering the goods and thereby take some of the fuel away from this anger. But it's likely that the occupation will still rankle, and that the calls from Iraqi nationalists and Islamic fundamentalists will continue to draw thousands of protesters into the streets to demand that the Americans go home.

> *"You can exercise power at the barrel of a gun for only so long against a populace demanding self-determination."*

If anyone thought this occupation of Iraq was going to be easy, send them to Mosul or Falluja. On April 15 [2003], a crowd of 2,000 to 3,000 Iraqis in Mosul was protesting against the American occupation and, in particular, against Iraqi opposition leader Mishaan al-Jabouri, who claimed to be the new governor of this city of 700,000 people. When al-Jabouri spoke to the crowd and praised the Americans, many in the crowd responded by throwing rocks at him, according to several news accounts. As the crowd got rowdier, the Marines opened fire, killing at least ten Iraqis and wounding dozens of others. One of the wounded was an eleven-year-old girl who had been watching the protest from the roof of a nearby building. She ended up with a chunk of shrapnel embedded in her lung. The next day, U.S. soldiers killed three more people in Mosul.

Then, on April 28 in Falluja, 200 people reportedly had gathered to protest the fact that U.S. troops had taken over a school, but then what happened is unclear. U.S. troops say they were fired on from the crowd, and then returned fire, killing at least thirteen. The protesters say no one from the crowd shot at the Americans. On the morning of April 30, as demonstrators were denouncing the shootings, U.S. soldiers killed two more demonstrators.

This is what occupation looks like.

The Importance of Oil

With some justification, many Iraqis suspect that the primary reason for Bush's invasion was to grab Iraq's oil.

If it wasn't about oil, how come one of the first things the U.S. soldiers did was to secure the oil fields?

If it wasn't about oil, how come U.S. troops guarded the oil ministry, while they stood idly by as looters rampaged through the national museum?

If it wasn't about oil, how come Philip J. Carroll, former head of Shell Oil Company of the United States, has been appointed to run the oil ministry?

If it wasn't about oil, how come Rumsfeld's favorite, [leader of the Iraqi National Congress] Ahmad Chalabi, is on record as saying, "American companies will have a big shot at Iraqi oil"?

If it wasn't about oil, how come Rumsfeld took less than a week to use oil as a weapon by turning off the spigot on the pipeline between Iraq and Syria?

"Some argue that it's too simplistic to say this war is about oil," Naomi Klein wrote in *The Nation* on April 23 [2003]. "They're right. It's about oil, water, roads, trains, phones, ports, and drugs." General Garner may end up privatizing all of these industries, Klein says, arguing that this is corporate globalization at gunpoint. Who needs the IMF [International Monetary Fund], the World Bank, and the World Trade Organization when the Pentagon can do the job?

Privatization of Iraq's Economy

Klein is on to something. "State Department blueprints sent to Congress before the war began laid out a vision for Iraq's reconstruction that would move that country aggressively toward 'self-managed economic prosperity, with a market-based economy and privately owned enterprises,'" *The Washington Post* reported.

The privatization of Iraq's economy will be a bonanza for U.S. corporations. Halliburton already received a no-bid contract for as much as $7 billion to help rebuild Iraq's oil industry, though the final amount may turn out to be much less than that. Still, it "could benefit once a privatized Iraq oil industry begins handing out oil-service contracts," *Business Week* said. [Construction firm] Bechtel landed a contract for $680 million, and "Bechtel could also benefit if Iraq's economy thrives and the country can embark on a massive rehabilitation program," *Business Week* added.

The person the Bush Administration has picked to oversee the agriculture sector in Iraq is Dan Amstutz, a former senior executive of Cargill, the largest grain company in the world. "Putting Dan Amstutz in charge of agricultural reconstruction in Iraq is like putting Saddam Hussein in the chair of a human rights commission," said Kevin Watkins, [the international organization] Oxfam's policy director, according to an article in *The Observer* of London. "This guy is uniquely well-placed to advance the commercial interests of American grain companies and bust open the Iraqi market, but singularly ill-equipped to lead a reconstruction effort in a developing country."

A lot of U.S. companies are trying to climb aboard the Iraqi "gravy train," one Administration official told *U.S. News & World Report*. "It will cost billions to rebuild Iraq," the magazine noted. "Lots of firms are getting in line." And they are all American. Bush, Rumsfeld, and Garner are in no mood to reward French, Russian, or German companies. (By the way, Garner's chief Iraqi deputy, Emad Dhia, is on leave from his job at the Pfizer pharmaceutical company.)

The United States as a Colonial Power

The United States in Iraq is acting like Britain in colonial India, or Britain in colonial Iraq eighty-six years ago, for that matter. "Our armies do not come into your cities and lands as conquerors or enemies, but as liberators," British General Stanley Maude said after capturing Baghdad from the Ottomans in 1917. Iraqis did not enjoy being under British rule, and nationalist and Islamic forces rose up in 1920. Britain brutally put down that revolt after calling in bombers from the Royal Air Force.

We can only hope that Bush's war for the "liberation" of Iraq doesn't end with strafings from the U.S. Air Force. But how Bush intends to rule this country of twenty-four million people is difficult to imagine. U.S. troops may be there for a long time, and every second they remain, they will be sitting ducks for snipers and suicide bombers.

The United States is now a colonial power in Iraq, and the history of colonialism is clear: At some point, the colonialists lose. You can exercise power at the barrel of a gun for only so long against a populace demanding self-determination.

Feverishly, Donald Rumsfeld has been working to get an Iraqi face to front for the U.S. occupation, and Iraqi fingers to pull the triggers. But that won't mask the reality—or the folly—of the occupation.

The U.S. Occupation of Iraq Will Increase Terrorism

by William Norman Grigg

About the author: *William Norman Grigg is a senior editor at* New American, *a biweekly newsmagazine.*

The [2003] invasion of Iraq put an end to Saddam Hussein's dictatorship, which was symbolized by the dreaded "four A.M. knock on the door." Why, then, are Iraqis—the supposed beneficiaries of liberation—still facing that proverbial police state calling-card, now delivered by coalition troops, rather than Ba'athist thugs?

The June 15th [2003] *New York Times* described a U.S. military raid on a gas station in Fallujah, an Iraqi city seen as a stronghold for anti-American guerrillas. The raid involved an Abrams battle tank, four Bradley fighting vehicles, and a small infantry unit. The U.S. troops rousted a group of truck drivers sleeping near the gas station. "We are searching for weapons," one soldier explained. "We have nothing but potatoes," replied one of the drivers.

In Ramadi, a small town roughly 60 miles west of Baghdad, "the families were still asleep when the [U.S.] armored column rumbled into their village at 5:15 A.M.," recorded an AP [Associated Press] dispatch from Iraq. "These are coalition forces," announced an Arabic-language warning broadcast from loudspeakers. "Please stay in your homes and open your doors. Thank you for your cooperation." Men and women were led out of their homes, bound with plastic handcuffs, and detained in a nearby home while troops searched the village. This weapons sweep netted a single rifle. Commented local resident Abdul Qader Fahd: "The resistance is going to increase. Dealing with civilians like this is terrorism."

According to Fallujah resident Jassim Mohammed, whose two adult sons were arrested by troops during a weekend raid: "We got rid of one problem and now we have a bigger one. . . . Even Saddam never did this to us."

"The U.S. army has changed from being a liberator to an offensive occupier," insisted Iraqi Fawzi Shafi, editor of the new weekly newspaper *Sot il-Hurriye* (Voice of Freedom). "Last Friday [June 13 (2003)] they came into my house with about 25 troops," complained Shafi to the *Christian Science Monitor.* "They searched during breakfast and scared the children. They insulted us by putting us [face-down] on the floor in front of our women."

Certainly American troops are not brutal, sadistic thugs like Saddam's secret police. But as the war to oust Saddam morphed into an occupation of indefinite duration, our troops found themselves caught in a familiar predicament. Ambushes by Iraqi guerillas and imported foreign Mujahadin [freedom fighters] have made more aggressive security measures necessary; imposing such measures exacerbates the resentment of Iraqi civilians, generating further attacks. It's a familiar, if tragic, dynamic.

> *"Under U.S. occupation . . . Iraq is becoming an even more dangerous incubator of terrorism."*

Terrorism's purpose, as Marxist theoretician Carlos Marighella pointed out in his notorious *Mini-Manual for Urban Guerrillas,* is to provoke a crackdown to create optimum conditions for a political revolution. "First the urban guerrilla must use revolutionary violence to identify with popular causes and so win a popular base," explained Marighella. "Then, the government has no alternative except to intensify repression. The police roundups, house searches, arrests of innocent people make life in the city unbearable."

This revolutionary prescription has led to nearly unending bloodshed in Northern Ireland and Palestine. It threatens to do so as well in Iraq.

Echoes of Vietnam?

The official rhetoric emanating from the administration has also taken on a familiar Vietnam-era cadence: To pacify resistance and ensure the protection of occupation troops, efforts are being made to win the "hearts and minds" of the Iraqis. Reported the June 16th [2003] *New York Times:* "American troops pressed forward today in a new campaign combining military raids against suspected supporters of Saddam Hussein with high-visibility relief projects for Iraqi civilians. Commanders said they hoped that the two-sided approach would help eradicate armed resistance against American forces."

Accordingly, only hours after U.S. troops conducted armed raids in Baghdad to search for weapons, "military engineers set out to build soccer fields for children there. . . . In other parts of town, soldiers were giving out free gasoline. . . ." As Army reserve engineer Carleigh McCroy observes, "It's kind of contradictory for them. You bomb them, and three roads over you're fixing the school."

While many Iraqis are doubtless grateful for such amenities, others have suffered inconsolable losses and are eager for revenge. Thuluya, a relatively prosperous village 40 miles northwest of Baghdad, "has been transformed" by the death of three civilians accidentally killed during a coalition military operation, reported the June 15th [2003] *Washington Post*. The once-supportive Sunni Muslim population there "speaks of revenge."

During an arms sweep, U.S. troops arrested about 400 Thuluya residents, releasing all but 50 of them several days later. One of those temporarily detained was taxi driver Hashim Ibrahim Mohammed, who—like many others under Saddam's rule—joined the Ba'ath Party hoping to improve his children's career prospects. According to his account, U.S. troops "entered his house after midnight . . . put him on the ground, a boot on his back, and tied his hands with plastic handcuffs," reported the *Post*. Tape was placed over his mouth and he was blindfolded. Fourteen of Hashim's relatives were arrested. Hashim's 15-year-old nephew, also named Hashim, was among the three civilians killed during the raid. "I think the future's going to be very dark," warned Rahim Hamid Hammoud, a local judge. "We're seeing each day become worse than the last."

The purpose of President [George W.] Bush's photo-op aboard the *U.S.S. Abraham Lincoln* was supposedly to place the president before throngs of cheering sailors as he announced the end of "major combat operations" in Iraq. The propaganda backdrop behind him declared: "Mission Accomplished." Six weeks later [in July 2003], thousands of U.S. troops are still engaged in deadly combat missions against irregular forces, including Saddam loyalists and imported foreign Mujahadin. On June 15th, the amnesty period for Iraqis to turn in their firearms expired—which will almost certainly mean a significant escalation in fighting as U.S. troops ramp up efforts to seize proscribed weapons.

But at least the Iraqis are freer now than they were under Saddam's late, unlamented regime, correct? To adapt one of [former U.S. president] Bill Clinton's notorious formulations, that would depend on what the meaning of "free" is. Jacob Hornberger, president of the Future of Freedom Foundation, points out: "The Iraqi people are now living under direct military rule, with foreign military commanders ruling by decree. Democratic elections are prohibited, and political rulers are being selected by military commanders. Iraqi citizens are being required to turn in their weapons to the military authorities. There is a mandatory 11 P.M. curfew, enforced by soldiers. There are warrantless searches of homes and warrantless seizures of criminal suspects; these are conducted not by the police but by army troops. Occupation troops are killing demonstrators and suspected criminals without a trial or due process of law."

Bring Them Home!

That this state of affairs is intolerable for long-suffering Iraqis is obvious. But it's nearly as bad for the American troops who carry out the occupation. Twenty-one-year-old Sergeant Jaime Betancourt, who lost four of his buddies in a Baghdad car bombing in March [2003], has been called on to enforce the curfew and patrol Baghdad's streets. "I think . . . the most scary thing [was] trusting civilians, especially after the car bomb," Betancourt told the June 15th *New York Times*. After serving in the invasion force and enduring the car-bomb attack, he observes, "We didn't want nothing to do with these people anymore."

Private First Class Matthew C. O'Dell, an infantryman in Betancourt's platoon, offered an even more pointed observation: "You call [Secretary of Defense] Donald Rumsfeld and tell him our sorry a**es are ready to go home. Tell him to come spend a night in our building." Similar sentiments could probably be expressed by many other U.S. troops described in the *Times* story, who had served as UN peacekeepers in Bosnia and Kosovo before being deployed in the Iraq occupation.

Danger, tragedy, and death are inevitable features of war, and confronting them is unavoidably part of a soldier's life. Our nation's independence and our personal liberties exist, in large measure, because brave, capable, honorable men enlist in our military and endure what most of us cannot even imagine. This is why it is a crime against our nation to waste our fighting men's lives in conflicts that have nothing to do with protecting our freedom and independence.

Saddam, despicable as he was, never posed a serious threat to our nation. Under U.S. occupation, with American troops being used to carry out a mission that will create anti-American hatred, Iraq is becoming an even more dangerous incubator of terrorism.

Chapter 3

Do the Iraqis Have a Good Quality of Life?

Chapter Preface

In an interview with the international organization Human Rights Watch, Settar Khalaf, a cattle herder living near Basra in southern Iraq, recounted a day in spring 1999. In a remote area where Khalaf regularly took his herd, he saw a bulldozer dig three trenches. The following morning he watched several buses and six government cars arrive on the site. Hiding close to the vehicles, Khalaf saw men in military attire exiting from the cars and removing prisoners, blindfolded and handcuffed, from the buses. According to his estimates, there were approximately one hundred people in the buses. The prisoners were led in a line to the trenches, into which they were placed one by one. Seconds later, the men in uniform began shooting at the prisoners with machine guns and pistols for several minutes. Then a bulldozer covered up the trenches.

This site became one of many mass graves that have been discovered in Iraq following the 2003 overthrow of Saddam Hussein's regime—evidence of the extreme brutality that many Iraqi people suffered under this dictatorship. Under Hussein's regime, Iraq's citizens suffered constant human rights violations, living in fear of arbitrary arrest, torture, and death. Today, with Hussein's government toppled, Iraqis no longer live in fear of being led away by his secret police; however, there is continued debate over what the quality of life is like in Iraq.

Iraq's people have a long history of suffering. According to the Coalition Provisional Authority, the American-led interim government in Iraq, over 250 mass graves have been reported in Iraq, but the hundreds of thousands of people thought to be buried in them are only part of the huge number of total Iraqis believed to have disappeared under Hussein's rule. Millions of people have reportedly gone missing as a result of executions, wars, and defections. In 1988 Hussein is said to have used chemical weapons against the Kurds, a minority ethnic group living in northern Iraq, killing an estimated five thousand innocent civilians living in the Iraqi town of Halabja, many of them women and children. The chemicals contaminated the food and water supply, and according to Kurdish physician Fouad Baban, the effects of the attack continue today, with high rates of miscarriage, infertility, and birth defects among Kurds living near Halabja.

Following the overthrow of Hussein's regime, many people believe that the quality of life in Iraq has improved dramatically simply because the people are free. Writer Amir Taheri states in the *National Review*,

> A society where people hardly spoke to one another, let alone to strangers, is bustling with talk, debates, disputes, and demonstrations for every cause under the sun. Thousands of banned books are on sale in the streets, and over 200

new newspapers and magazines have started publication. People are no longer afraid to turn on their radios and TVs as loud as they wish.

Yet others argue that although the people are free, the quality of life in Iraq is still very poor due to a devastated economy and infrastructure. In November 2003, approximately 70 percent of Iraqis were unemployed and desperate for work. The authors in the following chapter offer their views on what the quality of life is like in Iraq after the 2003 war.

The Fall of Saddam Hussein's Regime Has Given the Iraqis Freedom

by Steven Vincent

About the author: *Steven Vincent is a freelance writer living in New York.*

By late October [2003], there seemed widespread agreement in the Western press that the United States was failing in Iraq [after its 2003 invasion], where I had been living for the past month and a half. Saddam Hussein, I was reminded by television reports and pieces on the Internet, was still at large[1]; the weapons of mass destruction that had been the ostensible reason for American intervention were looking like figments of "sexed-up" intelligence reports, if not a plot by the Bush administration to deceive the American people; and, by precipitously overturning the rock of the Baathist regime, the U.S. had succeeded only in releasing thieves, kidnappers, rapists, terrorists, and suicide bombers to prey at will on the Iraqi people. With its faked reasons for embarking on military adventurism and its patent inability to fulfill its postwar promises, America had earned the enmity of the world. And rightly so.

In Baghdad, however, the picture could not have looked more different. Waiters smiled at me when I identified myself as an American, cabbies brushed their palms together in a good-riddance gesture as they declared, "Saddam gone, America great!," and on the campus of Baghdad University I was approached by a man who wished to tell me "how honored Iraqis are that the Americans came to rid us of a tyrant." Opinion surveys attested to the conviction of most Iraqis that their lives would improve over the next five years, and their desire that coalition forces remain in the country at least until law and order were restored. With additional numbers of Iraqi police on the streets, this was already happening—rates of all major crimes were dropping.

---

1. Hussein was captured by U.S. forces in December 2003.

As for those elusive weapons of mass destruction, in my six weeks in the country I met precious few Iraqis who even alluded to them. Instead, they were focusing, with relief and gratitude, on what was perhaps the major reason [George W.] Bush had cited for going to war—the removal of Saddam Hussein. "Even if those weapons turn out to be an excuse for America to invade Iraq, I say fine," remarked Nasser Hasan, a poet and former member of the Iraqi national chess team whose translation skills and insights I would find invaluable during my visit. "Whatever it took to finish Saddam." Or, as a painter named Muhammad Rassim put it, "in our minds, the end of Saddam Hussein was the reason for going to war."

Endless Tales of Cruelty

How bad was Saddam? The question may seem naive: the answer, after all, lies in innumerable journalistic stories and has been documented, in hideous detail, in human-rights reports for everyone to see. But to appreciate the depth of Iraqi suffering under his decades-long rule you have to visit the country and absorb the seemingly endless individual tales of brutality and violence. They, in their nightmarish sum, constitute justification enough for the war against Saddam.

My own direct education began on my first day. The twelve-hour drive from Amman, Jordan to Baghdad ran through the area west of the city known as the "Sunni Triangle"—the traditional stronghold of Saddam loyalists. Here, in towns like Ramadi and Faluja, was where Baathist holdouts and their foreign recruits were still ambushing U.S. soldiers. As we drove, stretches of lush greenery rose up inexplicably from the surrounding desert. An Iraqi-American traveling with me explained that, to reward his followers, Saddam had created this "Garden of Eden" by diverting water from the Euphrates. But, as with everything in Iraq, that was not the whole story. In the early 1990's, seeking to suppress a revolt in southern Iraq, Saddam had dammed, burned, and bombarded nearly 12,000 square miles of marshes, causing catastrophic ecological damage. "In his way," commented my traveling companion, "he both turned a desert into a garden and a garden into a desert."

Like most moderately informed Americans, I had read stories of Saddam Hussein's cruelty: the estimated 5,000 killed in the 1988 poison-gas attack on the Kurdish city of Halabja,

> *"To appreciate the depth of Iraqi suffering . . . you have to visit the country and absorb the seemingly endless individual tales of brutality and violence."*

for example, or the grisly 1999 murder of the Shiite cleric Sadeq al-Sadr (Saddam's thugs drove nails into the grand ayatollah's head after first raping his sister in front of him). I had tended to relegate such tales to a familiar catch-all category: more evidence of the sorry state of world affairs. Not until the fall of the tyrant and my decision to see postwar Iraq for myself did I begin reading the documents prepared over the years by Amnesty International, Human Rights Watch, and other monitoring groups. They were shocking.

Iraqi Deaths Under Saddam

The first thing I discovered was that it was nearly impossible to compute how many people the tyrant had actually killed, whether by direct or indirect means. In 1980, for example, Saddam initiated his eight-year war with Iran, leading to the combat deaths of perhaps 375,000 Iraqis; in 1987–88, the notorious Anfal campaign to suppress anti-government sentiment in the Kurdish-dominated area of northern Iraq managed to do away with 100,000 people (including the inhabitants of Halabja). In 1990, he invaded Kuwait, provoking Gulf War I, which resulted in perhaps another 100,000 Iraqi combat deaths. Then there were the untold thousands of lives lost in the aftermath of that war, when Saddam brutally put down Shiite revolts in the southern part of the country. As for Gulf War II, an accurate tally of Iraqi combat and civilian deaths is still unavailable, but we can add to the bloody account every loyalist killed by U.S. troops and every innocent Iraqi caught in a crossfire.

This does not include summary executions. The UN and human-rights groups have noted Saddam's habit of "cleansing" prisons by killing their inmates. The record is appalling: in 1984, 4,000 political prisoners killed at the Abu Ghraib jail, and 2,500 more between 1997 and 1999; from 1993 through 1998, 3,000 inmates killed at the Mahjar prison, often by machine

> *"It was nearly impossible to compute how many people the tyrant had actually killed, whether by direct or indirect means."*

gun. In the south, Saddam murdered more than 100 prominent Shiite clerics. In 1999, security forces fired into a demonstration and killed hundreds of civilians, including many women and children. "Nonjudicial" executions of criminals and army deserters, often by means of beheading, likewise ran into the thousands.

To dispose of the bodies, Saddmn resorted to the expediency of mass graves. More than 100 of these bleak sites have been unearthed from the Kurdish north to the Shiite south, with perhaps hundreds more waiting to be dug up. (In September [2003], British authorities unearthed some 25 bodies buried under a traffic island in Basra.) The discovery of these killing fields has generated heartbreaking television scenes, with images of people frantically untying parcels of bones for evidence of missing loved ones. In one haunting scene, a man held a small bag of skeletal fragments to his nose as if to inhale the scent of his murdered son.

Torture

But in the catalogue of Saddam's evil, perhaps the most gruesome entry concerned the use of torture. Favored methods included the disfigurement and branding of criminals, such as chopping off fingers or tearing out tongues that had uttered anti-Saddam thoughts. Other methods involved rape, electric shock, beating with an axe handle, the penetration of victims' limbs and chests with a power drill, or the gradual lowering of bound captives into a bath of acid. Men were fed alive into wood-shredding machines. A general who had earned Saddam's displeasure was devoured by rabid dogs. According to one macabre report, women prisoners were forced to eat chunks of their own flesh that Baathist thugs had sliced from their bodies.

> *"Saddam's tyranny was complete, total, inextricably intermixed with the living cells of Iraqi society like a cancerous tumor."*

Then there were the refugees: nearly 100,000 Kurds driven from their homes in the Anfal campaign; 500,000 Shiites rendered homeless by the destruction of the southern marshes. Beginning in 1969, Saddam deported from Iraq tens of thousands of so-called Kurd Failyi, or people with the ill luck to be both Kurdish and Shiite; at least 10,000 of these unfortunates who once lived in the area of Baghdad are still missing, their whereabouts unknown.

The list goes on, extending from the massively grotesque to the petty—people forced from jobs, or denied jobs, or harassed by security officials, or simply forced to live lives of self-censorship and fear. Saddam's tyranny was complete, total, inextricably intermixed with the living cells of Iraqi society like a cancerous tumor that, under the world's neglect, grew and grew until forcibly removed by the United States.

Still, these were only reports, and I needed to hear with my own ears the testimony of survivors. And so one of my first stops in Baghdad was the National Association of Iraqi Human Rights, located in the Mustansiriya district northwest of the city's center.

"I deserted from the army and spent five years hiding from Saddam Hussein," said Asad al-Abady, the association's deputy director. His was one of the milder cases of persecution I heard about over several afternoons seated on a hard sofa in his sparsely furnished office. Founded in 1996 in Jordan—where its current director still lives—the association has seventeen offices throughout Iraq, making it the oldest and largest of the country's four human-rights groups. Its purpose is to collect information and personal testimony on a range of issues, from the plight of Iraqi refugees to instances of torture, rape, and execution. The idea is eventually to present the findings to the new ministry of human rights and the ministry of justice.

When I asked Abady about the number of case histories his group had accumulated, he responded by holding up a single gray folder. "This is a Baath party list, made in 1987, of 33 people whom the regime arrested in 1980 and who were at that point still awaiting trial. Sixteen years later, we have no idea what happened to them." He dropped the folder into a cardboard box filled with similar folders and slid it across the floor. "If you knew the contents of this one box alone, you would faint." Then he took me to a dusty room on the building's second floor, where, illuminated by sunlight filtering through a filthy window, stacks of folders lay toppled by their own height and strewn about in unequal piles. "We have," Abady noted, "seventeen more rooms like this in our branches across the country."

A typical case involved an elderly woman named Maha Fattah Karah, whom they summoned to speak with me. Shrouded in black purdah, she settled into a chair in Abady's office and in animated Arabic (translated for my benefit by the poet Hasan) began her story. In the 1980's, her husband had fled to Iran to avoid arrest by Baathists, who claimed that he had been "unfaithful" to the regime. The party then confiscated Maha's home and belongings, throwing her into the street with her three children. A few years later, Baathists arrested her eldest son on the same charge of unfaithfulness and executed him—taking pains, Maha noted, to charge her for the price of the bullet. Hearing about his son's death, Maha's husband returned to Iraq, only to be seized by security agents, imprisoned for five years, and executed. He was buried in a graveyard, but the regime forbade Maha or her surviving children to visit it.

At this point, the woman became so shaken that Abady motioned me to stop questioning her. Rising from her chair, she stretched out her palms and began to plead. "I look to America," she sobbed. "I ask America to help me. I ask America not to forget me." Then, supported by two young men, she turned and left.

Mass Graves

Abady's office had by now become crowded with men. When I asked about mass graves, a murmur passed among them. According to one of them, a doctor named Abdul Hadj Mushtak, the group had discovered three huge burial sites just south of Baghdad, each containing between 14,000 and 17,000 skeletons. "Iraqis knew generally where these places were, but not exactly," Mushtak recalled. "Our investigators found them and alerted the U.S. authorities."

The story was taken up by Fadel Abbas Kazen, a lawyer who was one of the first on the scene at a killing field near the village of Emam Baker bin Ali. "Bones and skeletal remains lay just under the surface of the earth," he told me. "I watched as people began digging up bodies, some of them with clothing still hanging from the bones. Some people had been killed before being buried, but some had

"Right in Baghdad itself there were quite a few such people . . . who seemed to ignore the record of Saddam's crimes as they vented their anger against the war."

been buried alive." In some cases death had come so unexpectedly that women who had gone to fetch water from a nearby river were buried with basins still clutched in their hands. "Behind a nearby police station, we found another grave containing fifteen more bodies," Fadel continued. In the following days, he oversaw the reburial of some 670 skeletons. "In a thousand years, there have been few tyrants like Saddam Hussein," the lawyer finished, fingering his prayer beads.

A Life of Constant Terror

I heard this refrain numerous times in Iraq: Saddam's evil was in a category of its own. Because his regime lasted 35 years, because Iraq is a relatively small nation, because he was so open and boastful about his tyranny—and because the outside world seemed so ready to ignore his crimes—there seemed no way for Iraqis to escape his grasp. "I have lived my entire life with that man in power," said Rand Matti Petros, the twenty-six-year-old manager of an Internet cafe in Baghdad. "I wake up each morning terrified that I've been dreaming and he's not really gone."

The painter Rassim described to me how the mere act of talking with foreigners at an art exhibition could result in being hauled away for hours of questioning by the dread Mukhabarat secret police. (A sculptor by the name of Haider Wady related that he had had to fend off demands from the Mukhabarat to procure foreign women for them to "date.") Mushtak recalled how his teenage son had once blurted, "I hate Saddam Hussein!" to a group of close friends, only to find himself arrested a few hours later. The police demanded a million Iraqi dinars to free him, and then 200,000 more. "My wife and I never discussed politics in front of our children," he told me. "We never knew when one might accidentally reveal something to an informer."

A few people I met had suffered worse and lived to tell about it. One was a former high-ranking Shiite cleric whom I will call Ahmed. In the late 1990's, accused by the Baathists of collaborating with anti-government Shiite groups in Europe, he was arrested and imprisoned for several years. In prison he underwent torture. "My hands were tied behind my back and I was hoisted off the ground, sometimes for as long as three days." He went on to describe how his captors shocked him with electric wires charged by a hand-turned military generator and beat him with thick rubber cables. Ahmed was now a broken man: the right side of his body had lost much of its feeling and his right leg, withered by disease contracted in prison, was no thicker than a man's arm. Growing more agitated as he concluded his story, he confessed that the greatest damage from the torture was spiritual, that "it made me question my faith. Today, I am an atheist."

Denial of Saddam's Crimes

Stories likes these, defining the reality of Iraq under Saddam Hussein, made me begin to wonder how Iraqis were dealing with the fact that many outsiders seemed to question the value of their country's liberation. Among those I talked to, the prevalent reaction was sheer disbelief. "If they had lived for five minutes under Saddam they wouldn't think like this," expostulated an Iraqi translator for the U.S. military. Yet right in Baghdad itself there were quite a few such people: journalists, representatives of non-governmental organizations (NGO's), peace activists, and others who seemed to ignore the record of Saddam's crimes as they vented their anger against the war.

I met "humanitarian workers" in Baghdad who, even as they decried the U.S. "occupation" of the country, would fall into an embarrassed silence when I mentioned Saddam's atrocities, and "peace activists" who suggested that the terrible image the world has of Saddam Hussein was largely the creation of "U.S. propaganda." One Dutch photographer argued that Saddam's attack on Iran was no worse than "America's invasion of Vietnam" and that Baath-party members were mostly "guys just looking for jobs." When I tried to describe to a worker for a Canadian NGO some of the findings of the human-rights association, he shrugged and waggled his hand as if to say, "Yeah, yeah, we've heard all this before." Impatiently, he burst out: "Yours is the real rogue nation."

> *"Washington has given the Iraqi people, and perhaps the Middle East as a whole, something they never possessed before—a future."*

I asked Hasan what he thought of the seemingly worldwide resistance to acknowledging the horrible reality of Saddam Hussein's crimes. He began by reminding me that some Iraqis practiced their own form of denial: for the most part, these were small-business owners, older artists, and intellectuals who, while not actively collaborating with the Baathists, had nevertheless thrived on their support. (I had encountered a number of such individuals myself.) Then he turned for wisdom to Shakespeare. "People who 'forget' about Saddam are like Gertrude in *Hamlet*. She chose to 'forget' about the murder of her husband to get on with her life, and encouraged her son to do the same. But the voices of the dead will not be silent. Like the ghost of Hamlet's father, they will not rest until some sort of justice is brought to Iraq."

A Future of Freedom

Justice: ask an Iraqi and you will be told that, along with freedom and stability, justice is the third reason why America needs not only to be in Iraq but to stay there. Because of U.S. power, Iraqis already enjoy an independent judiciary and a police force no longer made up of thugs and gangsters. Though Saddam himself remains uncaught, the continued presence of coalition troops is a pledge that his henchmen and *fedayeen* will not escape unpunished or fall into the hands of a vengeful mob but will face the just retribution of law. It is by means such as these, my interlocutors urged upon me, that Washington has given the Iraqi people, and perhaps the Middle East as a whole, something they never possessed before—a future. "There are no barriers for us now," a young Iraqi said to me gleefully.

That is not true, of course; there are barriers aplenty. The work of reconstruction—political, social, and cultural no less than physical—is gargantuan, long-term, and beset with peril. But increasing its difficulty is the historical and moral amnesia exhibited by the anti-war camp toward the crimes of Saddam Hussein. Castigating the United States rather than the tyrant it deposed, refusing to acknowledge the great good our nation has accomplished, these peace activists, Western politicians, international journalists, and intellectuals threaten the rebirth of the country for whose fate they profess to care.

Living Conditions in Iraq Are Improving After the War

by Thomas J. Basile

About the author: *Thomas J. Basile is the senior press adviser to the Coalition Provisional Authority in Iraq.*

Editor's Note: The following excerpt is based on queries submitted to Thomas J. Basile at "Ask the White House," an online interactive forum where individuals can submit questions to Bush administration officials.

Ashleigh, from Clemson writes: Tom, how stretched is the U.S. military troops?
Tom Basile: Thank you for the question.

As Secretary [of Defense Donald] Rumsfeld has said, we have enough troops in Iraq to handle the job. In addition to the American presence, a number of Coalition partners including Great Britain, Poland, and Spain also have troops in Iraq performing vital functions.

What is important to note when talking about the numbers of troops needed, is that each week more and more Iraqis are working alongside Coalition forces to help secure the country. In just six months [since May 2003] nearly 100,000 Iraqis have answered this call to service. On some nights Coalition troops are conducting as many as 1700 joint patrols with security services like the Iraqi Police and Civil Defense Corps. Many of these Iraqi assets have already helped relieve American and Coalition forces in some roles such as facility and infrastructure protection.

The Coalition is also standing up a new Iraqi Army, the first battalion of which graduated from basic training last month [October 2003]. We are on target for training nearly 40,000 new Iraqi Army troops by next fall. These troops will assist Coalition forces and be prepared to help secure the country when sovereignty is transferred back to the Iraqi people.

Thomas J. Basile, "Ask the White House," www.whitehouse.gov, November 6, 2003.

Before and After War

Meghan, from Chatsworth, CA writes: What's it like in Bahgdad right now? What are the major noticable differences between March 18th [2003] (I think that was day before we started attacks) and now [in November 2003], as far as daily life goes? How's the general morale of the troops that you've been in contact with?

Basile: Excellent question Meghan.

There are many differences between now and prior to the conflict or just after liberation. I'd like to focus on a few. Prior to the conflict, the children in the dilapidated schools of this country were pledging allegiance to Saddam [Hussein]. Now they pledge their allegiance to Iraq. In the area of education, we have seen marked progress in creating an educational environment that will breed hope not hate. This was a country that did not have a

> *"In the area of education, we have seen marked progress in creating an educational environment that will breed hope not hate."*

funded school maintenance program for over a decade. Conditions in schools were so bad enrollment had dropped to nearly 50% of eligible children in some areas.

Today, the Coalition and its partners are working with the Iraqi people to renovate the schools of this country. To date we have completed more than 1600 renovations, delivered tens of thousands of school supply kits, and increased teacher salaries many times over. Today Parent Teacher Associations are popping up across the country and for the first time, parents and educators are coming together to ensure a better atmosphere for learning.

The other major difference is the seeds of democracy taking root throughout Iraq. Where freedom of association was once restricted, now people of all segments of the population are coming together to make decisions about their future. In Baghdad alone, residents have selected 88 neighborhood advisory councils to help communicate the needs of the population to the City and the Coalition. This type of stewardship, cooperation and accountability is a major change for a people that suffered under the thumb of dictatorship. And they are already improving their quality of life.

As for our troops—they are heroes. They are professionals who in my opinion understand the importance of this mission and are committed to seeing it through. They deserve the respect of all Americans for the outstanding job they continue to do here in Iraq and in the war on terror.

Iraqi People

Rob, from Evansville writes: I'd like to hear a personal observation about the Iraqi people. Perhaps one Iraqi person that has touched your life.

Basile: I have found that the vast majority of the Iraqi people are thankful for our assistance in liberating their country from Saddam. They are a noble and proud people with a rich history and a strong sense of nationalism. They are proud to be Iraqis.

A couple of months ago, I had the opportunity to sit down with the man who would go on to become the Chief the Iraqi Supreme Court. I sat in his plainly furnished office in downtown Baghdad and listened as he spoke about finally ending the days of cutting out tongues, branding, other tortures and government interference with the judicial process. His enthusiasm as he talked about human rights and restoring the great legal tradition of Iraq, once widely regarded as the most respected in the region, filled the room with energy. I walked away from that encounter with a belief I still hold—and hold stronger today than then—that the Iraqi people are ready for democracy.

There are those former regime loyalists that crave the power they once had and seek to halt this progress. While they may try, the Iraqi people I continue to meet every day are ready for this change.

Not Alone

Greg, from Middleton writes: As the sole superpower of the world, I understand the need for the U.S. to get involved in other areas of the world, but I think we need more support from other countries. I don't like the fact that we are doing this completely alone.

Basile: We are not alone in this effort. At this time, 30 countries in addition to the US have contributed to the Coalition effort in Iraq. They have sent troops, engineers, equipment funds and advisors necessary for the reconstruction effort. Every day I walk though the CPA [Coalition Provisional Authority] headquarters and see a new uniform or hear a new language I hadn't before. Further, at the recent [October 2003] Madrid Donor's Conference nations from around the world pledged more than $10 billion in financial support for the reconstruction effort.

"Where freedom of association was once restricted, now people of all segments of the population are coming together to make decisions about their future."

We have had broad international support from the beginning and that support continues to grow.

Iraqi Law Enforcement

Kate, from Pawtucket writes: I think I'm like most Americans and would prefer to see the Iraqis take control of their country as soon as possible. Personally, I would like to see that now. My question has to do with Iraq patrolling their own streets. How many Iraqis are doing this? Are there any Iraqi policemen? They need to take over.

Basile: The Coalition agrees with you about turning control over to the Iraqi people. The President and Ambassador [Paul] Bremer have said that the goal of the CPA is to put ourselves out of a job. We want to leave Iraq a nation free and at peace.

However, now is clearly not the time to pull out our presence. We are making great strides toward helping the Iraqis build a better nation. The Coalition has articulated a seven point plan for creating the institutions of democracy here.

> *"In towns, villages and cities across Iraq we are seeing people come forward to serve on city councils, district councils, and village advisory boards."*

In just the past few months, the governing council has convened, it has appointed ministers to run the day to day operations of government agencies, and the Iraqis are actively engaged in developing a process by which a constitution can be written.

Once the constitution is written and a government has been elected the CPA will cease to exist and sovereignty will be ceded back to the Iraqi people. It needs some time, but we are making progress every day.

As for the police, there are between 45,000 and 50,000 police on the streets right now in Iraq. They are conducting patrols with Coalition forces, enforcing laws and serving their people.

In Baghdad, nearly 80% of Iraqi Police stations are now in what we call a monitoring phase where Iraqis rather than MPs [military police] run the stations. The justice system is operating and the Iraqi police are interdicting crime every day. Some have already lost their lives in the line of duty to help secure Iraq.

Iraqis' Will

Rachel, from Newburyport writes: It is clear the Iraqi people don't want us in their country. Shouldn't we listen to the will of the people?

Basile: I have had the opportunity to travel throughout Iraq and I can say that the VAST majority of the Iraqi people are grateful for our assistance. Your view is not expressed by the average Iraqi on the street.

The Iraqis are a proud people and like any proud people, they would like to see the eventual departure of any occupying forces.

But the people I speak to, that includes members of the new Iraqi media, understand the importance of the Coalition's presence during this pivotal moment in their history.

Our presence is paving the way for an Iraq that will be a productive member of the free world.

Coverage of Accomplishments

Bill, from Colorado writes: It's absurd to compare our efforts in Iraq with how the [former president Lyndon B.] Johnson and [former president Richard]

Nixon administrations conducted battle in Vietnam. What would you say are the greatest accomplishments we've had in Iraq to date (after Saddam's removal) that you would like to see more coverage of?

Basile: Thanks for your question. I think one of the most striking differences and accomplishments in the last six months is democracy taking root in the country—in towns, villages and cities across Iraq we are seeing people come forward to serve on city councils, district councils, and village advisory boards. Many of these folks have already been elected by the local folks. They are working close with the Coalition to assess priorities, and to plan for the future of their communities. These councils are having great results. They are helping to improve infrastructure, helping set up jobs programs, and looking at various ways that they can improve the quality of life for their residents and they are learning that as leaders they are going to be held accountable for their actions. They are also learning as leaders that they need to be responsive to the members of their communities. The Coalition is working to train the councils on how to run meetings, parliamentary procedure, how to set up an agenda, how to set up subcommittees and how to promote community stewardship—these are things that were never done before and never done under the regime of Saddam Hussein.

Terrorism

Teddy, from Ocala, Florida writes: Some are saying that the U.S. presence in Iraq has actually increased terrorism. Obviously, you are not going to agree with that, but certainly Baghdad is not a peaceful place. How do we know that things are actually better? And furthermore, I don't get the notion that Iraq is the central front in the war on terror.

Basile: There are people in Iraq that are former regime loyalists and they are witnessing the progress and are trying to stop it. One of the reasons we have seen terrorist activity is because the terrorists are seeing success on the part of the Coalition and the Iraqis to create a better life here.

The markets are full with shoppers. The restaurants are full. There are new products in the stores. Children are going to school. The Universities are open. And we know things are getting better every day because we can see the Iraqi people are determined to see this reconstruction through for the betterment of their future. There is a return to normalcy to this country which can be seen everywhere—including Baghdad. Which is not to say there is not work to be done on the security front, there is.

> *"There is a return to normalcy to this country which can be seen everywhere—including Baghdad."*

But to talk to the people in Baghdad and in the majority of the country, they are going about their lives and are hopeful for the future. . . .

Day-to-Day Governing

Rick, from Washington, DC writes: Tom, Give us a sense of the day-to-day activities of the Provisional Authority staff and the working environment. Are most of you directly working with Iraqi citizens and officials?

Basile: Thanks for your question. In fact, we have many Iraqis working for the Coalition Provisional Authority, they work with us in offices, they serve as translators community and cultural liaisons and advisors. The Coalition recognizes that we need the help of the Iraqi people in order to help them rebuild the country and create the institutions of democracy that will enable this nation to flourish. We have formed very strong relationships with the Iraqis that we work with. It is an extraordinary experience to work at the CPA and to work so closely with the Iraqi people.

We work on a day-to-day basis with Iraqis from all segments of Iraqi society who believe and are working every day to ensure that when the CPA leaves Iraq they will leave a strong free nation for the Iraqi people.

As to the day-to-day activity, many of us work here in what is called the Republican Palace in Baghdad. The dedicated employees of the CPA—many work 16–18 hour days, they actively liaise with all of the Iraqi ministries, the Iraqi governing council, religious leaders, educators and businesspeople across the country.

It is an extraordinary experience to work at the CPA and to work so closely with the Iraqi people.

The Iraqi Press

Ashleigh, from Strasburg, PA writes: Dear Mr. Basile, How does the Iraqi press portray US forces and leaders? Do the Iraqi people appear to have the same thoughts and feelings toward America as their newspapers and news programs suggest?

Basile: I continue to be impressed with the burgeoning Iraqi press corps which is developing in the country. Prior to liberation, the media here was very tightly monitored and state run. Now we have over 170 newspapers in Iraq, there are new radio stations, the whole culture of investigative journalism is being established here amongst the journalists who are realizing that their work can have an impact on local officials. The Iraqi papers that we read on a daily basis appear to be fair and balanced. They are learning that as they report something in the city, council or coalition is stepping up to be responsive to the people who are in that area. Many of these papers are neighborhood papers which don't have wide circulation which is helpful because they are the eyes and ears of the Iraqi people—they help us address residents concerns and prioritize our projects for reconstruction. So we've seen a very balanced approach on behalf of the Iraqi press and they have been very appreciative of the Coalition's willingness to engage with them on a regular basis. We engage with them at press conferences and at city hall in Baghdad. For the first time in history members of the press go to city hall every week and meet with city officials and Coalition officials and go and ask questions and get answers. We do get criticized occasionally in some of the Iraqi media outlets, but it is a free country and they can do that now where they couldn't before. And it is another sign of democracy taking root in Iraq. . . .

Trust Versus Revenge

David, from South Brunswick writes: Do the people of Iraq trust their own that have become police officers and civil servants or is there a fear of revenge that has been embedded over the years?

Basile: Good question. One of the first things the coalition did after liberation is institute a de-Baathification policy and the purpose of the policy was to effectively strip the government of all the high-ranking Baath party officials. There is a perception that is held by some, that the people would like to see elements of the baath party return—but being here in Iraq, I can tell you there is no love lost between the people of Iraq and the

> *"For the first time in history members of the press go to city hall every week and meet with city officials . . . and ask questions and get answers."*

Baath party. This policy was overwhelmingly accepted and has been implemented over time. This will go a long way toward helping people build confidence in government again. You have to consider that the people of Iraq for thirty years lived under the thumb of a corrupt totalitarian regime where government officials served the regime—not the people. And that definitely bred a culture of mistrust for law enforcement and for the government.

Part of our job working with the new leadership in Iraq will be to help create institutions of government that will build confidence and trust among the people of this country. The Iraqi people lived in fear of the secret police and other enforcers and informants that worked for the regime and Saddam Hussein. The new Iraqi security forces are being established with an ear toward human rights, new codes of conduct and standards of professionalism and accountability that did not exist during Saddam's rule.

A prime example of change is the establishment of a new Inspector General's office in the Iraqi police force. It will take time for the people of Iraq to build strong relationships with the government officials but after decades of distrust we would never expect it not to.

Stemming the Tide of Deaths

Seth, from Atlanta, GA writes: How do you see the Coalition Provisional Authority's role changing in the next six months [from November 2003]? Can you stem the tide of needless deaths, or are you already anachronistic?

Basile: First off, the Coalition's role over the next six months will be to continue the progress we have made in the first six months. We will be accelerating an augmentation of Iraqi police and Iraqi security forces that will work alongside the coalition to better secure the country and to interdict terrorism.

We also will be continuing to move forward working with the governing council to develop a process by which the constitution for this country can be written and the institutions of this document be instituted so that sovereignty can be ceded back to the Iraqi people and the CPA's mission can be successfully completed.

I get the impression from your question that you do not believe coming into this country has been worthwhile and that those who lost their lives in the pursuit of the liberation of this country died in vain. I have seen firsthand brutality of the former regime. I have had the privilege of visiting Halabjah where Saddam Hussein gassed 5,000 people; where women and children were burned alive in the streets. The survivors recognize the value and contributions of the international community. I have been to the southern part of the country where Saddam's brutality sought to destroy a 5,000 year old culture when he decimated the marshes that sustain the marsh Arabs of southern Iraq. Those people also recognize the brutality of the regime and will never forget the contributions that we are making here to restore their livelihood and their culture. And I've also met the man on the street who was hauled out of his home at gunpoint in front of his family and brought to the torture rooms for charges he still does not know. All of these people would disagree with you. In removing Saddam Hussein, we freed the people and we are giving them hope for the future. And we are contributing to the peace and stability of the world.

The Position of Iraqi Women Has Improved

by the U.S. Department of State

About the author: *The U.S. Department of State is the primary U.S. foreign affairs agency. It works to promote peace and stability in the United States and throughout the world.*

Representatives from a delegation of Iraqi women leaders said their country's politics and infrastructure were much improved since Saddam Hussein's regime was ousted by Coalition forces in April [2003].

The women, some of whom serve on the Iraqi Governing Council or the Baghdad City Advisory Council, spoke to journalists at Washington's Foreign Press Center November 19 [2003].

Raja Khuzai, a Governing Council representative, said that due to the oppression of the Ba'thists, "every honest Iraqi was happy with the war and welcome[d] the war."

"You don't know a dictatorship unless you live in it," she said.

Lina Abood, a gynecologist and obstetrician, reminded the audience of the thousands of unknown Iraqis buried in mass graves after being killed by Saddam's regime, while Siham Hamdan, a university lecturer and member of Baghdad's Advisory Council, said she appreciated the new freedom the Iraqi people had to criticize or demonstrate against their government.

Another Governing Council member, Songul Chapouk, said that many welcomed the Coalition invasion due to a strong desire to be released from the former regime. "We couldn't release ourselves because we don't have the power," she said.

The four women said the economic and security situation has also improved for women since the fall of Saddam Hussein.

Khuzai said there was some media exaggeration about the security problems in the country, including the situation of women. "Everything is back to normal," she said, with colleges and schools open, and hospitals running 24 hours a day.

U.S. Department of State, "Iraqi Women Say Life in Iraq Has Improved Since Saddam's Ouster," www.usinfo.state.gov, November 19, 2003.

Hamdan added that many of her female colleagues had returned to their jobs "because of the improvement in the economical situations, increasing their salaries."

"It's enough for us, war and killing," said council member Chapouk. "We need safety. We need peace. . . . We have to move and to ask for help from all countries, because Saddam left us without anything. He damaged everything, and we need now to rebuild Iraq again."

Khuzai said that besides improving security, job creation was also an immediate concern. She suggested creating a program similar to U.S. President Franklin Roosevelt's Civilian Conservation Corps (CCC) that employed hundreds of thousands of Americans during the depression period of the 1930's.

> *"Iraqi women must be planners, implementers and beneficiaries of all reconstruction efforts in Iraq."*

She also called for microcredit and microlending programs for small Iraqi businesses.

The State Department's Senior Coordinator for International Women's Issues, Charlotte Ponticelli, hosted the briefing. She said it was important for Iraqi women to be "planners, implementers and beneficiaries of all reconstruction efforts in Iraq."

"[T]he Iraqi women have clearly expressed their strong desire to be at the table at the highest of decision-making levels," she said.

Siham Hamdan also said outsiders should not doubt the ability of the Iraqi people to lead themselves. "We need every help now to encourage us, to push us forward, and not to bring us backwards to Saddam's regime, to Saddam's dictatorship," she said.

"So let us give the chance for Iraqis, for the first time, after 35 years . . . [to] rule themselves," said Hamdan. "We have trust in our people. We have to have this trust. We don't have a lot of alternative; otherwise, we cannot accept a foreigner to rule us, even for one day."

Following is a transcript of the Iraqi women's delegation at the Foreign Press Center. . . .

These Brave Women

Charlotte Ponticelli: Thank you so much. . . . It really is a great pleasure to be here today at the Foreign Press Center, and to meet again with these truly distinguished Iraqi women leaders, some of whom I met, actually, for the first time during a recent trip to Baghdad. All of these women are dedicated to a better future for their families and their communities, and they are determined to make that future work for all Iraqis, men and women.

As President [George W.] Bush mentioned to these women who are here today, when he met with them earlier this week at the White House, the stories of the courageous leaders are "stories of human tragedy on the one hand and human hope on the other." Our discussions with this delegation over the past week are really a continuation of our ongoing dialogue with the women of Iraq. It's a dialogue that's already spawned great cooperation and ideas.

In our discussions with these brave women, both here and in Baghdad, several key issues have emerged. In addition to concerns about the security situation, the Iraqi women have clearly expressed their strong desire to be at the table at the highest of decision-making levels.

Songul and Raja on the Governing Council, and Siham on the Baghdad City Advisory Council, I think are great examples of the political leadership role that women can and should be playing in Iraq. They and the rest of the group have made it clear that it is also important that women be involved in the constitutional drafting process, and we support their aspirations.

Iraqi women must be planners, implementers and beneficiaries of all reconstruction efforts in Iraq. All Iraqis must be involved in running their country, women and men. There are plenty of willing and able women, as we can see today, women like Dr. Lina Abood, who runs a clinic in Baghdad. She's a general practitioner of obstetrics and gynecology and sees about 200 patients a week. She's an example of the contributions that women are making now, today, in Iraq.

As President Bush has said, the Iraqi people are plenty capable of governing themselves. We recognize that and we're here to support them

"We need now to rebuild Iraq again. And women can do this. And we will win in this job."

any way we can. We know that training, including leadership, organization and networking programs, is something that we can do, and will continue to do to assist them. We are also working with many interested Americans who are stepping forward and volunteering their time and their talents to assist the women of Iraq, and will be helping to make those connections.

I'll end now, because I want you very much to hear from these pioneering women themselves, and I'd like to turn to my friend first, Songul Chapouk, who would like to say a few words. Thank you.

War Is Harder on Women

Songul Chapouk: Thank you. I think it's a pleasure for me to be here again. I was here before, a month and half. I joined a conference in Washington Institute, and I went to foreign affairs and State Department. And again, now I am here with my group of women, and we are enjoying it here, to be here, and it's a pleasure for us to serve our country, because we know that Iraqi people need help, especially the women. They need help, because the war affected on women more than men.

And if you saw the women in the war, they are all without men, without their husbands. I was without my husband, because he had to go to work, and to save, to protect the company he worked in. And I was alone with my children, in home. I suffered, from the bombs, from killings. I saw people killing. For three wars we saw it.

It's enough for us, war and killing. We need safety. We need peace. How we can reach it if we not move? We have to move and to ask for help from all countries, because Saddam left us without anything. He damaged everything, and we need now to rebuild Iraq again. And women can do this. And we will win in this job, inshaliah. . . .

Raja Khuzai: Thank you. This is my first visit to U.S., and I am very pleased, and I have learned a lot. I'm the head of the delegation, 17 women, leaders, and different ethnic and religious groups. This—really this is an example of the Iraq, the one-nation Iraq, the new Iraq. I am proud with this group.

We have met top officials here and we have discussed the role of women, especially in the constitution, the drafting process, and the legislation as well. Also, I have raised the point of security and the role of creating jobs for the unemployed. I think creation of jobs is very important, and security. And I raised the example of President Roosevelt and the Depression period, which is the CCC. If we create massive civil works, it will work, it will help our community.

The other thing is the small businesses and microcredits and microlending. This will help the Iraqis. They have suffered. We need to help them. The other thing that now, in this time, we are ready for local elections only. And then after that, we may do the national elections. . . .

The Situation of Women After the War

Question: . . . If you were to draw a curve on, you know, the situation for women in Iraq, let's say, from four weeks ago, until today, how would it go? It is worse, better, is it the same? . . .

Khuzai: It's better.

Question: Well, over the past, let's say, month, two and half months.

Khuzai: It's increasing now to improvement. There is an improvement. . . .

Lina Abood: Well, my profession is I'm a Ph.D. in obstetrics and gynecology, and I was running a maternity hospital, so I think I'll comment on this subject. There is a vast difference from now since before the war. We are much better, and health-wise, especially the women. The family planning clinics are running, you know, better than six months ago, or let us say, eight months ago. Even during the war, I was running the family planning clinic. I didn't leave it.

> *"So many of my colleagues . . . just returned back to their jobs because of the improvement in the economical situations, increasing their salaries."*

Question: Would any of you care to comment on the labor situation for women?

Chapouk: Yes. I think women's condition is good now, because if you see in the schools, teachers are coming to school and students also. That's good. That's every day. I saw people that were leaving from home to school, and nothing happened. Even you saw if something happened. That wasn't happened to every day. It was just for a day. It wasn't for—it was for a day, not all the days. And people leaving their home safely and go to work. I saw many people. And my sisters. They are doctors. They are engineers and teachers, and I didn't heard from them any day that they left their job. They are working. Since the war, it is better.

> *"Colleges are open, schools are open, hospitals running 24 hours a day; everything is back to normal."*

Siham Hamdan: I want to add to that that so many of my colleagues, doctors, especially female, they just returned back to their jobs because of the improvement in the economical situations, increasing their salaries, and that's good. . . .

Security

Question: Thank you. This is Tulin Daloglu from Turkey's Star TV. I am just wondering whether you can bring the lives of women in Iraq much closer to us. Still the security is a serious threat. Immediately after the war, we read stories that women were scared to leave their houses because they were scared to be raped, but then there was the issue, the cultural issue, the religious issue that they are so ashamed to talk about this.

Now the security seems still a serious concern. I wonder how it is like in Baghdad. You're all coming from Baghdad, I assume. What is—how do you spend a day—not you, but maybe the women around you? Are they still afraid to leave their homes? Is rape still an issue? Do you have patients coming up, and are they now talking about it, or is it still, within this traditional and religious trend, a sacred issue that they do not talk? Can you directly refer to the issues of women that how they are doing in this difficult time?

Khuzai: Well, there is a lot of exaggeration about the security problem, and the women—about women, especially. I don't know why they concentrate and focus on women can't leave houses. This is an exaggeration. Well, my daughter is 21, and she is going to College of Pharmacy every day. I never worried about her. Okay?

Colleges are open, schools are open, hospitals running 24 hours a day; everything is back to normal. It's just the media. They focus on these negative things. They never focus on the positive things. Okay? And I, as an obstetrician, I never seen a case of rape—okay—till I was appointed as a Governing Council member in 13th of July [2003]. Okay? So really it's exaggeration. I don't know. It's the media. . . .

Abood: I want to answer this. Yeah. We can say some cases, I mean, shortly after the war, but now the conditions, there is a great improvement for myself and going to my clinic is, you know, easily, and I can stay there, and but for a limited time, but it's getting more and more improvement in Baghdad, especially. And these numbers of raped women and killing, it has been exaggerated after the war because, all of us, we are working in the hospitals and not seeing this large number of these cases. . . .

Question: Yeah. My name is Reha Atasagan with the Turkish Television. And my question is to members of the Governing Council, Mrs. Chapouk and Khuzai.

When you took over as the members of the Governing Council, did you believe that you represent Iraqi people, and how could you make decision on behalf of the Iraqi people when you are not elected? You said, you know, it took time for us to get the right decisions. So you were not representing the Iraqi people.

And, secondly, I mean, I don't believe when you say there is no security problem. I mean, the whole world is talking about this security. UN [United Nations] withdraw itself from Baghdad, and there is this great operation going on with the American forces. I mean, how can you—I mean, it's a kind of a denying that the security—we all wish there is security there, but, I mean, we don't see any security. . . .

Biased Media?

Chapouk: Yeah. About the American forces, I have American escort with me, and I didn't see any Iraqi people hurt them or hate them. When they saw them, they are very proud of them, and they shake hand with them, and they give them flowers, honestly. This is what I am there. And the security problem, I called my husband the last night. He said there is nothing.

And also, I called Kirkuk, where is my family, and I asked my sister whether my children going to school. Do you know I have a daughter, 13 years old? She go to school alone and by walk. Nobody ask her "why you are going?" Even her friends also. They are coming from far away, and they are coming by walk. Nobody against women. This is wrong.

And these people [who] are doing these things, they are not Iraqi. They are not Iraqi. They are doing something here, and here, and here, and to show the media that Iraqi security is bad. Why it is bad? I saw Iraqi policemen, they're working at night. They are very brave. And American forces, also they are protecting people, they're helping Iraqi people.

> *"These numbers of raped women and killing, it has been exaggerated after the war . . . we are working in the hospitals and not seeing this large number of these cases."*

What they have done, the media, let our media to be? Where is our media? We don't have media. Foreign media told you all, [Arab news media] al-Jazeera and Arabiya told you these things. We don't have our media. And if you go and everything, everything happened that there is a media zoo there.

I don't know. They make a deal with them? They meet in secret with them? I don't know. They pay for them to do all these things? There is many people trying to make all of these things for Iraqi people, and I think Iraqi people are strong.

> *"When the war happened, I was happy, and every Iraqi was happy because we want to [be] release[d] [from the Saddam Hussein regime]."*

And you said we are not elected. How you can make election in Iraq now? There is no—nothing. We don't have anything. How we can make election? We have to choose people to rule, and then if we find, if we make a counting of population, then it will be election for Iraqi people. We will not stay forever. We are ruling Iraq for just for the time [being], not all the time. And when they want us, elected us, we will stay. And if they not want us, we will leave. But our aim [is] to serve Iraq. If I don't go to serve Iraq, and she don't, who will serve Iraq, who will protect Iraq, who will govern Iraq? We need Iraqi people to go out, and to not be afraid.

Abood: Yeah. I want to answer. I can say that the security in Iraq now is affecting both men and women equally because we are suffering from only the terrorism attacks, not from other cases like robbery operations or killing or kidnapping or something else. So that's the critical situation here.

Khuzai: Well, I, myself, and all my colleagues in the Governing Council, we represent most of the Iraqis. And this is the thing, you know, it is a transitional period. How can you do it, you know? This is the only way. This is the only way. We can't do elections straightaway after the war. We need time. . . .

Released from Dictatorship

Question: . . . This is addressed to the first speaker, who made a really moving reference about impact of war on women and children, so on, so forth. So what were your thoughts on the eve of the war, before the war? Were you afraid of the coming war, and did you protest about it?

Chapouk: When the war happened, I was happy, and every Iraqi was happy because we want to [be] release[d]. It's enough for us. If American people must come to release us, and these forces, coalition forces, if they not came, who can release us from Saddam? We couldn't release ourselves because we don't have the power.

Then they came and the war start. Everybody in Iraq was happy because we will be free and we can—and every bomb come on the building of Saddam, we prayed for God to kill these people, to remove these people, and we didn't protect ourselves. We have been in our homes. Iraqi people not afraid of war because the war was the right thing. It happened in Iraq, this war, because it was for freedom, for Iraqi freedom. And did you see the children when the forces came? Everybody was happy.

Khuzai: You don't know a dictatorship unless you live in it, so nobody here knows what dictatorship means. Dictatorship, we lived in it: Well, you can't talk, you just can't criticize the government. You can't criticize Saddam or his sons. If you do so, and somebody hear you, the least punishment is cutting of the tongue; otherwise, you will be executed. So every Iraqi, every honest Iraqi, was happy with the war and welcomes the war.

Abood: I think all of you saw the mass graves, and there are a number of thousands of people that are not—they are, until now, missed, and we don't know their fate. They are just dissolved by an acidic materials or just cutted into pieces into the river of the Tigris. I want you to know this information.

The Former Regime Inflicted Lasting Damage on the Iraqi People

by David Brooks

About the author: *David Brooks is a contributing editor for the* Atlantic Monthly, *and a regular commentator on National Public Radio, CNN's* Late Edition, *and* The NewsHour with Jim Lehrer.

In the early 1990s, while covering the decline and fall of the Soviet Union, I observed a curious phenomenon. The inside of every apartment I visited was tidy and clean. But every building's vestibule, hallways, and stairs were filthy and rancid. The floors looked as if they'd never been mopped; lights were burned out; the air reeked of urine. I started asking people why they didn't get together to clean up the hallways. After all, I'd say, there are four or five families living on your floor. A half hour's shared work and it would be done.

They'd give various reasons: The neighbor on this side is an alcoholic. The neighbor on that side we never see. But the real reason was that after seven decades of living under totalitarianism, they didn't know whom they could trust; they didn't know if their neighbors belonged to the secret police. By that time citizens were no longer being sent off in large numbers to the gulags for minor or manufactured crimes, but the bonds of normal society had been destroyed. People's souls had been damaged by decades of terror and mass murder.

Decades of Repression in Iraq

Memories of that time came to me as I looked at images of our soldiers in Iraq during the early days of the war [in spring 2003]. The soldiers were thrust among people who have been living with random violence, invisible but constant surveillance, arbitrary law, and brutal repression for more than three decades. In short, the Iraqis have been living on the dark side of the moral universe. I hope our soldiers aren't thinking that the people they encounter have been undamaged by their experience, or that they will respond to events in the ways Americans would.

And I hope that we at home aren't underestimating the weirdness of what the soldiers encounter. During the first days of the war many Americans assumed that it would be over, as so many said, "in a flash." This is a natural impulse, common at the start of wars. We realize that what we're embarking on is a terrible enterprise, so we want to believe that it will be easy and short—that the boys will be home for Christmas, as they used to say.

It almost never works out that way. But part of our dream this time was that the average Iraqi would react to our invasion as we thought we might react under similar circumstances. As soon as the military power of the United States became apparent to the Iraqis, we imagined, millions of them would rise up to seize freedom and overthrow tyranny. They'd see that Saddam was doomed and quickly switch to the winning side.

Effects of a Brutal Totalitarian Regime

I got caught up in those hopes as much as anybody else, even though, because of my experience in the former Soviet Union, I had little excuse. In addition, I'd read [historian] Hannah Arendt. In *The Origins of Totalitarianism* (1951) she drew a crucial distinction between tyranny and totalitarianism. In a tyranny, she wrote, the leader lives apart from the people. He exploits them for whatever money, power, and position his lusts require, but he doesn't try to reshape who they are. In a totalitarian state, Arendt argued, the leader gets inside people's heads. He constructs a regime that is everywhere, one that seeks to obliterate spontaneity, creativity, and individual initiative, and to dictate thought. The result is not over-politicization but a perverse depoliticization of life. People come to understand that they cannot think a political thought, because the wrong one could get them executed. They lose the habits of citizenship. Society becomes atomized. Individuals experience psychological isolation and loneliness, because they can't be sure that even their own family members won't betray them. They fall into a passivity induced by the impossibility of freedom. All they have is their perpetually whipped-up nationalism and the omnipresence of their dictator.

> *"As events in Iraq unfold, we need to remember that every segment of Iraqi society has been profoundly affected by [Saddam Hussein's] regime."*

If Saddam's regime had been merely a tyranny, perhaps the Iraqis would have risen up at the start of the war, as we hoped. But the ideology of the Baath Party was formulated by intellectuals who studied in Paris in the 1930s. They combined a deep admiration for Nazi ideas with a respect for Leninist party structure. Saddam himself especially idolized [Communist leader Joseph] Stalin, and the regime he established was an Arab amalgam of the most brutal twentieth-century totalitarianisms, with an Islamic element added in the final decade. As events in Iraq unfold, we need to remember that every segment of Iraqi society has been profoundly affected by that regime.

The Oppressors

Let's start with the oppressors. According to estimates from Human Rights Watch, Saddam's forces have killed or caused the disappearance of some 290,000 Iraqis. Thousands more were killed during ethnic-cleansing campaigns against the Kurds and the Shiites. Killing that many people and processing their corpses requires a huge apparatus. Saddam was careful to implicate as many people as possible: for example, he ordered civilian advisers to serve on firing squads, so that they, too, would have blood on their hands. The people who manned that apparatus are not unhurt by what they did.

What is it like to be an official in a government that rules by terror? What sort of taste for sadism grows in one's heart? What does murdering fellow citizens, even neighbors, do to one's soul? How has a person who has performed such deeds justified them, and is that person likely to give up that justification simply because American troops appear?

"The Iraqi people . . . will be dealing with the psychological and spiritual aftershocks of the country's trauma for a long time."

One has probably been regarded with fear and trembling by everybody else, and may have developed a lust for blood and violence. "When we are cruel to others, we know that our cruelty is in order to bring them back to their true selves, of which they are ignorant," Michel Aflaq, a founder of the Baath Party, once wrote.

The Fedayeen Saddam have probably experienced the same sensations that motivated members of the Gestapo and the KGB—the desire to inflict pain, the feeling that one is so powerful in serving one's cause, and so superior to others, that one can maim and kill at will. Earlier [in 2003] the U.S. State Department reported that members of the Fedayeen went on a beheading spree, lopping off the heads of more than 200 women in the name of stamping out prostitution. Their zealous cruelty brings to mind an SS guard Arendt described in her book. "Usually I keep on hitting until I ejaculate," the guard told an interviewer. "I used to be perfectly normal. That's what they've made of me."

The Subjects

And what of the subjects of Saddam's regime? What is it like to have one's mind invaded without respite by such a man and his propaganda? What is it like to live a life dominated by fear, by the knowledge that at any moment an official might rape one's daughter or kill one's son? What is it like to live in a society of emotionally wounded people who have lost friends and family to the regime, to the war against Iran, to the first Gulf War?

My *Weekly Standard* colleague Matt Labash learned of one incident that, though shocking to an American sensibility, is merely typical of Saddam's Iraq. A man was arrested for a minor infraction, beaten, and detained; finally he was told he was being released. Baath Party officials escorted him from the jail to his home, where his family joyfully gathered around him. Then the officials shot him in the head.

Hannah Arendt is famous for her phrase "the banality of evil," but she was also struck by the radicalism of evil—by humankind's ability to be evil in ways that destroy all norms, all expectations, all sense of order. When Baath Party officials took children hostage to force their brothers and fathers to fight against the United States this spring [2003], they were committing the sort of crime that Arendt had remarked on in other totalitarian regimes. "The alternative is no longer between good and evil, but between murder and murder," she wrote. "Who could solve the moral dilemma of the Greek mother, who was allowed by the Nazis to choose which of her three children should be killed?"

Lasting Damage

One simply doesn't recover from experiences like these. At the start of the war the prominent Iraqi intellectual Kanan Makiya began posting a diary on *The New Republic*'s Web site. In one entry he described an Iraqi friend who had suddenly flown into a rage over a trivial slight. The man had relatives who had been murdered, Makiya pointed out; he himself had been starved and tortured. "Try to imagine the worst and still you will not come close to the physical pain this man has suffered," Makiya wrote, addressing fellow exiles.

And remember while you are trying to imagine what this person went through, that this is the human raw material that you want to build democracy for.

Every day in the last five weeks of my travels I have come across such damaged and wounded people, people who breathe nationalism, sectarianism, without knowing that they are doing so, and people who are deeply chauvinistic and suspicious toward their fellow Iraqis. These are the facts of life for the next generation in this poor, unhappy and ravaged land. Don't even think of coming back to it after liberation if you are not prepared to deal with such facts.

Makiya holds fervently to the vision of an Iraqi democracy. He has devoted the past three decades of his life to making this vision a reality. But he knows that the blood shed during thirty-five years of Saddam's rule will not wash away in a lifetime or two. The Iraqi people, along with any nations that try to help rebuild Iraq, will be dealing with the psychological and spiritual aftershocks of the country's trauma for a long time.

Perhaps the most sickening aspect of the Iraqi drama has been Saddam's popularity in various parts of the world. Here is a man responsible for the deaths of more Muslims than any other person in recent history. But Palestinians carrying his photograph marched in his support, and so did large numbers of people in other Arab countries. Majorities in Europe told pollsters that Saddam's threat to peace was equal to or less than that of [U.S. president] George [W.] Bush.

Part of this reaction is pure anti-Americanism. But part of it is the strong if secret admiration that many people have for cruel power and unabashed strength. Totalitarianism exists, Arendt said, because it solves certain psychological problems: it eliminates uncertainty and it casts politics in a maximalist, seemingly heroic role. It will survive, if not in Iraq, then in North Korea, or in a terrorist cell somewhere. And as bizarre as it may seem to us, there will always be people willing to fight and die in order to preserve it.

The Iraqi People Are Being Oppressed by the United States

by Nicole Colson

About the author: *Nicole Colson is a reporter for the weekly* Socialist Worker *newspaper.*

During his "top gun" photo-op aboard the *USS Abraham Lincoln* in May [2003], [President George W.] Bush declared an end to major combat in Iraq, saying, "In the battle of Iraq, the United States and our allies have prevailed. . . . In the images of celebrating Iraqis, we have also seen the ageless appeal of human freedom. Decades of lies and intimidation could not make the Iraqi people love their oppressors or desire their own enslavement."

Bush was right: Lies and intimidation can't make the Iraqi people love their oppressors. But the past four months [May–August 2003] have shown that the liar, intimidator and oppressor of Iraq's people is none other than Washington itself.

For Bush, the summer has seen a string of embarrassing revelations—most prominently, the fact that his administration fabricated a lie about Iraq's supposed attempts to purchase "yellowcake" uranium from Niger in order to build a nuclear weapon. For National Security Advisor Condoleezza Rice, the claim about Iraq's purchase of uranium was "just one small justification" for going to war. In one sense, Rice is right. The faked Niger story was just one lie out of dozens that Washington told over and over again in order to whip up support for their war for oil and empire. These fabrications included, most famously, [British prime minister] Tony Blair's assertion, now under some scrutiny in Britain, that Iraq could deploy its weapons of mass destruction in 45 minutes. The aim from the start was not to merely topple Saddam Hussein, but to occupy the country, seize control of its oil and use the country as a strategic base to extend tighter U.S. dominance over the region. It was never about "liberation."

All is not going as smoothly as Bush and his neoconservative advisers predicted. The truth can be seen now in the "new" Iraq—a country with a ruined economy, critical shortages of electricity, food and water, a brutal occupying army and a growing resistance to the occupation that is beginning to make things uncomfortable for the Bush administration both at home and abroad. More U.S. soldiers have died from armed resistance since Bush's May [2003] declaration than during the declared war, and discontent among soldiers is on the rise.

Today [in September 2003], as more and more pundits and ordinary citizens begin to talk of "quagmires" in Iraq (evoking images of Vietnam), the Bush administration has been forced, at least temporarily, to rethink how best to pursue their continued drive for military and economic domination around the globe. This article will examine the status of Iraq under the occupation, the development of resistance and the implications for the Bush administration.

The Face of Occupation

In August, L. Paul Bremer, III, the U.S.-appointed overseer of Iraq, gave the now-standard line about the benefits of U.S. conquest: "Each Iraqi is free to choose his or her own path. This is the meaning of the coalition's military victory. A new Iraq means new freedom." Today, however, freedom is a scarce commodity in Iraq—along with electricity, water, food and democracy. A quick look at the Bush administration's latest report on Iraq, "Results in Iraq: 100 Days Toward Security and Freedom," shows a nearly delusional gap between White House rhetoric about "liberated" Iraq and the on-the-ground reality of what is an iron-fisted occupation.

Under the rule of the Coalition Provisional Authority (CPA), the U.S. and UK rulers running Iraq, the White House claims that "major strides" are being made in security, economic stability and democracy. The report lauds the fact that oil production is up, electricity is being distributed "more equitably," water is functioning at pre-war levels, health services are recovering and the Iraqi Interim Council is now governing. On every account, there is a huge gap between the stated "progress" of the U.S. occupation and the reality. When the report was released, the *New York Times* was moved to comment that, "The biggest problems have been airbrushed out of the White House report, making it read more like a Bush campaign flier than a realistic accounting to the American people."

The Iraqi economy remains in ruins, with at least 50 percent—and by some estimates as many as 80 percent—of Iraqis without work. One solution to the unemployment crisis

> *"The liar, intimidator and oppressor of Iraq's people is none other than Washington itself."*

would be allowing Iraqis to rebuild their country, yet for all the Bush administration's promises about rebuilding Iraq for the benefit of the Iraqi people, today the main beneficiary of U.S. reconstruction in Iraq is the gaggle of politically connected U.S. corporations—like Bechtel and Halliburton—which continue to win multimillion-dollar contracts in the bid to privatize every last arena of Iraq's infrastructure. In the latest outrage, it is now being reported that WorldCom Inc.—which has never successfully built a wireless network and is best known for its corporate accounting scandals—is in line to win a $900 million Pentagon contract to build a cell phone system for occupied Iraq.

Jodie Evans, a peace activist and organizer with the International Occupation Watch Center, summed up the attitude of U.S. reconstruction officials this way after returning to the U.S. from Baghdad in July [2003]:

> I met the man who was hired to create a new civil government in Baghdad, to bring Baghdad back to order. His name was Gerald Lawson. . . . I asked him what he knew about Iraqis. He knew nothing, and didn't care to know anything. He didn't know their history, their government, didn't speak a word of Arabic and didn't care to learn. . . . He works for a corporation created by ex-generals. Their job is to create the new Iraqi government structure.
>
> We met the man whose job is to make sure the hospitals have what they need. . . . He is a veterinarian. . . . I met the guy in charge of designing the airport, where major jumbo jets are supposed to land. He had never designed an airport before.

Evans' comments paint a portrait of stunning arrogance on the part of the U.S. toward rebuilding a country that has been devastated over 13 years by war and blockade.

In Baghdad, a 15-minute walk from where Paul Bremer has set up shop in a luxurious, air-conditioned former presidential palace in Baghdad, shopkeeper Shamsedin Mansour summed up the frustration that many Iraqis

> *"The main beneficiary of U.S. reconstruction in Iraq is the gaggle of politically connected U.S. corporations."*

must feel with their U.S. occupiers: "We have had no electricity for six days. Many of our people are suffering from heart problems because of the heat. We live with as many as 42 people in a house and do not have the money to buy even a small generator. Without light at night, it is easy for gangs of thieves with guns to take over the streets, and the shooting keeps us awake. If we try to protect ourselves with arms, the Americans arrest us."

Today, electricity still has not been fully restored in the country—at a time when the midday temperature routinely hits 120 degrees-plus. In early August [2003], U.S. officials announced that production of electrical power was going down, not up, and admitted that even when war damage to the power grid is repaired, the country will produce 30 percent less electricity than it needs.

Clean water is also hard to come by in Iraq. In Baghdad alone, one post-war survey found that 40 percent of the water network was damaged, and that there were over 500 separate breaks in the distribution system. Chronic water shortages are also a consequence of the power cuts. Even when there is water, it is often not safe to drink. For weeks after the end of major combat, Baghdad did not have a single functioning sewage treatment plant—because of the damage caused by years of U.S. bombing and United Nations–imposed sanctions. Following the war, the World Health Organization reported a spike in cases of cholera and child diarrhea, due primarily to the lack of potable water. In one post-war assessment, UNICEF [United Nations Children's Fund] found that seven out of 10 children in Baghdad suffered from diarrhea, due primarily to contaminated water.

> *"There are . . . hundreds of examples of daily brutality and humiliation that ordinary Iraqis are subjected to under the heel of the U.S. occupation."*

The CPA says that it can have the water system fully operational by the beginning of Ramadan in October [2003], but the sewage system is a different matter, because the main sewage treatment plants were stripped bare in post-war looting, and because the country's sewage plants rely on electricity to operate.[1]

Today, the CPA cynically blames Saddam's "underinvestment," as well as looting and sabotage, for the delays in restoring essential services to Iraqis. But Iain Pickard, a British coalition spokesman, let slip the real reason for delays in early August [2003]. "The U.S. contractors have their own agenda and that is Washington's agenda," Pickard stated bluntly.

That agenda doesn't seem to include getting Iraq's hospitals up and running in a timely manner, either. Today, Baghdad hospitals remain bleak places, plagued by constant problems with electrical and water supplies, as well as irregular deliveries of basic supplies like oxygen and anesthetics. According to Jim Haveman, the senior U.S. adviser to the provisional Iraqi Health Ministry, the main goal is to simply prevent epidemics.

Even Iraq's oil industry—the most sought-after piece of the economy by the U.S.—remains in tatters. At its peak, and including routes through both Syria and Saudi Arabia that are now closed, Iraq's oil export infrastructure could handle output of around six million barrels per day. However, chronic power outages and sabotage have affected the oil industry as well; in mid-August [2003] the Iraqi oil ministry reported that power cuts had halved oil exports from southern Iraq and copper theft from electricity lines threatens to shut down exports from the region completely.

Prior to the war, the Bush administration repeatedly argued that Saddam Hussein used the proceeds of the oil-for-food program to enrich his own regime rather than provide food and other necessities for the people of Iraq. Yet, because the war and subsequent occupation have disrupted what was an advanced and well-run system of food distribution, malnutrition has gone up, not down. According to UNICEF, a post-war assessment found that in Baghdad, acute

---

1. As of early 2004 some improvements had been made to the water, electrical, and sewage systems, with U.S. funds budgeted for further repairs.

malnutrition had nearly doubled from 4 percent a year ago, to almost 8 percent. At least one out of five Iraqi children continue to suffer from chronic malnutrition, and in late June [2003], UNICEF reported that a staggering 100 percent of the Iraqi population had become dependent on food aid—where 60 percent were dependent on food aid before the war.

Many Iraqi women now enjoy less freedom than prior to the war. There are reports of a rash of kidnappings and rapes, and in response, some women are staying indoors, avoiding schools and have taken to wearing the veil. In May [2003], the humanitarian group Save the Children reported that school attendance of girls had dropped by half. "Under Saddam, we were only afraid of Uday," said Baghdad resident Zeman Arkan, who has been forced to give up going to work because her family cannot ensure her safety during her commute. "Now, it's worse than under Saddam. There's no security for us."

To the extent that any reconstruction is in the works, it is the kind that will line the pockets of U.S. corporations. The oil contracts are now well-known, but there are others in on the action. The Bush administration awarded Abt Associates, for example, a $43.8 million contract to "assist in stabilizing and strengthening the health system in post-conflict Iraq." In return, according to journalist Robert Fisk, Abt has declared that medical equipment must meet U.S. technical standards—meaning that all new hospital equipment must come from the U.S.

The Brutality and Arrogance of Occupation

Beyond the utter failure of coalition forces to provide for the daily material needs of the Iraqi people, there are the hundreds of examples of daily brutality and humiliation that ordinary Iraqis are subjected to under the heel of the U.S. occupation.

Although Iraqi casualties rarely merit attention in the U.S. news media, U.S. troops continued to sweep through major cities in June and July [2003], conducting a series of brutal raids to disarm Iraqi civilians and round up what the Pentagon claims are "Saddam loyalists." In Operation Ivy Serpent, a U.S. sweep carried out in July, troops killed at least four Iraqis and arrested another 50 people.

For the most part, the Iraqis who have been caught up in U.S. sweeps are not high-ranking members of the Baath Party. Many are simply victims of faulty U.S. intelligence, or happen to be in the wrong place at the wrong time. In late July, for example, five people were killed in Baghdad's Mansour district by the elite "Task Force 20," the U.S. special forces team in charge of hunting down Saddam Hussein. Troops opened fire on several cars that mistakenly failed to stop for a U.S. roadblock. One car contained a disabled man named Mazin, his wife and teenage son. According to witnesses, a bullet from the volley of shots fired at the car passed through the windshield and blew off the right half of Mazin's head. "We consider the Americans now as war criminals," said Mahmoud al-Baghdadi, a 32-year-old baker. "They claim to be fighting terrorism, but they cannot defend freedom by killing disabled people."

In this case, the U.S. refused to issue an apology. While acknowledging that several innocent civilians had been killed in the botched raid, the U.S. would not accept blame. According to Lt. Gen. Ricardo Sanchez, the head of allied forces in Iraq, "Apologies are not something that we have within military processes. . . . We acted on intelligence that we believed was sufficient."

The utter brutality of raids like this have given the U.S. forces in Iraq a bad reputation and provoked such outrage that, just days later, Sanchez was forced to backpedal. Announcing that the military would be scaling back their raids, Sanchez told reporters that: "It was a fact that I started to get multiple indicators that maybe our iron-fisted approach to the conduct of ops was beginning to alienate Iraqis." He added that local Iraqi leaders working with coalition forces had said that they were unable to support the humiliating methods troops were using in conducting raids to round up those suspected to have ties to the former regime. The Iraqis' message, Sanchez said, is that "when you take a father in front of his family and put a bag over his head and put him on the ground, you have had a significant adverse effect on his dignity and respect in the eyes of his family."

The indignity of the treatment of Iraqis by U.S. troops doesn't end there. According to reports by Amnesty International, many of the thousands of Iraqis being held captive by the U.S. military are kept in what amounts to concentration camps and are subjected

> *"Many of the thousands of Iraqis being held captive by the U.S. military are . . . subjected to conditions that qualify as torture."*

to conditions that qualify as torture. "Detainees continue to report suffering extreme heat while housed in tents; insufficient water; inadequate washing facilities; open trenches for toilets; no change of clothes, even after two months' detention," Amnesty said.

Amnesty also said it had received several reports of cases of detainees who have died in custody, "mostly as a result of shooting by members of the coalition forces." There are reliable reports that some children have also been rounded up and subject to similar treatment.

"If You Keep Them Hungry, They'll Do Anything for Us"

Army Col. David MacEwen, who helps coordinate civic works in Iraq, explained the "carrot and stick" methods employed by the occupation forces: "During 'peninsula strike' [a huge operation of raids and arrests of more than 400 Iraqis in June (2003)] we worked very hard for every combat action to have a 'carrot' that followed. We'd do a cordon and search in one area and then make sure the next day that LPG [cooking gas] was available, or that a pump at a water plant was working."

The message to the Iraqis seems to be: If you want clean water, don't resist. If you want the things you need to live, don't resist. Activist Jodie Evans commented on what seems to be a deliberate strategy on the part of coalition forces to subject Iraqis to an iron-fisted occupation in the hopes that it will crush the spirit of resistance. Recounting a meeting with a man whose job was to collect intelligence for [U.S. administrator in Iraq] Paul Bremer, Evans said: "That professor I spoke to, the one doing the intelligence for Bremer, I told him that I had spoken to countless Iraqis and all of them felt this chaos was happening on purpose. . . . He basically said this was true, that chaos was good, and out of chaos

> *"The hollow promises of democracy are being exposed every day, and as the occupation continues, it will provoke more outrage and resistance among ordinary Iraqis."*

comes order. So what the Iraqis were saying—that this madness was all on purpose—this intelligence guy didn't discredit. He said, 'If you keep them hungry, they'll do anything for us.'"

For ordinary Iraqis, this is the reality of occupation. The hollow promises of democracy are being exposed every day, and as the occupation continues, it will provoke more outrage and resistance among ordinary Iraqis—resistance that the U.S. has, in many cases, responded to in the most brutal way.

Take the recent shootings in Sadr City, a slum in northeast Baghdad occupied by Shiites. According to residents, on August 13 [2003], a U.S. Blackhawk helicopter attempted to tear down an Islamic flag from a telecommunications tower. When 3,000 angry residents poured into the streets in protest, U.S. troops opened fire on the crowd killing at least one and wounding several more—including a 12-year-old boy who was shot in the face.

The U.S. claims that troops were fired upon, but the incident was so outrageous that the U.S. military was forced to apologize. "We deeply regret what has happened today. What occurred was a mistake and was not directed against the people of Sadr City," said Lt. Col. Christopher Hoffman in a letter distributed to locals. But it was not a mistake, it was the logical consequence of the U.S. occupation.

That logic was on display again on July 29 [2003], as some 1,000 Iraqis marched to the former presidential palace in Baghdad to protest unemployment. The protest, organized by the Union of Unemployed People in Iraq (UUPI), called for jobs for Iraqis and for unemployment insurance. At the palace, now used by U.S. occupation forces, the demonstrators staged a sit-in. As the sit-in continued into a second day, the protest was attacked in the early hours of the morning by U.S. troops. Ghasam Haadi, the UUPI's president, and 19 others were arrested. After a meeting with a protest delegation, the detained protesters were released, but according to the UUPI, on the fifth day of the sit-in, August 2, U.S. troops arrested 55 members of the group. They were only released when the UN intervened on their behalf.

Chapter 3

The New Rulers of Iraq—Who's Really in Charge?

Yet another "stride" forward that the Bush administration points to in its 100-day occupation report is, "For the first time in the lives of most Iraqis, a representative government is being established and human rights and freedom are being enshrined."

Even as the U.S.-appointed, 25-member governing council of Iraqis held its inaugural meeting July 13 [2003], ultimate control over Iraq—including veto power over the council's decisions—still rests with Paul Bremer. But it's not as if the council is likely to challenge Bremer's authority. It is made up of men like U.S. puppet Ahmad Chalabi of the Iraqi National Congress (INC), an embezzler who hadn't set foot inside Iraq for 45 years until April, and Wael Abdul-Latif, the U.S.-appointed governor of the oil-rich southern city of Basra. The council is so divided that it took more than two weeks to decide who would be in charge—with members finally deciding that the council presidency would rotate among nine different members.

While the Iraqi Interim Governing Council may get to do a few things, like come up with a new currency or declare new holidays, the reality is that Paul Bremer has veto power over all of the council's decisions. Right in the midst of the coverage of the new council, an anonymous "senior administration official" was quoted in the *New York Times* responding to the idea that other countries might want to have a share in the decision as to how Iraq's future oil revenues are spent. "It still hasn't entirely sunk into the international community," said the official, "but the CPA is the government of Iraq. There are already unfortunate misunderstandings on that, but I cannot underline that often enough. The CPA is the government of Iraq."

Meanwhile, out in the streets of Iraq, the U.S. occupiers are increasingly turning to the very thugs that they're supposedly opposed to—former secret police under Saddam Hussein's regime—to keep order.

In late August [2003], it was reported that occupation officials had embarked on a campaign to quietly recruit and train former members of Saddam Hussein's security forces in order to help isolate and identify those participating in anti-U.S. resistance. "What we need to do is make sure they are indeed aware of the error of their ways," an anonymous senior American official was, incredibly, quoted as saying. As the *Washington Post* put it: "U.S. officials . . . said they recognized the potential pitfalls in relying on an instrument loathed by most Iraqis and renowned across the Arab world for its casual use of torture, fear, intimidation, rape and imprisonment."

The contradiction is galling. As left-wing author and activist Tariq Ali commented: "The only explanation provided by Western news managers to explain the resistance is that these are dissatisfied remnants of the old regime. This week Washington contradicted its propaganda by deciding to recruit the real remnants of the old state apparatus—the secret police—to try to track down the resistance organizations." . . .

Iraqi People Should Be Free to Decide Their Future

Every day that U.S. troops remain in Iraq there will be more people who question why the Iraqi people are not free to decide their own fate. The Bush administration may be determined to wage its war on the world, but the arrogance of their occupation will continue to stoke outrage—both abroad and at home—that can fuel an opposition strong enough to stop their war machine.

The Position of Iraqi Women Has Not Improved

by Zainab Salbioff, interviewed by *off our backs*

About the authors: *Zainab Salbioff is the founder and president of Women for Women International.* Off our backs *is a news journal written by and about women.*

Zainab Salbioff, recently back from a trip to Iraq in May [2003], was interviewed June 13 [2003] by *off our backs* intern Maryam Moody and collective member Karla Mantilla. Salbi is the founder and President of Women for Women International, a foundation that provides assistance to women in Bosnia, Afghanistan, Rwanda, Kosovo, Pakistan, Colombia, Nigeria and Iraq. Salbi, a native of Baghdad, grew up during the Iran-Iraq War and came to the United States to complete her education.

Conditions Before the War

off our backs: Could you tell us a little bit about what the conditions of women were in Iraq before the war?

Zainab Salbioff: There are different eras that women went through in Iraq. The ones who grew up in the 1950s, 60s, and 70s had much more access and liberty than the women who grew up in the 80s and the 90s.

My mother's generation, for example, is a generation who had enjoyed not only access to higher education but were very active in the public work force and enjoyed a great level of independence in terms of traveling abroad, alone, doing whatever they wanted to do in their lives. There were women who were active in organized women's groups in the 50s and the 60s, there were women active in their political parties—we had multiple parties in Iraq then. There were women ministers in the 50s, the first woman judge was assigned in 1956 in Iraq.

This situation changed in the 80s and the 90s, and particularly in the 90s. In the 80s we had a war. At that time women were, again, promoted in the public sphere, but it also was an era in which Saddam Hussein took over. So while economically women were promoted to be very active participants in the public sphere and the economy, because the men were fighting, the government, Saddam's regime particularly, utilized sexual violence against women to recruit them for political gains. The sexual violence targeted women who the government wanted to recruit into the secret service. For example, if you refused, then you would be raped, the rape would be videotaped, and the tape would be used as blackmail against you. This way you not only had to spy on your husband and your brothers and family members, but also recruit other females to join the secret service.

> *"The political parties in Iraq, the vast, vast majority, if not almost all of them, do not have women. Nor have they addressed the issues of women's participation."*

Sexual violence and rape were used particularly against women who belonged to families from the political opposition. The government in general felt that women were at their disposal. So, you go to any public place, whether it's a restaurant or a club or a university, and if any member of the former regime liked any of the women, then they showed that they felt they had complete access to her, regardless of her commitments or her desires or whether she agreed or not, regardless if she's married or not. Simply put, owning the country meant owning the women of that country as well.

The 90s had the character of a different era as a result of the sanctions and a continuation of the same regime. In many ways, women's rights deteriorated. You can find middle-aged women who are educated—can read and write—whose daughters are illiterate. That is completely the reverse of what you see in other countries. There is no sector in Iraq that is prohibited to women. Women have access to all levels of education. But due to the repression of the regime and then the economic sanctions, there began to be problems. First salaries became very low—so a teacher's salary was $2.00 per month. A lot of women who had a choice to do other work besides going out in the public sphere and being at risk of harassment, chose to stay home. Others did not have that choice. As a result, many of them took their daughters out of school. And a lot of the educated middle class women decided to stay home instead of going out to work because of the unfriendly atmosphere in the public sphere, low salaries, economic hardships, and the sexual harassment that women face.

After the War

How have things changed as a result of the United States bombing Iraq? What's going on with them today, right now?

Iraq is going through a reconstruction process in terms of government, politics, economics—everything. It is very critical that women get involved in the process and have a very real and active role—not just a symbolic one. That is something that a lot of women in Iraq feel very strongly about.

I returned from Iraq about a month ago [in 2003] and many women from the different socio-economic classes, from different ethnic/religious groups were saying, "We want an active participation at all levels of this society and government. We don't want just to be singled out to a women's ministry. We want to be part of the defense ministry, the sports ministry—everything—across all sectors in both the government and non-governmental structure."

Although this is what women are saying, there has been very little participation by women at the different levels. The two main American-hosted political gatherings after the war—held in Nasriyah and Baghdad—had only a handful of women compared to a few hundred men. The political parties in Iraq, the vast, vast majority, if not almost all of them, do not have women. Nor have they addressed the issues of women's participation.

I was there at a couple of political conferences. When women stood up and said, "What about our participation? We want women's role in the new Iraq," all the men stood up and clapped. So there is the momentum that this is something we want, that this is something we're committed to. But when it comes to action, we haven't seen it.

Who decided who got invited to the Nasriyah and Baghdad meeting?

It's under American leadership.

Do you think the issue of not including women is a problem of the coalition forces?

I think actually it's both the coalition forces and the Iraqis. All groups have expressed a verbal commitment to promote women's rights, or women's participation in the reconstruction of Iraq—from the U.S. State Department to the House of Representatives to Iraqi political parties. But there has not been much action. As a practical woman, I want action.

There has been some improvement since I left. For example, [Paul] Bremer [the U.S. appointed civil administrator of Iraq] met with some 40 Iraqi women to create a conference to promote women's participation in Iraq. That is all good. But what we don't want is an Afghanistan experience in which all women are funneled into a single women's ministry.

The question is not only how to include women, but how to make sure that gender issues are actually considered in the reconstruction of Iraq. For example, where does gender come in when we talk about the police retaining all the food distribution, all economic reconstruction, and all governmental reconstruction?

> *"The question is not only how to include women, but how to make sure that gender issues are actually considered in the reconstruction of Iraq."*

Food distribution, for example, was occurring mostly through the mosques. And while in principle there is nothing wrong with that, you have to look at gender effects. Have the people who are distributing the food thought about how to make sure women don't get marginalized in the process, so that women do not fall through the cracks through these methods of distribution? There are now a lot of women who are required to dress in specific ways, women who had not previously worn the veil and now have to so they can get food packages. And because of the security risk, every time they leave the home to get to food or whatever they may need, they risk their safety.

Trafficking in Women

Do women have the ability to care for children?

The women I interviewed, especially single heads of households, were actually much more vulnerable than the rest of the population. They now have to walk their kids to school, wait for them at school, and then walk them back because of safety issues.

> "We at least had a sense of normalcy [under Saddam Hussein] even if we were living in a constant state of fear, we had a sense of a normal life."

Also, according to *The Economist*, there is now a market in Baghdad for trafficking women. The lack of safety and security is the number one priority that we have. When I was there, there was even a woman that was kidnapped from her own kitchen. Women are the biggest targets in terms of safety.

What kinds of groups or people are targeting women for such trafficking or for other purposes?

No one knows if this is an organized effort or if this is a random ad hoc effort. No one knows if the women are being trafficked inside of Iraq or outside of Iraq. There haven't been many women rescued who can talk about that, so no one knows. What we do know is that it's becoming a major, major issue. And that it is something that women had not faced in Saddam's time. Of course, the vulnerability of being sexually harassed and prey to Saddam and his cronies if they wanted you—that was a big deal. But on the day-to-day level, there was a sense of security that women could leave the house and walk or drive and go to work or wherever. And now that sense of safety is gone.

How do women feel about the war happening in general? Do you have any sense of that?

I went to Iraq in December–January of this year [2002–2003] to sort of get an assessment of a pre-war Iraq. The number one fear of [the] people was the war, and the number two fear of my people was the looting and the chaos in the aftermath of the war. And both of these things happened. As someone who lived in a war, it's not an easy experience. It's something that I feel like people in the U.S. do not understand. The media have not done a fair job of conveying the magnitude of war. Regardless of whether it is a just or unjust war, it is not an easy thing to support because on a personal level, you suffer so much. That's what a lot of Iraqis told me before the war. They did not want to suffer again. They have already suffered through twenty years of war—they did not want to go through it again.

War and sanctions.

Yes, war and sanctions. Actually, the war really never ended—I mean there has been war in Iraq in the last ten years, bombing every month as a result of the first Gulf War [in 1991].

Which most Americans didn't know.

Absolutely. Having said that, everyone is also very grateful and very excited that Saddam left. I had people run behind me saying, "Please tell Mr. [George W.] Bush thank you." Having gone through the war, we suffered but still we are so happy that Saddam is out. We cannot believe it. I just wrote a sixteen-page report titled "Please Tell Mr. Bush." But they never stop the sentence there. And they always continue the sentence by saying, "But we need the security issues to be addressed, we need a government, we need the chaos and anarchy stopped. We need to live our normal lives again, we cannot continue like this." So it's a conflicted feeling.

Now, as in all wars, women generally are the ones to keep the family going. They are the practical ones who have to think about food, electricity, and education for their kids. It's hard to keep life going. Women don't get excited and say, "Yippee, let's have a war." But they are excited that Saddam is out of the country. They do not see one consistent picture, but they exist parallel to each other.

Frustration with America

Are women fairly annoyed that the United States didn't provide better for services and security after the war?

Women, and the rest of the country, are very frustrated with the United States, in my opinion, for not providing what they perceive as being the basic precautions or preparations to eliminate the looting, chaos and anarchy. A lot of people asked me, "How could the two most powerful countries in the world who could win the war in one month, not have prepared for the day after?" Women particularly are frustrated because of the lack of security and how it's impacting their lives. I mean, you have women who have been oppressed by Saddam's regime and are saying "but you know what? We at least had a sense of normalcy even if we were living in a constant state of fear, we had a sense of a normal life. We could work."

> *"We can make a model out of how Iraqi women can participate in an active and progressive way in the reconstruction of a country."*

I met a single mother who lived in a small room with her daughter on the rooftop of her building. She has a small income-generating business making traditional frozen food. But she is so frustrated right now. She has to walk her daughter to high school every day and bring her back. She can't run her business because they have no electricity. She had less money than her rent, which was due in a week, and she has food to last only a week: She is very frustrated, saying, "How could you do that to us? I mean, yes, thank you so much for liberating us from Saddam. But how could you, leave us in this state? You should not have done it if you were not prepared for it."

Is there a sense at all that Americans conducted the war for self-interest?

Yes. At least that's what a lot of people say. They think there was a self-interest in there—that oil was an incentive. But the Iraqis are also very practical about it. They say, "that's fine, we got rid of Saddam. If the war was the only means to get rid of Saddam, and if the oil was the incentive, then that is fine with us, but at least help rebuild the country." They're saying, "Okay, I know what you want. I know why you did it. But at least give us some benefit from the process." The frustration is not because they don't think Americans are there for their own interest, but because they don't think Americans are addressing ours, and that Americans are leaving Iraq in a very chaotic and anarchic situation without addressing very practical and immediate needs.

Is there concern that what will happen in Iraq is like what happened in Afghanistan [after the United States ousted the ruling Taliban in 2001]? That it'll be a hot issue for while and then will be totally abandoned?

The concern is from this end more than from the Iraqi end. We are afraid for women and the development sectors. Women for Women International has offices in Afghanistan, Bosnia and Rwanda. For us, it's as important that we keep paying attention to these countries who faced war not only a year ago, but ten years ago. These countries still need help, and the women there still need a lot of issues to be addressed.

Iraqis look at things differently. A lot of Iraqis are saying—from the richest to the poorest—if this situation does not improve within six months to a year, we will pick up the guns and fight America. They are that angry. Regardless of how you feel about the war, we can now say, okay, it's behind us. So let's at least address the future in a healthy way. Let's not lose the future. We can make a model out of Iraq. We can make a model out of how Iraqi women can participate in an active and progressive way in the reconstruction of a country. Or we can do a mediocre job and we lose everything.

Chapter 4

How Should Iraq Be Reconstructed?

Chapter Preface

On January 15, 2004, approximately six months after the conclusion of the 2003 war, tens of thousands of Shiite Muslims shouting "no to America" marched through the southern Iraq city of Basra in a call for early elections of a new Iraqi government. Under direct elections, the Shiites, who compose approximately 60 percent of Iraq's population, could gain control of Iraq's government for the first time in decades. However, Iraq's Sunni Muslims, who have dominated the government throughout Iraq's history, fear that direct elections will minimize their influence in government. As Iraqi reconstruction proceeds, the effects of direct elections on Iraq's various ethnic groups is one of many conflicts complicating the rebuilding process.

The Shiites—Arab Muslims who follow the Shiite branch of Islam—have long comprised the majority of Iraq's population. However, since its creation in 1921, Iraq has been governed by a Sunni Arab minority. While the Sunnis constitute less than 20 percent of the country's population, their claim to rule has been backed by the preponderance of Sunnis over Shiites in the wider Arab world and by the support of Arab Sunni leaders outside Iraq, including the rulers of Saudi Arabia, who view Shiism as heresy and have felt more comfortable with Sunni rule next door. Even Western powers, including the United States, have supported Sunni rule in Iraq, viewing its secular nature as a counterweight to the fundamentalist Shiite-controlled government in neighboring Iran. During Sunni leader Saddam Hussein's thirty-year rule, the Sunnis enjoyed favoritism and domination in Iraq, and the Shiites were largely repressed.

Since the overthrow of Hussein's regime in 2003, that Sunni dominance is under direct threat for the first time. The composition of the Governing Council of Iraqi politicians, appointed by the U.S. Coalition Provisional Authority (CPA), the U.S.-led interim government in Iraq, reflects the Shia Muslim numerical majority in Iraq. Of the twenty-five members on the new council, only five can be described as Arab Sunni.

This dramatic reversal has caused the Sunnis to fear a grim future. "It is asking for trouble," says Mudar Shawkat, a leader of the Iraqi National Congress. Shawkat, a Sunni, says it is unacceptable to suddenly change a balance that has existed for such a long time. "Arab Sunnis have been involved in the Iraq establishment for hundreds of years," he says. "They will never accept that somebody puts them aside." To counter the threat of domination by rival Shiites, on January 5, 2004, the Sunnis formed a national council, demanding that the rights of Sunnis in the new government be equal to those of Shiites.

As the CPA and the interim Governing Council oversee the political transition to a self-governing Iraq, they face the difficult challenge of balancing the rights of Shiite and Sunni Muslims, in addition to other groups in Iraq. Yitzhak Nakash, associate professor of Middle Eastern history, believes that the future Iraqi government will be Shiite-dominated, and will face the difficult task of reconciling the interests of Iraq's many factions:

> The Bush administration will need to reach out to the Shiite Arab majority, which represents 60% of the country's population, while taking measures to ensure that a change of regime in Iraq will not expose the Sunni minority to Shiite revenge and tyranny. . . . Ultimately, the key to Iraq's future will lie with its Shiite majority. . . . Shiite political leadership will need to unite secularists and Islamists, urban and rural dwellers, Shiites living inside Iraq as well as those who will return from exile. It must also be capable of reaching out to Iraq's non-Shiite communities.

However, many people fear that if the Shiite majority takes power in Iraq, an Islamic theocracy modeled after Shiite-dominated Iran will be established, oppressing the people of Iraq.

The challenge of creating a new Iraqi government that balances Shiite and Sunni interests is only one of the many difficulties faced by those trying to reconstruct Iraq following the 2003 war. The authors in the following viewpoints debate some of the conflicts related to Iraqi reconstruction.

Democracy Should Be Established in Iraq

by Daniel L. Byman and Kenneth M. Pollack

About the authors: *Daniel L. Byman is an assistant professor in the Security Studies Program at Georgetown University and a nonresident senior fellow at the Saban Center for Middle East Policy at the Brookings Institution in Washington, D.C. Kenneth M. Pollack is director of research at the Saban Center and the author of* The Threatening Storm: The Case for Invading Iraq.

What should the government of Iraq after Saddam Hussein look like? The U.S. government has worked feverishly to address the problem—creating working groups and planning cells, formulating options, and discussing ideas with U.S. allies while pundits and analysts in the media, think tanks, and academia have further identified this issue as a vital one to ensure that peace in Iraq and in the region is secured.

Democracy lies at the heart of all of these discussions. President George W. Bush himself declared, "All Iraqis must have a voice in the new government, and all citizens must have their rights protected." As members of a prosperous democratic society, U.S. citizens innately believe that democracy would be good for Iraqis too. The most optimistic have even offered a vision of a future Iraq as a "City on the Hill" for the Arab world that would inspire democracy throughout the Middle East and beyond.

Yet, skeptics abound. [Editor] Adam Garfinkle, for example, argues that even trying to build democracy in the Arab world would not only fail but also further stoke anti-Americanism in the process. Overall, critics raise at least five related objections to creating a democratic Iraq that seem damning at first blush. First, they contend that acceptable alternatives to democracy exist for Iraq that, if hardly ideal, are more feasible and more likely to ensure the stability and cohesiveness of the country. Second, they argue that Iraq is not ready for democracy. Third, they state that Iraqi society is too fragmented for democracy to take hold. Even if Iraq held elections or had other outward institutions of democracy, in

Daniel L. Byman and Kenneth M. Pollack, "Democracy in Iraq," *Washington Quarterly*, Summer 2003, p. 119. Copyright © 2003 by The Center for Strategic and International Studies and the Massachusetts Institute of Technology. Reproduced by permission.

practice such a system would yield an illiberal result such as a tyranny of the Shi'a majority. Fourth, they insist that the transition to democracy in Iraq would be too perilous and the resulting government too weak; thus, the institutionalization of democracy, particularly a federal form of it, would fail. Critics often conjure a vision of an Iraq beset by civil strife with rival communities seeking revenge on one another while neighboring armies trample the country. Finally, they assert that the United States is too fickle, and the Iraqis too hostile, to give democracy the time it would need to grow and bear fruit.

> *"Perhaps the most compelling reason to invest in building democracy in a post-Saddam Iraq is that the alternatives are far worse."*

Overall, primarily for these five reasons, the doubters do not so much question the desirability of democracy in Iraq as they do its feasibility.

Claiming that building democracy in Iraq after the U.S.-led war to depose Saddam would be easy or certain—let alone that doing so might solve all of the problems of the Middle East overnight—would be foolish. Nevertheless, the arguments advanced by skeptics exaggerate the impediments to building democracy and ignore the potential impact that a determined United States could have on this effort. Iraq is hardly ideal soil for growing democracy, but it is not as infertile as other places where democracy has taken root. Iraq's people are literate, and the country's potential wealth is considerable. A properly designed federal system stabilized by U.S. and other intervening powers' military forces could both satisfy Iraq's myriad communities and ensure order and security. Creating democracy in Iraq would require a long-term U.S. commitment, but the United States has made similar commitments to far less strategic parts of the world. Creating a democracy in Iraq would not be quick, easy, or certain, but it should not be impossible either.

No Other Choice

Perhaps the most compelling reason to invest in building democracy in a post-Saddam Iraq is that the alternatives are far worse. Those who oppose such an effort have offered two alternatives: an oligarchy that incorporates Iraq's leading communities or a new, gentler dictatorship. Although not pleasant, skeptics of democracy argue that the United States must be "realistic" and recognize that only these options would avoid chaos and ensure Iraq's stability. That either of these approaches could offer a stable and desirable alternative to the lengthy process of building democracy from the bottom up, however, is highly doubtful. . . .

Difficult but Not Impossible

The second principal criticism leveled by the skeptics of democracy for Iraq is that Iraq is too much of a basket case for it ever to become a democracy. As Middle East expert Chris Sanders argues, "There isn't a society in Iraq to turn into a democracy"—a view shared by a range of experts interviewed by journalist James Fallows. This pessimism contains grains of truth. Building democracy in Iraq will not be easy, straightforward, or guaranteed; others have failed under more propitious circumstances. Moreover, building democracy in Iraq will be a long and laborious process, if it succeeds at all. No particular reason, however, exists to believe that creating a workable democracy in Iraq would be impossible. In this respect, the skeptics have exaggerated the obstacles.

The claim that the historical absence of democracy in Iraq precludes its development today can be easily refuted by the fact that many democracies that have developed within the last 20 years—some with more problems than others—lacked a prior democratic tradition. Any new democracy has to start somewhere. After World War II, many Americans and Europeans believed that Germans were unsuited to democracy because they were culturally bred—if not genetically predisposed—to autocracy, and they pointed to the failure of the Weimar Republic as proof. The same claim was made about several East Asian countries, whose Confucian values supposedly required a consensus and uniformity inimical to democracy. White South Africans similarly argued that their black compatriots were somehow unequipped to participate in the democratic process. The British often said the same about India before independence. Since the fall of the Soviet Union, democracy has broken out across Eastern Europe, and in some cases it has been a relatively quick success (e.g., Poland, Estonia, the Czech Republic, and Hungary)

> *"Iraq . . . has a number of advantages that would contribute to a successful democracy-building effort."*

and in other cases a disappointment (e.g., Belarus). In virtually all of these countries, however, and in dozens of others around the world, democracy may remain a work in progress, but it is not hopeless.

Iraq's Foundations for Democracy

The various socioeconomic indicators that academics use to assess the probability of democracy succeeding also suggest that Iraq has a reasonably good foundation to make the transition. . . . In key categories such as per capita income, literacy, male-to-female literacy ratio, and urbanization, Iraq's numbers are comparable to those of many other states that have enjoyed real progress in the transition from autocracy to democracy, such as Bangladesh, Kenya, and Bolivia.

Critics correctly point out that the above statistics are correlates, not causes; simply possessing a certain gross domestic product (GDP) or literacy rate does not automatically lead a country to democracy. Yet, the same uncertainty about what causes democracy also applies to what hinders it. Scholars have some insights into the process, but time and again history has surprised us. Democracy has sprung up in the most unlikely of places: sub-Saharan Africa, Latin America, and South as well as Southeast Asia.

Some noteworthy democratic successes in the Kurdish part of northern Iraq further belie the criticism that Iraq cannot become democratic. Beset by infighting and economic dislocation, among other problems, the Kurds have nonetheless established a reasonably stable form of power sharing. Corruption and tribalism remain problematic, but Iraqi Kurdistan has progressed greatly. At local levels, elections have been free and competitive, the press has considerable freedom, basic civil liberties are secure, and the bureaucracies are responsive to popular concerns and surprisingly accountable. Pluralism—if not full-fledged democracy—is working in Iraqi Kurdistan and working well.

Iraq, in fact, has a number of advantages that would contribute to a successful democracy-building effort; namely, it is perhaps the best endowed of any of the Arab states in terms of both its physical and societal attributes. In addition to its vast oil wealth, Iraq also has tremendous agricultural potential. Prior to the Persian Gulf War, its population was probably the best educated, most secular, and most progressive of all the Arab states. Although it has been devastated economically [since 1991], Iraq has many lawyers, doctors, and professors. Together, they could constitute the base of a resurgent Iraqi middle class and thus an important building block of democracy.

Moreover, across the Middle East, popular stirrings indicate the desire for democracy among many people throughout the region. Within the strict parameters of Syrian control, Lebanon once again has a fairly vibrant pluralistic system, while Jordan, Morocco, Kuwait, Qatar, Bahrain, and Yemen have all instituted democratic changes that appear to be building momentum for greater reforms. If poorer, more traditional societies in the Middle East can take steps toward democracy, surely Iraq can take them as well.

Lessons from Other Recent Interventions

A further advantage Iraq would have over other states in a transition to democracy is that U.S. resources would back it up, hopefully along with the assistance of the United Nations and other international organizations. During the last 15 years, numerous efforts to establish democracy after a major international intervention suggest that the same is possible for Iraq. In 1996, after the Dayton peace accords were signed, NATO [North American Treaty Organization] and the UN [United Nations] created an extensive new program to rebuild Bosnia. Early efforts were disjointed, but the program improved over time. Although Bosnia was hardly a model democracy, by as early as 1998 the U.S. Department of State could brag that Bosnia's GDP had doubled, unemployment was falling, basic services had been restored throughout the country, an independent media was thriving, and public elections had been held for all levels of government.

The Bosnia model was refined and reemployed in Kosovo in 1999 after hostilities ceased, where it worked better because lessons learned in Bosnia were heeded. In particular, the UN Interim Administration Mission in Kosovo planned and coordinated the efforts of international organizations better. The same approach was even more successfully applied in East Timor, where a functional—albeit nascent—democracy is essentially now [in 2003] a reality.

> *"If poorer, more traditional societies in the Middle East can take steps toward democracy, surely Iraq can take them as well."*

Panama provides another interesting example of U.S. efforts to build democracy. Like Iraq, Panama before 1989 had never experienced anything other than pseudodemocracy in the form of meaningless elections that the ruling junta invalidated whenever it desired. After the U.S. invasion in 1989, the United States instituted Operation Promote Liberty to rebuild Panama economically and politically. Although postinvasion reconstruction in Panama had its fair share of mistakes and inadequacies, Panama today is not doing badly at all. Getting there took roughly 10 years, but it happened.

None of the examples above offers a perfect model for a post-Saddam Iraq. Yet, together they indicate that intervening forces can reduce strife and foster power sharing and that reform movements can blossom in seemingly infertile ground.

Imagining a Democratic Iraq

Still others who argue against the possibility of democracy in Iraq claim that the nation's unique problems, such as its dangerous neighborhood or explosive communal mix, will pervert elections, freedom of speech, or other democratic building blocks and thus produce illiberal results. Even states with the right foundation can fail if the constitutional system it develops does not match its needs. The failure of the Weimar Republic in Germany, for example, was at least in part the result of a poorly designed democratic system, not the inability of Germans to be democratic. The very features of Iraqi society that make it so difficult to govern and make it unlikely that any system other than a democratic one could ensure stability also demand a democratic system capable of dealing with its serious internal contradictions.

The greatest obstacle to democracy in Iraq is the potential for one group—particularly Iraq's majority Shi'a community—to dominate the country. This problem is not unique to Iraq; it has plagued democracies since their modern inception. As James Madison wrote in 1787:

> Complaints are everywhere heard from our most considerate and virtuous citizens, equally the friends of public and private faith, and of public and personal liberty, that our governments are too unstable, that the public good is disregarded in the conflicts of rival parties, and that measures are too often decided, not according to the rules of justice and the rights of the minor party, but by the superior force of an interested and overbearing majority.

For Madison, the answer was to be found through the cross-cutting identities of U.S. citizens, but Saddam's manipulation of Iraq's ethnic, tribal, and religious divisions have weakened, but not obliterated, such bonds. Thus, the fear is that Iraq's Shi'ite community, which comprises more than 60 percent of the population, might use free elections to transform its current exclusion from power to one of total dominance. Knowing this, Sunni Arabs, and perhaps the Kurds as well, might oppose a majority rule–based system. Thus, the key for an Iraqi democracy will be to fashion a system that addresses the potential problem of a tyranny of the majority.

Envisioning a form of democracy able to cope with Iraq's political problems is, in fact, quite possible. Perhaps surprisingly, a democratic system with some similarities to the U.S. system would appear to best fit the bill. Iraq needs a democratic system that encourages compromise and cooperation among members of otherwise well-defined groupings. Features of Iraqi democracy should include:

- Defining the rights of every individual and limiting trespasses by the central government. In particular, the freedom of language and of religious expression should be expressly noted.
- Declaring that all powers not reserved to the federal government be vested in local governments to constrain the central government further.
- Creating an additional set of checks and balances within the structure of the federal government to limit its powers and particularly to limit the ability of any group to manipulate it to repress other members of Iraqi society.
- Electing a president indirectly, to ensure that different communities have a say in who is chosen. In particular, Iraq should look to other systems (such as Malaysia's) that strive to ensure that candidates are acceptable to multiple constituencies and are not simply imposed on the country by the largest group.
- Employing a system of representation in the legislature that is determined by geography—not pure party affiliation as in many parliamentary systems—to encourage cooperation across ethnic and religious lines.

This last point is an important one in thinking about Iraqi democracy. Although the locations of communities are fairly well correlated to geography (i.e., the Kurds live in the north, the Shi'a in the south, and the Sunnis in the west), there are also important regions of overlap. In Baghdad and in large chunks of central Iraq, Sunni, Shi'a, and Kurds all live together. By insisting on a system of geographically determined representation, Iraqi legislators elected from these mixed districts would have an incentive to find compromise solutions to national problems to try to please their mixed constituencies rather than just one particular community of Iraqis. . . .

A key difference from a U.S.-style system would be embracing the reality of Iraq's separate and diverse ethnic, tribal, and religious communities—and both working with them and weakening their political influence at the same time. If the electoral system is properly designed, it can also foster moderation, leaving firebrands isolated and out of power. One technique championed by scholar

Donald Horowitz is to create political incentives for cross-community cooperation. Malaysia, for example, has successfully overcome tension between Malays, ethnic Chinese, and ethnic Indians using an integrative model that relies on electoral incentives to foster cooperation. Malaysia's system succeeded in part because the country had experienced ethnic violence in the past, which its political leaders then sought to avoid—a possible parallel to Iraq.

Shepherding the Transition

Because a newborn Iraqi democracy organized on the model sketched above would inevitably begin from a position of weakness, the international community, particularly the United States, must play midwife for democracy to flourish. Even if all goes well, the new government will need years to gain the trust of its people, demonstrate its ability to maintain order and broker compromises, and foster the maturation of democratic institutions. Indeed, the fourth criticism of democracy in Iraq is that even a government designed to ensure that all of Iraq's communities have a voice will not be able to withstand the challenges it will face in its critical early years.

Because [Iraqi leader Saddam Hussein] nurtured intercommunal hatred, minor provocations could spiral out of control and spark internecine conflicts in the early months after his fall. As has frequently occurred elsewhere around the world, chauvinistic leaders of all of Iraq's communities might exploit a weak, new government by using their newfound freedoms of speech and assembly to stir up hatred without any penalty. Some groups, particularly the Kurds, might take advantage of a new state's weakness to press for secession. Those who became rich and powerful under the Ba'th regime might use their initial advantages to ensure their continued dominance by ignoring election results. Americans expect losers in elections to leave office gracefully—or at least just to leave. This expectation of a peaceful departure, however, is not universal. Building democratic institutions depends on creating mutual expectations of cooperation and nonaggression both among leaders and the electorate, but developing these expectations requires time and peace to take root.

> *"Intervening forces can reduce strife and foster power sharing and . . . reform movements can blossom in seemingly infertile ground."*

A weak federal government that was not protected by the United States would also increase the danger of regional strife. Iraq's neighbors have a history of meddling and could take advantage of any weakness to protect their own interests. Turkey may intervene economically, politically, or militarily to ensure that Iraqi Kurds remain weak and do not support Kurdish insurgents within Turkey itself. Ankara already maintains several thousand troops in Iraq to fight its own Kurdish insurgency. Iran may champion its partisans within Iraq's Shi'a community, either by providing them with armed support from Iraqi dissidents residing in Iran or by covertly working with Iraqi Shi'a leaders. Different communities may organize in response to, or in support of, perceived meddling, even when little exists.

These concerns are real, but they are not unmanageable. Critics tend to overlook the success of other international efforts at performing precisely this role in democratic transitions elsewhere around the world. The UN, the United States, and the coalition of U.S. allies will have to help the new Iraqi government fend off these challenges until it has developed the institutional strength to handle them itself. Minimizing the risks of civil strife, meddling neighbors, and other barriers to successful institutionalization will require the United States to push for and then staunchly back an international effort to address Iraq's political, diplomatic, and security efforts. . . .

The Singular Importance of the United States

Although the reconstruction of Iraq should be undertaken within a UN or some other international framework that reassures both the Iraqi people and the rest of the world, the United States nonetheless must actively lead the effort. If Washington shirks this responsibility, the mission will fail.

A security force composed mostly of allied troops or run by the UN in Iraq—as opposed to a strong command structure under UN auspices as was established in East Timor—would lack credibility. Iraq's neighbors, particularly Iran, might play off of fissures in the coalition's relationships to bolster their own influence. Internally, if control of the peacekeeping mission is split among different coalition members, different peacekeeping forces would employ different tactics and rules of engagement, allowing hard-liners in some sectors to foment discord.

Taking the reins of postconflict reconstruction in Iraq does not mean that the United States need retain large forces in Iraq forever. As soon as the security situation is calm and under control, the United States should place its operations under the UN's aegis (though not its control), hopefully as part of a larger international reconstruction effort for Iraq's political and economic sectors. This situation, in turn, should last for several years as the UN, nongovernmental organizations, and multinational security forces gradually devolve the functions of government to a new Iraqi regime—with security last on the list.

"The key for an Iraqi democracy will be to fashion a system that addresses the potential problem of a tyranny of the majority."

Only when a new democratic government has demonstrated that it can govern should the international community, including the United States, turn to a purely supportive role. Even then, the new regime may need U.S. help to ensure security. We can hope for a quick transition, but we should plan for a long one. . . .

Staying the Course

A final argument against democratization for Iraq is that the United States' own lassitude will lead to an early withdrawal, leaving Iraq's democracy still-born. The claim that the United States would not be willing to sustain a lengthy commitment has been made—and disproven—repeatedly. In his new history of U.S. decisionmaking about Germany after World War II, [historian] Michael Beschloss relays countless incidents in which senior U.S. policymakers, including President Franklin D. Roosevelt, asserted that the American people would not be willing to keep troops in Europe for more than one or two years. Beschloss quotes then-Senator Burton Wheeler (D-Mont.) charging that the American people would not tolerate a lengthy occupation of Europe, which he called a "seething furnace of fratricide, civil war, murder, disease, and starvation." Similar statements are made about Iraq today by those who claim that the United States will not be willing to do what is necessary to help democracy flourish in Iraq.

In 1950, who would have believed that the United States would maintain troops in South Korea for more than 50 years? Before the U.S. intervention in Bosnia in 1995, many pundits claimed that occupying the Balkans, with its ancient ethnic and religious hatreds, would plunge the country into a quagmire, forcing the United

> *"Full-blown democracy in Iraq offers the best prospects for solving Iraq's problems over the long term."*

States out, just as had happened in Lebanon and Vietnam. Yet, seven years later, U.S. forces are still in Bosnia. They have not taken a single casualty, and there is no public or private Bosnian clamor for them to leave. Furthermore, Iraq is far more important to the United States than Bosnia. Given the vital U.S. interests in a stable Persian Gulf, fears of U.S. fickleness seem sure to prove just as baseless for Iraq as they have for Germany, Japan, Korea, and Bosnia.

The Strategic Importance of a Stable, Democratic Iraq

Full-blown democracy in Iraq offers the best prospects for solving Iraq's problems over the long term for several reasons. Democracy would provide a means for Iraq's ethnic and religious groups for reconciling, or at least create political mechanisms for handling divisions by means other than force. It would create a truly legitimate Iraqi government—one that did not repress any elements of the Iraqi people but instead worked for all of them. For the first time in Iraq's history, the government would serve to enrich its citizenry rather than enrich itself at its citizenry's expense.

Failure to establish democracy in Iraq, on the other hand, would be disastrous. Civil war, massive refugee flows, and even renewed interstate fighting would likely resurface to plague this long-cursed region. Moreover, should democracy fail to take root, this would add credence to charges that the United States cares little for Muslim and Arab peoples—a charge that now involves security as well as moral considerations, as Washington woos the Muslim world in its war on terrorism. The failure to transform Iraq's government tarnished the 1991 military victory over Iraq; more than 10 years later, the United States must not make the same mistake.

Iraq Is Not Ready for Democracy

by Patrick Basham

About the author: *Patrick Basham is a senior fellow at the Cato Institute's Center for Representative Government in Washington, D.C. He writes and speaks extensively on comparative politics, democratization, political parties, campaigns, and elections.*

President George W. Bush is rolling the democratic dice in Iraq and gambling that the formation of democratic institutions there can stimulate a democratic political culture. If he is proved correct it will mean a democratic first, for what Bush seeks to achieve in Iraq has never been accomplished before. On the contrary, the available evidence strongly suggests that the relationship between institutions and culture works the other way around.

A political culture shapes democracy far more than democracy shapes the political culture. The building blocks of a modern, democratic political culture are not institutional in nature. The building blocks are not elections, parties, legislatures and constitutions. Rather, they are found amidst supportive cultural values and apt economic conditions.

[Head of U.S. Central Command] Gen. Tommy Franks clearly did his homework before engaging Iraq in military combat, but there are red faces throughout the Bush administration over the lack of preparation for the political challenge of post–Saddam [Hussein] Iraq. Vivid demonstrations of religious fervor and undemocratic intent, viewed in tandem with clerics who have taken the political initiative by gaining control of numerous villages, towns and sections of major cities, caught U.S. political leadership completely off guard.

Whether it's setting up Islamic courts of justice or applying pressure against liquor distributors, music stores, cinemas and unveiled women, religious fundamentalists have taken advantage of the free-for-all that is postwar Iraq to browbeat their communities into a stricter Islamic way of life. Meanwhile, in northern Iraq, Kurds have forced Arabs from homes and land originally confiscated from the Kurds during Saddam Hussein's tenure.

To pour fuel on this fire, Ba'athist gangs rapidly have reorganized and with violent consequences. In a very revealing move, Ambassador Paul Bremer, head of the U.S.-led Coalition Provisional Authority, canceled local elections after concluding that the likely outcomes would be unfavorable to U.S. interests. A classified State Department report warned that "anti-American sentiment is so pervasive that Iraqi elections in the short term could lead to the rise of Islamic-controlled governments hostile to the United States."

In all likelihood Bush will be gravely disappointed with the result of his effort to establish democracy in Iraq. Mounting evidence strongly suggests that Iraq's democratic journey will be slow, treacherous and littered with setbacks.

It is true that a fairly high level of popular support exists in Iraq for the concept of democracy. Most Iraqis superficially agree with [former British prime minister] Winston Churchill that democracy may have its problems but it is better than any other form of government. But that is not enough. In practice, overt support for democracy is a necessary, but not a sufficient, condition for democratic institutions to emerge. In fact, individual-level lip service to democracy is only weakly related to a truly liberal democratic society.

The long-term survival of democratic institutions requires a particular political culture that solidly supports democracy. A liberal democracy requires a framework of liberal political norms and values, as well as the foundation of a pluralistic civil society. Hypothetical support for representative government provides neither sufficient stimulus nor staying power for democracy to take root.

Essential Cultural Factors for Democracy

What are the specific cultural factors that play an essential, collective role in stimulating and reinforcing a liberal democracy? The first is political trust. This is the assumption that one's opponent will accept the rules of the democratic process and surrender power if he or she loses an election. The second factor is social tolerance, i.e., the acceptance of traditionally unpopular minority groups, such as homosexuals. The third factor is popular support for gender equality. Fourth is a widespread recognition of the importance of basic political liberties, such as freedom of speech and popular participation in political decision-making at all levels.

Unfortunately in Iraq most of these critical ingredients are either absent or were diminished by years of benign or deliberate neglect. In Iraqi society, prevailing levels of political

> *"Mounting evidence strongly suggests that Iraq's democratic journey will be slow, treacherous and littered with setbacks."*

trust, social tolerance, gender equality and political activism fall far short of what is found in all successful democracies.

Like other societies, the condition of Iraqi democracy is tied to the respective political culture. A political culture, in turn, is clearly related to the respective level of economic development, specifically rising living standards and the independence of a large, thriving middle class. Democratization is much more likely to occur—and to take hold—in richer, rather than in poorer, nations.

Leading political scientists have demonstrated that as a person's values change, that person's political behavior supports more stable levels of democracy. In practice, a high standard of living legitimizes both the new democratic institutions and the new democracy's political class. Iraq will not be a stable democratic nation until it is much wealthier.

Iraqi Culture Far from Democracy

Like many of its Arab neighbors, Iraq has failed to come to terms with the modern world. More than 75 percent of Iraqis belong to one of 150 tribes. Significant numbers of Iraqis subscribe to many of the medieval conventions of Islamic law—from unquestioning obedience to tribal elders to polygamy, revenge-killings and blood money paid to the relatives of persons killed in feuds.

"Before elections take place, the tangible foundations of a free, open and civil society need to be built."

Iraqi political culture still is dominated by identity politics—the elevation of ethnic and religious solidarity over all other values, including individual liberty. In this deeply paternalistic political culture, political leaders frequently are portrayed as larger-than-life, heroic figures able to rescue the masses from danger or despair.

In such an environment most people adopt a political passivity that acts as a brake on the development of ideas such as personal responsibility and self-help central to the development of economic and political liberalism. Consequently, political freedom is an alien concept to most Iraqis.

At present, Iraq's educated middle class can contribute modestly to the democratization of their country, but it does not constitute a critical mass capable of moderating and channeling the political debate. Ironically, Ba'ath Party members have lost their party but most have kept their jobs as they collectively constitute the most skilled, yet undemocratic, constituency in Iraqi politics.

In reality Iraq looks closer to anarchy than democracy. How did the White House stumble into this dangerous predicament? Ironically, the Bush administration accepted the antiwar argument that Iraq was too secular a country to foster a populist, religious-based antipathy to U.S. interests.

But the notion of a secular Iraq requires considerable qualification. During the last 35 years Iraq's outward appearance of religious moderation largely reflected the Hussein regime's preference for institutionalized thuggery over religious fanaticism. The Ba'athist Party that provided Saddam's political backbone was philosophically and operationally fascist, inspired more by the muscular Arab nationalism adapted from European Nazism than by dreams of an Islamic afterlife.

Saddam himself sprang politically from Iraq's minority Muslim sect, the Sunnis, whose moderation is measured relative to Iraq's Shia Muslim majority—a sizable proportion of which adheres to the faith promulgated by Iran's fundamentalist Islamic leadership.

Intense Rivalries

Does the Shia community's numerical strength foreshadow serious problems for a democratic Iraq? At the very least, the explosion of Shia sentiment vividly illustrates the complex nature of Iraqi society. There exist centuries-old religious and ethnic hatreds, as well as intense, frequently violent, tribal and clan rivalries.

Historically, no Iraqi government, including Saddam's, has survived without significant tribal support. During the 1990s the two dominant Kurdish political organizations fought a very bloody four-year civil war. While their recent rhetoric is more political than militaristic, a leading Kurdish politician proudly asserts, "We still believe in tribes. Tribes are the way forward, not political parties."

Today [in 2003], popular debate is focused more on past injustices than on future possibilities. Therefore, Iraq's new political institutions must be designed to prevent the long-suppressed but currently better organized, more motivated and better financed fundamentalist Shia from exacting revenge upon the Sunnis and ignoring the legitimate needs of the Kurds and Christians. It is going to take a highly skilled navigator successfully to map a course through the diverse currents sweeping Iraq's domestic politics.

Iraqi politics is truly something of a hornet's nest. The extensive political maneuvering among opposition groups is a serious obstacle to implementing representative government. Each group wants to benefit from the end of the Saddam era, preferably at the expense of its rivals.

In the very long term, perhaps the Iraqi democratic reconstruction project will be successful. But it will be a good deal harder than White House theorists originally expected because this project is not just about establishing electoral democracy—it really is about establishing liberal democracy.

There is a real danger in holding national elections too soon. Before elections take place, the tangible foundations of a free, open and civil society need to be built. It is one thing to adopt formal democracy but quite another to attain stable democracy. It is critically important that Iraq's first national election not be its last.

Bush may need to compromise his democratic ideals with a healthy dose of pragmatism. What may be desirable in Iraq in the short to medium term is democracy lite, i.e., democratic gradualism. One must appreciate that the United States is attempting to sow the seeds of 21st-century political institutions in the soil of a 15th-century political culture. In coming seasons, a bountiful democratic harvest in Iraq is a very unrealistic prospect.

The United Nations and Arab Organizations Should Be Given a Greater Role in the Reconstruction of Iraq

by Bryane Michael

About the author: *Bryane Michael teaches economics and management at Oxford University, United Kingdom.*

In March 2003, the United States declared war on Iraq because of Baghdad's refusal to comply with UN [United Nations] weapons inspections. The goal of the war was to remove Iraqi President Saddam Hussein from power and precipitate a pro-market, pro-democracy "regime change." The regime did change— Saddam Hussein was replaced by the Coalition Provisional Authority and the recently [in July 2003] installed Governing Council. Supporters of the war in the U.S. government and in the Washington-based conservative think tanks spurred on the Bush administration, arguing for extensive U.S. intervention to establish democracy, the ending of a cycle of poverty engendered by Hussein's antidevelopmental and predatory policies, and the creation of an oasis of pro-Western political and economic stability in the Arab world.

Yet, if the U.S. presence in Afghanistan—which started some 17 months earlier [in October 2001]—is any predictor of U.S. engagement in Iraq, the promise of a U.S.-led, democratically based economic development seems distant. By September 2002, America had spent $13 billion on the Afghanistan war effort, in contrast with only $10 million in humanitarian assistance. Preference for spending on war rather than peace does not augur well for an ambitious rebuilding effort in Iraq.

As Afghanistan and Iraq show, the current system of international development is unable to deal with military-induced humanitarian crises. Iraq could

Bryane Michael, "Losing Iraq by Failing to Rebuild It," *World & I*, October 2003, pp. 38–43. Copyright © 2003 by News World Communications, Inc. Reproduced by permission.

turn into a large-scale "development disaster" that the current system of international development cannot accommodate. The present system is based on unilateral U.S. action that largely ignores the United Nations and spends much more on war than peace.

In each instance of U.S. intervention in the Arab world, there is talk of a new Marshall Plan.[1] In Iraq, it was U.S. Agency for International Development chief Andrew Natsios who compared the reconstruction effort to the famed post–World War II reconstruction plan. Yet, instead of heralding a new Marshall Plan portending economic development, U.S. intervention appears to lead to long-term humanitarian crisis. If America hopes to move from ineffective unilateralism to sustainable development for the Arab world (and elsewhere), it will need to engage in the enlightened self-interest of multilateral action through the United Nations and Arab organizations.

Upcoming Development Disaster

The humanitarian effects of the Iraqi war have been dire, representing the next stage of a development disaster spanning more than a decade. According to the United Nations, 13 years of economic sanctions have already exhausted Iraq's economy and resulted in at least 800,000 children being chronically malnourished. The International Physicians for the Prevention of Nuclear War says that the Gulf War in 1991 resulted in over 100,000 civilian causalities; by the time of the latest war in Iraq, only 41 percent of the Iraqi population had access to potable water. The most recent war has brought increasing hardship for the Iraqi population. According to a July 9 [2003] Reuters article, over 6,000 Iraqi civilians were killed, and a recent World Food Program report asserts that 20 percent of Iraqis suffer from chronic poverty. In many cases, women, children, and the elderly are the most dramatically affected. Basic infrastructure, such as transportation and electricity, in many parts of Iraq have been crippled. Disrupted water and sanitation systems create an environment for the spread of cholera and dysentery. Medical facilities are overwhelmed and underresourced. The result is widespread looting and an overall lack of security.

In the short term, security is the most pressing problem preventing reconstruction and development in Iraq. Yet, security will be difficult to restore given the wide range of divisions in Iraq that create a free-for-all grab for resources. Social divisions between Kurds (mostly concentrated in the northeast) and Shiite and Sunni Muslims (who held minority rule under Saddam) are often

> *"The humanitarian effects of the Iraqi war have been dire, representing the next stage of a development disaster spanning more than a decade."*

---

1. After World War II the United States provided Europe with money for rebuilding through a program called the Marshall Plan.

compounded by political divisions between ethnic and regional factions. Added to these tensions are the skirmishes between Iraqi insurgents and coalition forces.

In Afghanistan, lack of security caused by warlord-centered feudalism has already led to a near collapse of development efforts—a road that Iraq looks likely to travel. In the long term, the country's developmental prospects are conditioned on its ability to accumulate capital, effective labor, and technology. By the late 1980s, Iraq had established some light industry and electronics industries with the help of French and Soviet investment. But after the war, much of this investment was crippled. Most current investment focuses on petroleum, which contributes neither to the Iraqi human or industrial capital stock.

Development Disaster Spreads

In Iraq, the development consequences of the war are direct and apparent. In other Arab and developing countries, the war's deleterious effects will be less visible. From a historical perspective, oil prices are relatively high due to disruptions in Iraqi supply and general uncertainty. In the short term, this will be a boon for oil-producing Arab countries. In the long run, though, oil from Iraq would increase beyond the current UN sanction level as U.S. companies participate in the rehabilitation of Iraq's oil sector, adding an additional 5–6 million barrels a day of capacity in upcoming years. Given that Iraq is the second-largest oil producer after Saudi Arabia, the result would be increasing quantities and lower prices for world oil.

> *"The regime change occasioned by the Iraqi war has not been one in Iraq so much as in the system of international development."*

Oil price changes will lead to international income redistribution, possibly causing important economic and political changes in the Arab world. In Saudi Arabia, lower oil prices have led to falling per capita incomes by 60 percent since 1980. Such incomes are likely to fall further and income disparities are likely to grow, leading to social tensions and pressures for reform. Long-term adjustment to falling oil prices will probably require development finance to promote the diversification of Middle Eastern economies.

Aside from oil, the Iraqi war has led to economic instability affecting Turkey, Syria, Israel, and Palestine and has generated uncertainty throughout the Arab world. The war will certainly affect the results of World Bank and International Monetary Fund discussions on economic reform as adjustment leads to restrictive monetary and fiscal policy, putting in jeopardy disadvantaged groups and undermining Middle Eastern economic development.

Paying for Change

According to U.S. officials, the United States envisions a postwar Iraq involving an extended American military presence administering the country and providing economic, humanitarian, and reconstruction assistance. According to Mark Stoker, defense economist at the International Institute for Strategic Studies, if Iraq is to attain a per capita gross domestic product equal to that of Egypt or Iran, reconstruction aid would need to total about $20 billion. If occupation as well as reconstruction costs are tabulated, Congressional Budget Office estimates place the cost of occupation anywhere between $17 billion to $45 billion per year, resulting in a total estimated minimum cost of $75 billion and a maximum cost of up to $500 billion.

> *"The failure of development assistance in Iraq is a strong indication of the need to redesign the system of international development."*

Other experts provide similar estimates. William Nordhaus, in a Yale University study, has put reconstruction and nation building at $100–600 billion over the next decade, while former presidential economic adviser Lawrence Lindsay places the figure at $100–200 billion.

In all likelihood, the United States will be unwilling or unable to pay such a large reconstruction and development bill for two reasons. First, global economic recession has reduced Washington's ability to collect taxes. [As of October 2003] global GDP [gross domestic product] growth has fallen about 2 percent since 2000. The IMF [International Monetary Fund] estimates that a $10-a-barrel rise in the price of oil (an "oil shock") sustained over a year could reduce global gross domestic product by 0.6 percent. The IMF's April 2003 *Economic Outlook* notes a number of "transmission mechanisms" for oil-shock effects on output and growth, including lower consumer and business confidence and depressed investment.

Second, the U.S. administration has taken on a number of other commitments that will reduce funds available for Iraqi postwar reconstruction. The cost of continuing American involvement in Afghanistan is likely to require, according to Afghan President Hamid Karzai, at least an additional $15–20 billion in aid. In March 2002, President [George W.] Bush promised a $5 billion increase in development aid as part of a "new compact for development."

The regime change occasioned by the Iraqi war has not been one in Iraq so much as one in the system of international development. Before the war, many pundits and journalists claimed that unilateral action by Washington would signal the death of the United Nations and the multilateral system. While such claims have turned out to be an exaggeration, the current system of international development has undergone a serious blow. Indeed, the international development regime was already limping before the war, as shown by the steadily falling level of wealthy nations' assistance to the developing world. Of that assistance, America is a small donor as measured by its less than 0.1 percent of GDP (compared to Denmark, with more than 1 percent of its GDP in aid).

Yet, such aid—even multilateral aid—has been largely dominated by U.S.

policy. During the Cold War era, the United Nations was increasingly marginalized, as the United States preferred to use the United Nations to articulate its geopolitical interests and shift forums to the World Bank and IMF when it could not get its way in the United Nations. As geopolitics moves from the clash of economic ideologies embodied in the communism-capitalism divide to the clash of civilizations embodied in the Christianity-Islam divide, the multilateral system appears to be getting even weaker. The fact that the United States is limiting UN activity in Iraq to humanitarian assistance, and the funds it provides to the United Nations are telling (the United Nations appealed in June [2003] for $259 million to carry on its work in Iraq). The United Nations has been engaged in some important activities—such as delivering 100,000 metric tons of food, providing vaccines for about a quarter of a million children, assessing 10 percent of the total medical facilities in Iraq, and issuing a preliminary repatriation and reintegration plan to assist up to half a million Iraqi refugees. Yet these activities are only a drop in the bucket.

The World Bank and IMF have been similarly restrained from engaging in Iraqi reconstruction. At present, both institutions have not officially declared any support but stand ready to play their "normal role" and have sent fact-finding missions. Yet, even with the full engagement of the relatively large resources of the World Bank and IMF—especially for infrastructure and capacity building—it is unclear how effective their spending could be in averting the upcoming development disaster. The results of spending in Afghanistan have been less than spectacular, and World Bank and IMF lending could simply lead to the debt spiral in which many developing countries today find themselves. Even if the World Bank and IMF could cancel Baghdad's outstanding debts (which are equal to 150 percent of Iraq's GDP), it is unclear where productive capacity would come from.

Averting Disaster

What can be done to assuage Iraq's development disaster?

• The United Nations should be strengthened and given a role in planning and implementing Iraqi reconstruction. Former National Security Adviser Samuel Berger, writing for the Brookings Leadership Forum, has noted that the United States "should energize NATO [North Atlantic Treaty Organization], not just structurally, but in mission." Energizing defense-oriented organizations such as NATO would be a step in the wrong direction. The future of development should be rooted squarely in peace, not war.

• While the IMF and World Bank should be given a key role, it should be confined to providing technical assistance and grants. More loans would further impoverish Iraq in the long run.

• Arab institutions need to be strengthened, not just in Iraq but across the Arab world. Investment and grants can be administered in cooperation with the largest members of the Union of Arab Banks, and local consultants could be used in the reconstruction and development effort. Such policies would strengthen the Iraqi and Middle Eastern private sectors and assist with the longer-term goal of political stability and economic growth. Extensive Middle Eastern involvement in Iraqi reconstruction—especially by groups such as the Arab Fund for Economic and Social Development and the Arab Gulf Program for United Nations Development Organizations—would further promote the regional integration needed for sustained economic growth and cooperation with the West.

• Oil companies operating in Iraq should be "bailed in," contributing to reconstruction. Such bail-ins not only encourage the development of long-term productive investment but ease the burden on the public purses of Western donors.

In sum, the failure of development assistance in Iraq is a strong indication of the need to redesign the system of international development. Until the international community—and especially the United States—grants a greater role to the United Nations and Middle Eastern organizations, there is little hope of preventing the upcoming development disaster.

The United Nations and Arab Organizations Should Not Be Given a Greater Role in the Reconstruction of Iraq

by Reuel Marc Gerecht

About the author: *Reuel Marc Gerecht, a contributing editor to the* Weekly Standard, *is a resident fellow at the American Enterprise Institute.*

The organizing principle behind the American occupation of Iraq, so advises a chorus of influential voices, ought to be the foreign policy equivalent of financially syndicating risk. America's budget deficit is too big, the costs of administering and reconstructing Iraq too high, and the killing of U.S. soldiers in the country too frequent for the United States to bear alone the burden of transforming Iraq into a stable, democratic country. A [2003] post-conflict reconstruction report issued under the auspices of the Center for Strategic and International Studies asserts that "the scope of the challenges, the financial requirements, and rising anti-Americanism in parts of Iraq argue for a new coalition that includes countries and organizations beyond the original war-fighting coalition."

Delaware's Senator Joseph Biden, the senior Democrat on the Foreign Relations Committee, wants to see "French, German, . . . Turkish patches on [soldiers'] arms sitting on the street corners, standing there in Iraq" doing common duty and giving the United States "legitimacy as well as some physical cover." "Our troops are stretched very thin," echoes Carl Levin of Michigan, the senior Democrat on the Senate Armed Services Committee, adding, "We must end the feud with Germany and France and with the United Nations." Nebraska's Republican senator, Chuck Hagel, desperately wants to see "more United Nations involvement and more Arab involvement [in Iraq]. Time is not on our side. Every day we are losing ground." And Democratic presidential hopeful John Kerry, the junior senator from Massachusetts, is dismayed at the unilateralist "hubris" of the Bush administration. "We need to internationalize this. We need to do it now, and we need to do it openly, and we need to do it in order to defuse the [Iraqi] sense of occupation and protect the troops."

Dangers of an International Occupation

Irrespective of whether we should seek to have Europeans, Pakistanis, or Indians dying with or in lieu of Americans, irrespective of whether murderous hardcore Baathists and Sunni fundamentalists would feel less "occupied" and less murderous seeing Turks in their country, and irrespective of whether the economically stressed, antiwar countries of the European Union would actually give meaningful financial aid to Iraq, the idea of a "new coalition" to oversee the reconstruction of Iraq is entirely unwise. It would probably encourage the worst political and cultural tendencies among Iraqis, even among those who are profoundly pro-Western. It could easily send a signal throughout the Middle East and beyond that the

> *"If the [George W.] Bush administration cedes some political control in Iraq . . . it will likely open up a Pandora's box of competing Iraqi interests."*

Bush administration doesn't have the stomach to transform Iraq, let alone the region.

In the Muslim Middle East, . . . where the rulers and the ruled are constantly assessing American strength and purpose, multilateralism, when it is so evidently cover for a lack of patience and fortitude, is never a virtue. However long the United States stays in Iraq, the cost in American lives and dollars will likely go up, not down, the more we "internationalize" the occupation. The men who are killing U.S. soldiers, and other foreigners, want to drive the United States and other Westerners out of the country. When Washington talks about the need to share the pain, what these men hear is that America wants to run. And however commendable may be the idea of a joint American-European project in the Middle East through which we can lessen the rancor between us, greater European participation in Iraq's reconstruction is much more likely to fray U.S.-European relations than enhance them. It will be hard to blame the Iraqis for the ensuing troubles. It's not their fault if Washington doesn't read Islamic history.

Opening a Pandora's Box

For the last 300 years in the Middle East, ever since the Ottomans discovered their severe and ever-increasing military inferiority vis-à-vis the West, Muslims have tried to play one Westerner off against another. Englishmen against Frenchmen, Frenchmen against Austrians, Englishmen against Russians, Germans against everybody, Soviets against Americans, and now, *inshallah*, the European Union against the United States. If the Bush administration cedes some political control in Iraq to the United Nations in an effort to win greater international assistance, it will likely open up a Pandora's box of competing Iraqi interests at a time when Washington wants, above all else, to ensure that Iraqis cooperate as cohesively and as expeditiously as possible, with each other and with us. Even though the United States will surely remain the predominant occupation force in Iraq—and will unquestionably bear the responsibility for failure regardless of any new "coalition"—the possibilities for serious Iraqi (or European) mischief could increase significantly if the United Nations, French, Germans, or Russians started more aggressively critiquing American actions.

Just consider the difficulties the Bush administration has had pre- and postwar because of the profound and petty differences between the State Department, the Central Intelligence Agency, and the Pentagon. Though diminished, those differences persist. And they have had at times baleful repercussions for the post-Saddam administration of Iraq, confusing Iraqis about what American intentions really are. Now imagine layered on top of this U.S. debating society Europeans, Arabs, Pakistanis, and so on, all with their own national and cultural predilections.

Arab Assistance

It ought to be self-evident that Washington would not want any military or security assistance from any Muslim state that is not a functioning democracy, which essentially rules out everyone but Turkey. The Arab Sunni states, all ruled by dictators or princes, have to varying degrees an interest in *not* seeing a stable, democratic, Shiite-dominated Iraq born in their midst. America's toppling of Saddam Hussein may possibly provoke an intellectual and political earthquake in the Middle East, but we can be certain that the states of the Arab League, which refused to recognize the legitimacy of Iraq's new governing council, will try hard to preserve the status quo. And the Turks have an awful reputation in Iraq, both among the Kurds, who have long-standing ethnic troubles with their northern neighbors, and among the Arab Shia, especially their clergy, who see the Turks as propagators of a secularism hostile to Islam. The Bush administration went to great lengths to keep the Turks out of northern Iraq during the war. Having Turkish soldiers at Iraqi street corners would be one of the swiftest ways of torpedoing the country.

European Assistance

Intentionally or not, the Europeans could cause as much trouble as the Arabs or Turks. When I visited the French embassy in Baghdad in June, the French diplomats there were knowledgeable, friendly, intrepid, linguistically qualified, and better traveled within Iraq and considerably more plugged-in to the local Baghdad scene than their overly protected American counterparts. But they were also French, which means many of their basic political-cultural assumptions about Iraq, the war, the Arab world, Iran, Islam, democracy, and the role of the United States in the region and beyond were different, often significantly different, from mainstream American assumptions. Now, in the fullness of time, the French way of looking at the world may prove more accurate than the American perspective. But post-Saddam Iraq is not the place to test the relevancy of the *pensée unique.*

> *"Only the Americans and the Iraqis have the desire and the means to bring about [an Iraqi democracy]."*

Far too many of the assumptions about politics and culture regularly articulated by France's foreign minister, Dominique de Villepin, who is always ready to describe the *Götterdämmerung*, that President [George W.] Bush is on the verge of provoking, are simply antithetical to the views of the Bush administration and probably even to those of the Near East Bureau of the State Department. Inviting the French into Iraq—and the same could be said for the Germans and the Russians—would mean fundamental compromises over how we view the world and the Middle East. Post-Saddam Iraq is unquestionably a laboratory for new, potentially revolutionary ideas. But it ought not be a theme park where Eurocentric officials, diplomats, and think-tankers try out new strategies for bridging the America–Old Europe divide. Iraq and the Middle East are much too important to be held hostage to France and Germany.

Too much American-European "cooperation" would also needlessly damage our reputation with the Iraqis. Though the Western press corps prefers to dilate upon the foundering affection between Iraqis and Americans, Iraqi sentiment toward the Europeans, particularly among the Kurds and the Arab Shia, isn't fond. Wrongly or not, many Iraqis view the Europeans, especially the French and the Germans (and the United Nations), as sympathetic to Saddam Hussein's regime. It would be nonsensical for the Bush administration to want to have the French alongside them in Iraq. As the Iraqi oil industry slowly gains strength, the French will try to regain some footing inside the country, possibly even at the price of sending a token unit from the French Foreign Legion. Whether President Jacques Chirac and his foreign minister can swallow their pride and principles for profit is a more difficult question.

Establishing a Democracy

None of this means, however, that the Iraqis who detest the French or the Russians or the United Nations would fail to use any of these parties against the American administration in Iraq if by doing so they could advance their own interests. The process of drafting Iraq's new constitution over the next 12 months [in 2003 and 2004] may turn out to be a bruising affair, as the various groups in the country try to advance their concerns. This battling will likely be healthy, revealing the seriousness of the Iraqis' constitutional intent. The Arab Sunnis, Arab Shia, and Kurds could naturally try to introduce outside parties into the internal Iraqi debate to gain advantage or protect their flanks. The United States is going to have a discreet (one hopes), front-row, judge-and-jury seat. The U.S. officials who oversee this affair may be tested severely, as the Iraqis wrangle among themselves about what belongs in a constitution.

This process can only be made messier if more Europeans and the United Nations play political roles. (There is, on the other hand, nothing wrong with the Europeans or the United Nations increasing their humanitarian assistance.) The Iraqis don't need any more temptations to faction and fractiousness. The Americans don't need non-Iraqi distractions. Only a successful conclusion to the constitutional process will bless American efforts in Iraq. In the eyes of the Iraqi people, legitimacy springs from there, not from the members of the United Nations or its Security Council. The French, Germans, Russians, Turks, and the Arab League cannot give what they do not possess. Nor can they save American soldiers' lives. But the gradual creation of a functioning Iraqi democracy can, and only the Americans and the Iraqis have the desire and the means to bring that about.

Iraq Should Control Its Own Reconstruction

by the *Nation*

About the author: *The* Nation *is a weekly newsmagazine dedicated to the critical discussion of political and social issues.*

The quagmire in Iraq seems to deepen by the week, with the guerrilla resistance growing stronger and more sophisticated. The past month [November 2003] has been particularly sobering for the United States: five American helicopters downed, more than eighty American soldiers killed, and more departures among the nongovernmental organizations and international bodies needed to help in reconstruction.

In response to these events and to a new CIA report warning of the growing disaffection of the Iraqi people, the Bush Administration has unveiled an "Iraqization" strategy that moves up the date for turning over some control to an Iraqi governing body to June [2004] and that speeds up the process of training Iraqi police and security forces. Also anticipated is the first withdrawal of US troops next spring [2004], several months before the presidential election.

The new Bush policy seems more an exercise in political expediency—an attempt to put an Iraqi face on the US occupation while preparing the way to cut and run if the going gets tough—than a serious plan for fostering Iraqi democracy, stabilizing the country or bringing US troops safely home. Indeed, as Jalal Talabani, current president of the US-appointed Governing Council, made clear to the *Washington Post*, the United States will still be pulling the strings even after the handover, with American troops remaining as "invited guests."

American Difficulties

The Administration seems to believe it can get more Iraqis to join its efforts without ceding, in the near term, any real sovereignty. But without such sovereignty the Iraqi troops the United States is training, as well as the selected Iraqi leaders, will continue to be seen as collaborators and will have little effectiveness in repelling guerrilla attacks—whether by Saddam loyalists or by those simply opposed to the US occupation—or in establishing their own authority. As foreign policy columnist William Pfaff has recently observed, security and sovereignty cannot be separated: "You cannot have one without the other."

After having waged war on the basis of deception and outright lies, and after arrogantly rebuking the other United Nations Security Council members for their call for more international control, the Bush Administration bears responsibility for the fact that there are no good or easy

> *"We cannot will a stable, democratic Iraq into being. . . . Only the Iraqis can do that— on their own terms and in their own time."*

options in Iraq. Those who say we must "stay the course"—even when they mean by that a genuine effort to rebuild Iraq's infrastructure and provide safety for its people—ignore the reality on the ground. American forces, especially in the Sunni triangle, are doing little to provide security for postwar reconstruction and nation-building while provoking ever-greater hostility with their expanding "search and destroy" missions. They are increasingly targets, as are those Iraqis and citizens of other nations (like the nineteen Italians who died in a recent attack) who are cooperating with the United States. More US troops will do little to change that dynamic. Indeed, if history is any guide, this is a war we cannot win, even if the guerrillas represent remnants of a despised regime and lack broad support among Iraqis.

Letting Iraq Determine Its Own Future

The better, and ultimately more responsible, alternative is an immediate restoration of Iraqi sovereignty—ideally through a process overseen by the UN—combined with an orderly but rapid withdrawal of US troops. Only by setting forth a clear, firm timetable for both to be accomplished—within months—can Washington hope to break the momentum of the guerrilla war and transform the logic of the situation in Iraq from one of occupation to one of restoring self-determination. And it is only by signaling that it is willing to relinquish control—political and economic—that the United States can hope to re-engage the UN. This commitment to Iraqi sovereignty also means that it will be Iraqis, not the officials running Washington's crony contracting process, who determine the nature of Iraq's economic system and oversee the process of awarding contracts for reconstruction. Accompanying these changes could be a new effort to establish a truly multinational force that would provide an interim Iraqi government with assistance in reconstruction, security and preparations for elections. But these developments must be the product of, not the precondition for, the restoration of Iraqi sovereignty.

The future of Iraq should not be turned into a question of whether America has the stomach to stay the course. It is a question of giving Iraqis a chance to determine their own future, with whatever assistance they choose: the UN, the Arab League or other international bodies.

Yes, there is a danger that Iraq will slide further into chaos or civil war if US forces are withdrawn. But in our neoimperial delirium, we have forgotten one of the lessons of the twentieth century: that no people, no matter how dispirited by years of dictatorship, will tolerate occupation—whatever its intentions—for long before the occupiers themselves become the targets of revolt and the source of instability. We cannot will a stable, democratic Iraq into being, even with double or triple the US forces there now. Only the Iraqis can do that—on their own terms and in their own time.

Appendix of Documents

Document 1: Speech by Saddam Hussein

The following excerpt is from a speech made by Saddam Hussein to the Iraqi people on August 8, 2002, to mark the fourteenth anniversary of the Iran-Iraq War. In his speech, Hussein states that Western threats do not frighten him and that Iraq is ready to repel any attack made against it.

In the name of Allah

The most compassionate, the most merciful

Nay, we hurl the truth against falsehood, and it knocks out its brain, and behold, falsehood doth perish!

Our great people, our valiant men and women, our men of the heroic armed forces, our Arab brethren, fellow believers, wherever you may be, peace be upon you. . . .

One of the lessons of recent and distant history is that all empires and bearers of the coffin of evil, whenever they mobilised their evil against the Arab nation, or against the Muslim world, they were themselves buried in their own coffin, with their sick dreams and their arrogance and greed, under Arab and Islamic soil; or they returned to die on the land from which they had proceeded to perpetrate aggression. This has been the case with all empires preceding our present time. If this is what history tells us about its judgement on all times and eras of the past without exception, can we then describe those who are trying to ignore history now except in the words which no wise or prudent person would wish to be described with?

This is the inevitable outcome awaiting all those who try to aggress against Arabs and Muslims. If anyone wants to learn from history, anyone with greed and arrogance combined in himself, he ought to remember this fact and think again. Otherwise, he will end up in the dust-bin of history, as twentieth century politicians would say.

We always stood, and continue to stand, to learn from all such lessons, whenever the horns of aggression loomed large against us. We never faced, nor will face, any aggression relying basically on our force of arms, or our muscles and the muscles of our people, but rather on the strength of our faith, in the belief that

Allah always helps the faithful and their just cause to prevail over injustice. . . .

The forces of evil will carry their coffins on their backs, to die in disgraceful failure, taking their schemes back with them, or to dig their own graves, after they bring death to themselves on every Arab or Muslim soil against which they perpetrate aggression, including the Iraq, the land of Jihad and the banner.

We say this to refute the grumbling and sibiliation of those bragging their power, governed by the devil, their master in every evil act and crime which they perpetrate against the land of the Arabs and Muslims, while they wade in the rivers of innocent blood they shed in the world, believing that the people of the world should become slaves to Tyranny and its threats, both declared and executed threats. But if they wanted peace and security for themselves and their people, then this is not the course to take. The right course is of respect to the security and rights of others, through dealing with others in peace and establishing the obligations required by way of equitable dialogue and on the basis of international law and international covenants. . . .

There is no other choice for those who use threat and aggression but to be repelled even if they were to bring harm to their targets. Allah, the omni-powerful is above all power and shall repel the schemes of the unjust.

I say this even though I had preferred to avoid referring to it, under a different circumstance, as I have generally done so far. But I say it in such clear terms so that no weakling will imagine that when we ignore responding to ill talk, then this means that we are frightened by the impudent threats which will make those who have lost all ties with God the Compassionate, and all trust in their people, tremble and shiver; and so that no greedy tyrant will be misled into an action the consequences of which are beyond their calculations.

Allah is great . . . Allah is great . . . Allah is great.

Saddam Hussein, address to the nation of Iraq, August 8, 2002.

Document 2: Human Rights Abuses by Saddam Hussein

Many Iraqi people lived in constant fear under Saddam Hussein's regime, where arbitrary arrests, torture, and killings were common. This excerpt from a report by the British Foreign & Commonwealth Office is based on testimony of Iraqi exiles, and other evidence gathered by the United Nations and human rights organizations. It describes some of the human rights abuses in Iraq under Hussein's rule.

Torture

Torture is systematic in Iraq. The most senior figures in the regime are personally involved.

Saddam Hussein runs Iraq with close members of his own family and a few associates, most of whom come from his hometown of Tikrit. These are the only people he feels he can trust. He directly controls the security services and, through them and a huge party network, his influence reaches deep into Iraqi society. All real authority rests with Saddam and his immediate circle. Saddam is head of state, head of government, leader of Iraq's only political party and head of the armed forces.

Saddam presides over the all-powerful Revolutionary Command Council [RCC], which enacts laws and decrees and overrides all other state institutions. Several RCC decrees give the security agencies full powers to suppress dissent with impunity. An RCC decree of 21 December 1992 guarantees immunity for Ba'ath party members who cause damage to property, bodily harm and even death when pursuing enemies of the regime.

Saddam has, through the RCC, issued a series of decrees establishing severe penalties (amputation, branding, cutting off of ears, or other forms of mutilation) for criminal offences. In mid-2000, the RCC approved amputation of the tongue as a new penalty for slander or abusive remarks about the President or his family. These punishments are practised mainly on political dissenters. Iraqi TV has broadcast pictures of these punishments as a warning to others.

According to an Amnesty International report published in August 2001, 'torture is used systematically against political detainees. The scale and severity of torture in Iraq can only result from the acceptance of its use at the highest level.' Over the years, Amnesty and other human rights organisations have received thousands of reports of torture and interviewed numerous torture victims.

Although Iraqi law forbids the practice of torture, the British Government is not aware of a single case of an Iraqi official suspected of carrying out torture being brought to justice.

There is first-hand evidence that the Iraqi regime tortures children. In June [2002], a BBC [British Broadcasting Corporation] correspondent, John Sweeney, visiting the Kurdish safe haven of northern Iraq, reported the story of Ali, an Iraqi who used to work for Saddam's son Udayy. Some time after the bungled assassination of Udayy, Ali fell under suspicion. He fled north, leaving his wife and two-year-old daughter behind. The secret police came for his wife. They tortured her to find out where Ali was. When she did not tell them, they tortured the daughter, half-crushing her feet. When John Sweeney met Ali and his daughter two years later, she was still hobbling. Ali feared that his daughter had been crippled for life.

Mr Sweeney also met six other witnesses in northern Iraq with direct experience of child torture, including another of Saddam's enforcers—now in a Kurdish prison—who told him that an interrogator could do anything. 'We could make a kebab out of a child if we wanted to' he told Mr Sweeney and chuckled.

The Treatment of Women

Under Saddam Hussein's regime women lack even the basic right to life. A 1990 decree allows male relatives to kill a female relative in the name of honour without any punishment.

Women have been tortured, ill-treated and in some cases summarily executed too, according to Amnesty International. Su'ad Jihad Shams al-din, a 61-year-old medical doctor, was arrested in Baghdad on 29 June 1999 on suspicion that she had contacts with Shia Islamist groups. The soles of her feet were beaten during frequent torture sessions before she was released without charge or trial on 25 July 1999.

Human rights organisations and opposition groups continue to receive reports of women who have suffered psychological trauma after being raped by Iraqi personnel while in custody. Raping female political prisoners is part of the regime's policy. . . .

According to Amnesty International, in October 2000, dozens of women accused of prostitution were beheaded without any judicial process, together with men accused of pimping. Some of the victims were reportedly accused for political reasons and had not been involved in prostitution. Representatives of the Ba'ath party and the Iraqi Women's General Union witnessed the killings, carried out by members of the Saddam Fidayeen (the militia created in 1994 by Saddam's elder son, Udayy Hussein) using swords to behead victims in front of their homes.

Nidal Shaikh Shallal was fired from her government job and her husband was jailed for four months and tortured by Iraqi military intelligence. They later had their possessions confiscated and were expelled from their home by the Iraqi regime. On 18 October 2002, she told a meeting of the National Press Club in Washington about the situation of women in Iraq.

"The Iraqi woman has lost her loved ones—husbands, brothers and fathers," Shallal said. "The Iraqi woman has endured torture, murder, confinement, execution, and banishment, just like others in Iraqi society at the hands of Saddam Hussein's criminal gang."

"The heads of many women have been publicly cut off in the streets under the pretext of being liars, while in fact they mostly belonged to families opposing the Iraqi regime. Members of Saddam Hussein's gang have raped women, especially dissident women. The wives of dissidents have been either killed or tortured in front of their husbands in order to obtain confessions from their husbands. Women have been kidnapped as they walk in the streets by members of the gangs of Udayy and Qusayy [Saddam's sons] and then raped."

On a personal level, Shallal said her brother had been arrested in 1980. Her family still does not know what happened to him. Several of her cousins have been executed. 882 male members of her tribe, the Jibour, have been arrested. Their fates are unknown.

"Saddam Hussein: Crimes and Human Rights Abuses," Foreign & Commonwealth Office, London, November 2002.

Document 3: Persecution of the Kurds and the Shia

Under the Saddam Hussein regime, both the Kurds of northern Iraq, and the Shiites (Shia), Iraq's largest religious group, faced constant persecution. The following excerpt from a report by the British Foreign & Commonwealth Office describes some of the human rights abuses that these groups have experienced.

The Kurds

Under Saddam's rule, Iraq's Kurdish communities have experienced terrible suffering.

Documents captured by the Kurds during the Gulf War and handed over to the non-governmental organisation Human Rights Watch provided much information about Saddam's persecution of the Kurds. They detail the arrest and execution in 1983 of 8,000 Kurdish males aged 13 and upwards.

Amnesty International in 1985 drew attention to reports of hundreds more dead and missing, including the disappearance of 300 Kurdish children arrested in Sulaimaniya, of whom some were tortured and three died in custody.

In 1988, Iraqi government forces systematically razed Kurdish villages and killed civilians.

Amnesty International estimates that over 100,000 Kurds were killed or disappeared during 1987–1988, in an operation known as the Anfal campaigns, to quell Kurdish insurgency and activities.

The campaign included the use of chemical weapons. According to Human Rights Watch, a single attack on the Kurdish town of Halabja killed up to 5,000 civilians and injured some 10,000 more.

Persecution of Iraq's Kurds continues today [in 2002], although the protection provided by the northern No Fly Zone [established by the United Nations in 1991] has curbed the worst excesses. Saddam's regime is pursuing a policy of Arabisation in the north of Iraq to dilute Kurdish claims to the oil-rich area around the city of Kirkuk. Kurds and other non-Arabs are forcibly relocated from there to other parts of Iraq.

The UN Special Rapporteur reports claims by Kurdish opposition sources that 94,000 individuals have been expelled from their homes since 1991. Agricultural land owned by Kurds is said to have been confiscated and redistributed to Iraqi Arabs. Arabs from southern Iraq have been offered incentives to move into the Kirkuk area and, in disputes with their Kurdish neighbours, are always favoured by the authorities.

In addition, ethnic Kurds and Turcomans have been prevented from buying property and those who own property and wish to sell have to find an Arab buyer. Kurds have also been coerced into changing the ethnicity on their identity cards to Arab as part of this process. Turcomans are not even allowed to register as such. They must call themselves either Kurdish or Arab.

The Shia Community

The Shia community, who make up 60% of Iraq's population, is Iraq's biggest religious group. Saddam has ensured that none of the Shia religious or tribal leaders is able to threaten his position. He kills any that become too prominent.

In April 1980, a leading Iraqi Shia cleric, Ayatollah Muhammad Baqir al-Sadr, was executed. Many members of another leading clerical family, the al-Hakim, were arrested in May 1983 and executed. Another member of this family, Sayyid Mahdi al-Hakim, was murdered in Khartoum in January 1988.

More than 100 Shia clerics have disappeared since the 1991 uprising. Sayyid Muhammad Taqi al-Khoie was killed in a staged car accident in July 1994. Following the assassination in 1998 of two leading Shia clerics, Grand Ayatollah Shaykh Mirza Ali al-Gharawi and Ayatollah Shaykh Murtada al-Burujerdi, the UN Special Rapporteur reported his fears that this formed part of a systematic attack on the independent leadership of Shia Muslims in Iraq.

In early 1999, during a peaceful demonstration in response to the Iraqi regime's murder of the most senior Shia cleric in Iraq, Grand Ayatollah Sayyid Mohammed Sadiq al-Sadr, security forces fired into the crowd of protestors, killing hundreds of civilians, including women and children. Security forces were also involved in efforts to break-up Shia Friday prayers in Baghdad and other cities. Large numbers of Shia were rounded up, imprisoned without trial and tortured. In May 2001, two more Shia clerics were executed in Baghdad for publicly accusing the regime of the Grand Ayatollah's murder.

In response to attacks on government buildings and officials in southern Iraq during 1999, the Iraqi army and militia forces destroyed entire Shia villages in the south.

During the 1990s, Saddam pursued a policy of draining the marshes area of southern Iraq so forcing the population to relocate to urban areas where it was less able to offer assistance to anti-regime elements and could be controlled more effectively by the regime's security forces. As an UN Environment Programme report put it—'The collapse of Marsh Arab society, a distinct indigenous people that has inhabited the marshlands for millennia, adds a human dimension to this environmental disaster. Around 40,000 of the estimated half-million Marsh Arabs are now living in refugee camps in Iran, while the rest are internally displaced within Iraq. A 5,000-year-old culture, heir to the ancient Sumerians and Babylonians, is in serious jeopardy of coming to an abrupt end.'

"Saddam Hussein: Crimes and Human Rights Abuses," Foreign & Commonwealth Office, London, November 2002.

Document 4: United Nations Resolution 1441

As part of the cease-fire agreement following the Persian Gulf War, the United Nations mandated that Iraq must destroy all its biological and chemical weapons and the facilities to produce them. Following Iraq's continued noncompliance, the UN adopted Resolution 1441 in November 2002. The resolution, excerpted here, recognizes Iraq's failure to fulfill its disarmament obligations, and offers one more chance for compliance.

The Security Council, . . .

Recalling that its resolution 687 (1991) imposed obligations on Iraq as a necessary step for achievement of its stated objective of restoring international peace and security in the area,

Deploring the fact that Iraq has not provided an accurate, full, final, and complete disclosure, as required by resolution 687 (1991), of all aspects of its programmes to develop weapons of mass destruction and ballistic missiles with a range greater than one hundred and fifty kilometres, and of all holdings of such weapons, their components and production facilities and locations, as well as all other nuclear programmes, including any which it claims are for purposes not related to nuclear-weapons-usable material,

Deploring further that Iraq repeatedly obstructed immediate, unconditional, and unrestricted access to sites designated by the United Nations Special Commission (UNSCOM) and the International Atomic Energy Agency (IAEA), failed to cooperate fully and unconditionally with UNSCOM and IAEA weapons inspectors, as required by resolution 687 (1991), and ultimately ceased all cooperation with UNSCOM and the IAEA in 1998, . . .

1. *Decides* that Iraq has been and remains in material breach of its obligations under relevant resolutions, including resolution 687 (1991), in particular through Iraq's failure to cooperate with United Nations inspectors and the IAEA, and to complete the actions required under paragraphs 8 to 13 of resolution 687 (1991);

2. *Decides*, while acknowledging paragraph 1 above, to afford Iraq, by this resolution, a final opportunity to comply with its disarmament obligations under relevant resolutions of the Council; and accordingly decides to set up an enhanced inspection regime with the aim of bringing to full and verified completion the disarmament process established by resolution 687 (1991) and subsequent resolutions of the Council;

3. *Decides* that, in order to begin to comply with its disarmament obligations, in addition to submitting the required biannual declarations, the Government of Iraq shall provide to UNMOVIC [United Nations Monitoring, Verification and Inspection Commission], the IAEA, and the Council, not later than 30 days from the date of this resolution, a currently accurate, full, and complete declaration of all aspects of its programmes to develop chemical, biological, and nuclear weapons, ballistic missiles, and other delivery systems such as unmanned aerial vehicles and dispersal systems designed for use on aircraft, including any holdings and precise locations of such weapons, components, subcomponents, stocks of agents, and related material and equipment, the locations and work of its research, development and production facilities, as well as all other chemical, biological, and nuclear programmes, including any which it claims are for purposes not related to weapon production or material;

4. *Decides* that false statements or omissions in the declarations submitted by Iraq pursuant to this resolution and failure by Iraq at any time to comply with, and cooperate fully in the implementation of, this resolution shall constitute a

further material breach of Iraq's obligations and will be reported to the Council for assessment in accordance with paragraphs 11 and 12 below; . . .

11. *Directs* the Executive Chairman of UNMOVIC and the Director-General of the IAEA to report immediately to the Council any interference by Iraq with inspection activities, as well as any failure by Iraq to comply with its disarmament obligations, including its obligations regarding inspections under this resolution;

12. *Decides* to convene immediately upon receipt of a report in accordance with paragraphs 4 or 11 above, in order to consider the situation and the need for full compliance with all of the relevant Council resolutions in order to secure international peace and security;

13. *Recalls*, in that context, that the Council has repeatedly warned Iraq that it will face serious consequences as a result of its continued violations of its obligations;

14. *Decides* to remain seized of the matter.

"Resolution 1441," UN Security Council, November 8, 2002. www.un.org.

Document 5: Hans Blix's Statement to the United Nations

On February 14, 2003, UN Monitoring, Verification and Inspection Commission executive chairman Hans Blix addressed the United Nations concerning the status of weapons inspections in Iraq. In his speech, excerpted here, he stated that Iraq had accelerated its cooperation but that inspectors needed more time to verify its compliance.

Since we arrived in Iraq [in 2003], we have conducted more than 400 inspections covering more than 300 sites. All inspections were performed without notice, and access was almost always provided promptly. In no case have we seen convincing evidence that the Iraqi side knew in advance that the inspectors were coming.

The inspections have taken place throughout Iraq at industrial sites, ammunition depots, research centers, universities, presidential sites, mobile laboratories, private houses, missile production facilities, military camps and agricultural sites. At all sites which had been inspected before 1998, re-baselining activities were performed. This included the identification of the function and contents of each building, new or old, at a site. It also included verification of previously tagged equipment, application of seals and tags, taking samples and discussions with the site personnel regarding past and present activities. At certain sites, ground-penetrating radar was used to look for underground structures or buried equipment.

Through the inspections conducted so far, we have obtained a good knowledge of the industrial and scientific landscape of Iraq, as well as of its missile capability but, as before, we do not know every cave and corner. Inspections are effectively helping to bridge the gap in knowledge that arose due to the absence of inspections between December 1998 and November 2002.

More than 200 chemical and more than 100 biological samples have been collected at different sites. Three-quarters of these have been screened using our own laboratory analytical capabilities at the Baghdad Center (BOMVIC). The results to date have been consistent with Iraq's declarations.

We have now commenced the process of destroying approximately 50 liters of mustard gas declared by Iraq that was being kept under UNMOVIC [United Nations Monitoring, Verification and Inspection Commission] seal at the Muthanna site. One-third of the quantity has already been destroyed. The laboratory quantity of thiodiglycol, a mustard gas precursor, which we found at another site, has also been destroyed.

The total number of staff in Iraq now exceeds 250 from 60 countries. This includes about 100 UNMOVIC inspectors, 15 IAEA [International Atomic Energy Agency] inspectors, 15 aircrew, and 65 support staff.

In my Jan. 27 update to the Council, I said that it seemed from our experience that Iraq had decided in principle to provide cooperation on process, most importantly prompt access to all sites and assistance to UNMOVIC in the establishment of the necessary infrastructure. This impression remains, and we note that access to sites has so far been without problems, including those that had never been declared or inspected, as well as to Presidential sites and private residences. . . .

How much, if any, is left of Iraq's weapons of mass destruction and related proscribed items and programs? So far, UNMOVIC has not found any such weapons, only a small number of empty chemical munitions, which should have been declared and destroyed. Another matter and one of great significance is that many proscribed weapons and items are not accounted for. To take an example, a document, which Iraq provided, suggested to us that some 1,000 tons of chemical agent were "unaccounted for." One must not jump to the conclusion that they exist. However, that possibility is also not excluded. If they exist, they should be presented for destruction. If they do not exist, credible evidence to that effect should be presented.

We are fully aware that many governmental intelligence organizations are convinced and assert that proscribed weapons, items and programs continue to exist. The U.S. Secretary of State presented material in support of this conclusion. Governments have many sources of information that are not available to inspectors. Inspectors, for their part, must base their reports only on evidence, which they can, themselves, examine and present publicly. Without evidence, confidence cannot arise.

Hans Blix, "Briefing of the Security Council, 14 February 2003: An Update on Inspections," February 14, 2003. www.unmovic.org.

Document 6: Final Transitional Agreement

On July 13, 2003, the Coalition Provisional Authority (CPA) appointed the twenty-five-member Interim Governing Council to work with the CPA for the transition to Iraqi sovereignty. The following document outlines the agreement for the process of transition to a new Iraqi government.

1. The "Fundamental Law"

- To be drafted by the Governing Council [GC], in close consultation with the CPA [Coalition Provisional Authority]. Will be approved by both the GC and CPA, and will formally set forth the scope and structure of the sovereign Iraqi transitional administration.
- Elements of the "Fundamental Law":
  - Bill of rights, to include freedom of speech, legislature, religion; statement of equal rights of all Iraqis, regardless of gender, sect, and ethnicity; and guarantees of due process.
  - Federal arrangement for Iraq, to include governorates and the separation and specification of powers to be exercised by central and local entities.
  - Statement of the independence of the judiciary, and a mechanism for judicial review.
  - Statement of civilian political control over Iraqi armed and security forces.
  - Statement that Fundamental Law cannot be amended.
  - An expiration date for Fundamental Law.
  - Timetable for drafting of Iraq's permanent constitution by a body directly elected by the Iraqi people; for ratifying the permanent constitution; and for holding elections under the new constitution.
- Drafting and approval of "Fundamental Law" to be complete by February 28, 2004.

2. Agreements with Coalition on Security

- To be agreed between the CPA and the GC.
- Security agreements to cover status of Coalition forces in Iraq, giving wide latitude to provide for the safety and security of the Iraqi people.
- Approval of bilateral agreements complete by the end of March 2004.

3. Selection of Transitional National Assembly

- Fundamental Law will specify the bodies of the national structure, and will ultimately spell out the process by which individuals will be selected for these bodies. However, certain guidelines must be agreed in advance.
- The transitional assembly will not be an expansion of the GC. The GC will have no formal role in selecting members of the assembly, and will dissolve upon the establishment and recognition of the transitional administration. Individual members of the GC will, however, be eligible to serve in the transitional assembly, if elected according to the process below.
- Election of members of the Transitional National Assembly will be conducted through a transparent, participatory, democratic process of caucuses in each of Iraq's 18 governorates.
  - In each governorate, the CPA will supervise a process by which an "Organizing Committee" of Iraqis will be formed. This Organizing Committee

will include 5 individuals appointed by the Governing Council, 5 individuals appointed by the Provincial Council, and 1 individual appointed by the local council of the five largest cities within the governorate.

- The purpose of the Organizing Committee will be to convene a "Governorate Selection Caucus" of notables from around the governorate. To do so, it will solicit nominations from political parties, provincial/local councils, professional and civic associations, university faculties, tribal and religious groups. Nominees must meet the criteria set out for candidates in the Fundamental Law. To be selected as a member of the Governorate Selection Caucus, any nominee will need to be approved by an 11/15 majority of the Organizing Committee.
- Each Governorate Selection Caucus will elect representatives to represent the governorate in the new transitional assembly based on the governorate's percentage of Iraq's population.
- The Transitional National Assembly will be elected no later than May 31, 2004.

4. Restoration of Iraq's Sovereignty

- Following the selection of members of the transitional assembly, it will meet to elect an executive branch, and to appoint ministers.
- By June 30, 2004 the new transitional administration will be recognized by the Coalition, and will assume full sovereign powers for governing Iraq. The CPA will dissolve.

5. Process for Adoption of Permanent Constitution

- The constitutional process and timeline will ultimately be included in the Fundamental Law, but need to be agreed in advance, as detailed below.
- A permanent constitution for Iraq will be prepared by a constitutional convention directly elected by the Iraqi people.
- Elections for the convention will be held no later than March 15, 2005.
- A draft of the constitution will be circulated for public comment and debate.
- A final draft of the constitution will be presented to the public, and a popular referendum will be held to ratify the constitution.
- Elections for a new Iraqi government will be held by December 31, 2005, at which point the Fundamental Law will expire and a new government will take power.

"Agreement on Political Process," Coalition Provisional Authority, November 15, 2003. www.cpa-iraq.org.

Chronology

1920

The League of Nations places Iraq under British mandate.

1932

Iraq becomes an independent state and is ruled as a constitutional monarchy.

1945

Iraq joins the United Nations and becomes a founding member of the Arab League.

1958

The monarchy is overthrown in a military coup led by General Abdul Karim Qasim. Iraq is declared to be a republic and Qasim becomes prime minister.

1961

The Kurds in northern Iraq ask for complete autonomy in Iraq and a share of oil revenues. Qasim rejects the plan and Kurds revolt against the government.

February 1963

Qasim is assassinated as the Arab Socialist Renaissance Party (Baath Party) takes power. Colonel Abdul Salam Arif becomes president.

1964

A cease-fire is declared with the Kurds.

1966

Arif is killed in a helicopter crash and succeeded by his brother, General Abdul Rahman Mohammad Arif.

1968

A group of Baathists and military officers overthrows the Arif regime. Ahmad Hasan al-Bakr becomes president of Iraq.

1973

All foreign oil companies in Iraq are taken over by the government. Iran and Iraq are the region's major oil producers and vie for dominance.

1974

Iraq grants limited autonomy to the Kurds, but the Kurdistan Democratic Party rejects the plan. Fighting breaks out with the Kurds.

1975

The Kurds are defeated. At a meeting of the Organization of Petroleum Exporting Countries (OPEC), Iraq and Iran sign a treaty ending their border disputes.

July 1979

President Bakr resigns and Saddam Hussein assumes the presidency. Within days Hussein executes at least twenty potential rivals and members of the Baath Party and the military. Military skirmishes and propaganda war increase between Iraq and Iran.

1980

The Iran-Iraq War begins as Iran shells Iraqi border towns and Iraq attacks Iran.

1988

Iraq retaliates against the Kurds for supporting Iran, killing thousands with chemical weapons, and forcing thousands more to flee to Turkey. A cease-fire is declared between Iran and Iraq, ending eight years of fighting, which have left the Iraqi economy devastated.

1990

Iraq invades Kuwait, accusing it of violating oil-production limits set by OPEC. The United Nations calls for Iraq to withdraw and imposes heavy trade sanctions on the country.

January 1991

Under United Nations resolutions, a U.S.-led coalition of thirty-nine countries bombs Iraq, beginning the Persian Gulf War.

February 1991

The Iraqi army is defeated by coalition forces.

March 1991

Shiite and Kurdish rebellions break out in the north and south of Iraq, and thousands are killed by Iraqi forces.

April 1991

The UN Security Council declares the Persian Gulf War formally over. As part of the cease-fire agreement, Iraq must destroy all its biological and chemical weapons and the facilities to produce these weapons. A safe zone for the Kurds is established in northern Iraq, and Iraq is ordered to end all military action in this area. A safe zone is also established in the south to protect the Shiites.

May 1991

A UN Special Commission (UNSCOM) and the International Atomic Energy Agency (IAEA) begin attempts to verify that Iraq has destroyed all its prohibited weapons of mass destruction (WMD) facilities.

1992

Continuing sanctions on Iraq result in limited food supplies, high prices, inflation, and a poor infrastructure and health care system.

1994

Iraq recognizes Kuwait's borders and its independence.

1996–1997

Iraq impedes UN inspectors from entering Iraqi security service and military facilities.

1998

Iraq ends all forms of cooperation with UNSCOM and expels weapons inspectors.

1998–1999

Great Britain and the United States launch Operation Desert Fox, a campaign to destroy Iraq's suspected WMD programs. The UN Monitoring, Verification and Inspection Commission (UNMOVIC) is created to replace UNSCOM. Iraq does not recognize the commission.

August 2000

The Saddam International Airport in Baghdad is reopened for the first time in ten years.

October 2000

Iraqi officials attend an Arab League summit for the first time in ten years.

November 2002

The UN Security Council unanimously adopts Resolution 1441, which outlines an inspection regime for Iraq's disarmament. Iraq accepts the resolution and UN inspections resume.

December 2002

Iraq provides weapons inspectors with twelve thousand pages of information about the regime's chemical, biological, and nuclear weapons programs and declares that there are no weapons of mass destruction in Iraq.

February 2003

The United States, Great Britain, and Spain state that Iraq has failed to comply with Resolution 1441 and ask the UN Security Council to approve the use of force against the country. France, Germany, and Russia oppose the use of force and request that inspections be intensified.

March 17, 2003

Without UN support, U.S. president George W. Bush issues an ultimatum that either Saddam Hussein and his sons leave Iraq within forty-eight hours or the United States will pursue military action against Iraq.

March 19, 2003

A U.S.-led campaign against Iraq begins as American missiles hit targets in Baghdad. U.S. and British ground troops enter Iraq from the south.

April 9, 2003

In Baghdad a giant bronze statue of Saddam Hussein is toppled. This event is viewed by many as the symbolic crumbling of his regime.

May 1, 2003

Bush declares an end to major combat operations in Iraq. The UN Security Council approves a resolution backing the U.S.-led administration of Iraq. The United States abolishes the Baath Party and institutions of the former regime. Trade sanctions against Iraq are lifted.

July 2003

Iraq's twenty-five member Interim Governing Council (IGC), appointed by American and British officials, meets for the first time. American administrator Paul Bremer retains ultimate authority. Saddam's sons Uday and Qusay Hussein are killed by U.S. troops. U.S. forces in Iraq face guerrilla-style warfare from Iraqis opposed to the occupation.

August 2003

U.S. and British casualties in Iraq reach 298.

September 2003

Attempts to find WMD in Iraq continue to be unsuccessful. UN inspector Hans Blix says Iraq probably destroyed all its WMD more than a decade ago.

October 2003

According to an interim report by David Kay, the lead investigator searching for weapons of mass destruction in Iraq, no WMD have been found. The UN Security Council approves an amended resolution on Iraq that gives legitimacy to the U.S.-led administration of the country, but it stresses that power should be transferred to Iraqis as soon as possible.

November 2003

The number of U.S. and British deaths in Iraq reaches 510. The Bush administration agrees to transfer power to an interim government early in 2004.

December 13, 2003

Saddam Hussein is found hiding in a hole near his hometown of Tikrit and is captured by U.S. forces.

February 2004

Violence in Iraq escalates with increasing casualties among both Iraqis and coalition forces.

March 2004

The IGC reaches an agreement on an interim constitution, and calls for nation-wide elections by January 31, 2005. Four American civilian contractors in Iraq are killed and their corpses mutilated and dragged through the streets in protest of the U.S.-led occupation.

April 2004

Photographs showing the apparent abuse of Iraqi prisoners by both British and American troops cause worldwide outrage.

May 2004

U.S. and British casualties in Iraq reach more than eight hundred. The number of wounded U.S. soldiers is more than four thousand.

Organizations to Contact

The editors have compiled the following list of organizations concerned with the issues debated in this book. The descriptions are derived from materials provided by the organizations. All have publications or information available for interested readers. The list was compiled on the date of publication of the present volume; names, addresses, phone and fax numbers, and e-mail addresses may change. Be aware that many organizations take several weeks or longer to respond to inquiries, so allow as much time as possible.

American Enterprise Institute (AEI)
1150 17th St. NW, Washington, DC 20036
(202) 862-5800 • fax: (202) 862-7177
Web site: www.aei.org

The American Enterprise Institute is a scholarly research institute dedicated to preserving limited government, private enterprise, and a strong foreign policy and national defense. Its publications on Iraq include articles in its magazine *American Enterprise* and books, including *Study of Revenge: The First World Trade Center Attack and Saddam Hussein's War Against America.* Articles, speeches, and seminar transcripts on Iraq are available on its Web site.

Arms Control Association (ACA)
1726 M St. NW, Washington, DC 20036
(202) 463-8270 • fax: (202) 463-8273
e-mail: aca@armscontrol.org • Web site: www.armscontrol.org

The ACA is a national membership organization that works to educate the public and promote effective arms control policies. It publishes the magazine *Arms Control Today.* Documents and articles on nuclear, chemical, and biological weapons in Iraq can be found on its Web site.

Brookings Institution
1775 Massachusetts Ave. NW, Washington, DC 20036
(202) 797-6000 • fax: (202) 797-6004
e-mail: brookinfo@brook.edu • Web site: www.brookings.org

The Brookings Institution is a think tank that conducts research and education in foreign policy, economics, government, and the social sciences. Its Saban Center for Middle East Policy develops programs to promote a better understanding of policy choices in the Middle East. Articles on Iraq can be found on the organization's Web site and in its publications, including the quarterly *Brookings Review.*

Center for Strategic and International Studies (CSIS)
1800 K St. NW, Suite 400, Washington, DC 20006
(202) 887-0200 • fax: (202) 775-3199
Web site: www.csis.org

The center works to provide world leaders with strategic insights and policy options on current and emerging global issues. It publishes books including *The "Instant" Lessons of the Iraq War*, the *Washington Quarterly*, a journal on political, economic, and security issues, and other publications, including reports that can be downloaded from its Web site.

Education for Peace in Iraq Center (EPIC)
1101 Pennsylvania Ave. SE, Washington, DC 20003
(202) 543-6176
e-mail: info@epic-usa.org • Web site: http://epic-usa.org

The Education for Peace in Iraq Center works to improve humanitarian conditions in Iraq and protect the human rights of Iraq's people. It opposed both international economic sanctions and U.S. military action against Iraq. Articles on Iraq are available on its Web site.

The Heritage Foundation
214 Massachusetts Ave. NE, Washington, DC 20002
(202) 546-4400 • fax: (202) 546-8328
e-mail: info@heritage.org • Web site: www.heritage.org

The Heritage Foundation is a conservative public policy research institute. Its position papers and reports on Iraq include "Turning Back the Terrorist Threat: America's Unbreakable Commitment," "Forging a Durable Post-War Political Settlement in Iraq," and "The Road to Economic Prosperity for a Post-Saddam Iraq."

Hoover Institution
Stanford University, Stanford, CA 94305-6010
(650) 723-1754 • fax: (650) 723-1687
Web site: www.hoover.stanford.edu

The Hoover Institution is a public policy research center devoted to advanced study of politics, economics, and political economy—both domestic and foreign—as well as international affairs. It publishes the quarterly *Hoover Digest*—which often includes articles on Iraq—as well as a newsletter and special reports.

Iraq Action Coalition
7309 Haymarket Lane, Raleigh, NC 27615
fax: (919) 846-7422
e-mail: iac@leb.net • Web site: www.iraqaction.org

The Iraq Action Coalition is an online media and activists' resource center for groups who oppose both international economic sanctions and U.S. military action against Iraq. It publishes books and reports on Iraq, including *Iraq Under Siege: The Deadly Impact of Sanctions and War*. Its Web site includes numerous links to other organizations opposed to the war against Iraq.

Iraq Foundation
1012 14th St. NW, Suite 1110, Washington, DC 20005
(202) 347-4662 • fax: (202) 347-7897
e-mail: iraq@iraqfoundation.org • Web site: www.iraqfoundation.org

The Iraq Foundation is a nonprofit, nongovernmental organization working for democracy and human rights in Iraq, and for a better international understanding of Iraq's potential as a contributor to political stability and economic progress in the Middle East. Information on its projects as well as other information on Iraq can be found on its Web site.

Middle East Forum
1500 Walnut St., Suite 1050, Philadelphia, PA 19102
(215) 546-5406 • fax: (215) 546-5409
e-mail: info@meforum.org • Web site: www.meforum.org

The Middle East Forum is a think tank that works to define and promote American interests in the Middle East. It supports strong American ties with Israel, Turkey, and other democracies as they emerge. It publishes the *Middle East Quarterly*, a policy-oriented journal. Its Web site includes articles, summaries of activities, and a discussion forum.

Middle East Institute
1761 N St. NW, Washington, DC 20036-2882
(202) 785-1141 • fax: (202) 331-8861
e-mail: mideasti@mideasti.org • Web site: www.themiddleeastinstitute.org

The institute's charter mission is to promote better understanding of Middle Eastern cultures, languages, religions, and politics. It publishes numerous books, papers, audiotapes, and videos as well as the quarterly *Middle East Journal*. It also maintains an Educational Outreach Department to give teachers and students of all grade levels advice on resources.

Middle East Media Research Institute (MEMRI)
PO Box 27837, Washington, DC 20038-7837
(202) 955-9070 • fax: (202) 955-9077
e-mail: memri@memri.org • Web site: www.memri.org

MEMRI translates and disseminates articles and commentaries from Middle East media sources and provides analysis on the political, ideological, intellectual, social, cultural, and religious trends in the region.

Middle East Policy Council
1730 M St. NW, Suite 512, Washington, DC 20036-4505
(202) 296-6767 • fax: (202) 296-5791
e-mail: info@mepc.org • Web site: www.mepc.org

The Middle East Policy Council was founded in 1981 to expand public discussion and understanding of issues affecting U.S. policy in the Middle East. The council is a nonprofit educational organization that operates nationwide. It publishes the quarterly *Middle East Policy Journal*.

Middle East Research and Information Project (MERIP)
1500 Massachusetts Ave. NW, Washington, DC 20005
(202) 223-3677 • fax: (202) 223-3604
Web site: www.merip.org

MERIP is a nonprofit, nongovernmental organization with no links to any religious, educational, or political organizations in the United States or elsewhere. Its mission is to educate the public about the contemporary Middle East with particular emphasis on U.S. foreign policy, human rights, and social justice issues. It publishes the bimonthly *Middle East Report*.

U.S. Department of State, Bureau of Near Eastern Affairs
2201 C St. NW, Washington, DC 20520
(202) 647-4000
Web site: www.state.gov/p/nea

The bureau deals with U.S. foreign policy and U.S. relations with the countries in the Middle East and North Africa. Its Web site offers country information as well as news briefings and press statements on U.S. foreign policy.

Washington Institute for Near East Policy
1828 L St. NW, Suite 1050, Washington, DC 20036
(202) 452-0650 • fax: (202) 223-5364
e-mail: info@washingtoninstitute.org • Web site: www.washingtoninstitute.org

The institute is an independent, nonprofit research organization that provides information and analysis on the Middle East and U.S. policy in the region. It publishes numerous books, periodic monographs, and reports on regional politics, security, and economics, including *PeaceWatch*, which focuses on the Arab-Israeli peace process, and *Democracy and Arab Political Culture and Radical Middle East States and U.S. Policy.*

Bibliography

Books

Yossef Bodansky	*The High Cost of Peace: How Washington's Middle East Policy Left America Vulnerable to Terrorism.* Roseville, CA: Prima, 2002.
Joseph Braude	*The New Iraq: Rebuilding the Country for Its People, the Middle East, and the World.* New York: Basic Books, 2003.
Richard Butler and James C. Roy	*The Greatest Threat: Iraq, Weapons of Mass Destruction, and the Crisis of Global Security.* New York: Public Affairs, 2001.
Patrick Clawson, ed.	*How to Build a New Iraq After Saddam.* Washington, DC: Washington Institute for Near East Policy, 2002.
Toby Dodge	*Inventing Iraq: The Failure of Nation-Building and a History Denied.* New York: Columbia University Press, 2003.
Toby Dodge and Steven Simon, eds.	*Iraq at the Crossroads: State and Society in the Shadow of Regime Change.* Oxford, UK: Oxford University Press, 2003.
William Dudley, ed.	*Iraq: Opposing Viewpoints.* San Diego, CA: Greenhaven Press, 2003.
Dilip Hiro	*Iraq: In the Eye of the Storm.* New York: Thunder's Mouth Press, 2002.
Dilip Hiro	*Secrets and Lies: Operation Iraqi Freedom and the Collapse of American Power in the Middle East.* New York: Thunder's Mouth Press, 2004.
Christopher Hitchens	*A Long Short War: The Postponed Liberation of Iraq.* New York: Plume, 2003.
Leon M. Jeffries	*Iraq: Issues, Historical Background, Bibliography.* New York: Nova Science, 2003.
Lawrence F. Kaplan and William Kristol	*The War over Iraq: Saddam's Tyranny and America's Mission.* San Francisco: Encounter Books, 2003.
Jean E. Krasno and James S. Sutterlin	*The United Nations and Iraq: Defanging the Viper.* Westport, CT: Praeger, 2003.
Juman Kubba	*The First Evidence: A Memoir of Life in Iraq Under Saddam Hussein.* Jefferson, NC: McFarland, 2003.
David W. Lesch, ed.	*The Middle East and the United States: A Historical and Political Reassessment.* Boulder, CO: Westview, 2003.

Bibliography

| Bernard Lewis | *What Went Wrong: The Clash Between Islam and Modernity in the Middle East.* New York: HarperPerennial, 2003. |

| Sandra Mackey | *The Reckoning: Iraq and the Legacy of Saddam Hussein.* New York: W.W. Norton, 2002. |

| Norman Mailer | *Why Are We at War?* New York: Random House, 2003. |

| Kenneth M. Pollack | *The Threatening Storm: The Case for Invading Iraq.* New York: Random House, 2002. |

| Micah L. Sifry and Christopher Cerf, eds. | *The Iraq War Reader: History, Documents, Opinions.* New York: Touchstone Books, 2003. |

| Harlan Ullman | *Unfinished Business: Afghanistan, the Middle East, and Beyond—Defusing the Dangers That Threaten American Security.* New York: Citadel Press, 2002. |

Periodicals

| Tony Blair | "Iraq's Full Disarmament Necessary to Avoid War," *Canadian Speeches*, March/April 2003. |

| Patrick J. Buchanan | "The Wages of Empire," *Los Angeles Times*, February 23, 2003. |

| Peter Christoff | "Never Again? A Modest Proposal: The Question of Why We Went to War Remains Unanswered," *Arena Magazine*, August/September 2003. |

| David Corn | "Now They Tell Us: Postwar Truths and Consequences," *Nation*, May 19, 2003. |

| Con Coughlin | "The Savage Sunset of Saddam Hussein," *American Spectator*, January/February 2003. |

| Bob Drogin | "The Vanishing—What Happened to the WMD?" *New Republic*, July 21, 2003. |

| *Economist* | "Walking on Eggshells; Post-War Iraq," July 5, 2003. |

| *Economist* | "Whose War Is it Anyway?" September 13, 2003. |

| Michael Elliot | "The War That Never Ends," *Time*, July 7, 2003. |

| George Evans | "Witnessing Iraq's Last Revolution," *Contemporary Review*, October 2003. |

| Reuel Marc Gerecht | "How to Mix Politics with Religion," *New York Times*, April 29, 2003. |

| Jennifer A. Gritt and William Norman Grigg | "Weapons of Mass Delusion," *New American*, May 19, 2003. |

| Gene Healy | "Libertarian Interventionism: Will It Liberate?" *Liberty*, November 2003. |

| *International Socialist Review* | "End the Occupation," September/October 2003. |

| Faisal Istrabadi | "Democracy in Iraq," August 6, 2002. www.iraqfoundation.org. |

Derrick Z. Jackson	"Owning Up to Deceptions on the Iraq War," *Liberal Opinion*, October 13, 2003.
John B. Judis	"Below the Beltway: Sifting Through the Rubble," *American Prospect*, October 1, 2003.
Paul Kerr	"Controversy Grows Surrounding Prewar Intel.," *Arms Control Today*, September 2003.
Daryl G. Kimball	"Iraq's WMD: Myth and Reality," *Arms Control Today*, September 2003.
Laura King	"After the War/Fearing the Future; Women Fear Their Rights Will End with Hussein Era," *Los Angeles Times*, April 27, 2003.
Jim Lacey	"Hide and Seek . . . and Seek: Where'd Those Weapons of Mass Destruction Get To?" *National Review*, June 16, 2003.
Arthur Macewan	"Is It Oil?" *Dollars and Sense*, May/June 2003.
Timothy W. Maier	"Horror Stories: Millions of Secret Police and Intelligence Files Seized by U.S. Forces Detail the Unspeakable Atrocities Sanctioned by Saddam Hussein," *Insight on the News*, May 13, 2003.
Rania Masri	"The Corporate Invasion of Iraq," *International Socialist Review*, July/August 2003.
Oil Daily	"Bush Under Pressure to Recover Cost Through Iraqi Oil," September 16, 2003.
John O'Sullivan	"Where We Stand: The Situation in Iraq and How to Go Forward," *National Review*, September 29, 2003.
John Pilger	"Bush's Vietnam," *New Statesman*, June 23, 2003.
Ted Rall	"Bring Home the Troops," *Progressive Populist*, September 1, 2003.
Romesh Ratnesar with Simon Robinson	"Life Under Fire," *Time*, July 14, 2003.
Pamela Ann Smith	"Bush and Blair Scramble for Oil," *Middle East*, August/September 2003.
Mark Steyn	"Iraq: What Must Be Done Now," *Spectator*, June 7, 2003.
Zainab Al-Suwaij	"Iraq's Silenced Majority," *New York Times*, May 23, 2003.
Amir Taheri	"Iraq as It Stands: There Is Good News, and Bad News, and a Country Given a Chance," *National Review*, October 13, 2003.
Kenneth R. Timmerman	"The Hunt Is On for Saddam's Weapons," *Insight on the News*, May 13, 2003.
Srdja Trifkovic	"The Iraq Quagmire," *Chronicles*, November 2003.
Nathan Vardi	"Desert Storm," *Forbes*, June 23, 2003.
Scott L. Wheeler	"The Link Between Iraq and Al-Qaeda," *Insight on the News*, October 14, 2003.

Index

Kagan, Robert, 58
al Karbuli, Riyad Abbas, 57
Karzai, Hamid, 51, 163
Katz, Mark N., 68
Kay, David, 45
Kellogg Brown & Root, 14
Kelly, David, 44
Kerry, John, 167
Khuzai, Raja, 115, 116, 118, 119, 121, 122
Kirk, Mark, 60
Klein, Naomi, 90
Kosovo, 149–50
Kristol, William, 58
Kurds, 69, 71, 81, 97, 149, 152

law enforcement, Iraqi, 109–10, 113–14
Lemann, Nicholas, 40
Levin, Carl, 166
Liberia, 85
Lindsay, Lawrence, 163

Macewan, Arthur, 13
MacEwen, David, 133
Madison, James, 150
Mahajan, Rahul, 50
Makiya, Kanan, 126
Malaysia, 152
Marighella, Carlos, 93
Marshall Plan, 161
mass graves, 103–104
Maude, Stanley, 91
McCain, John, 35
McCrot, Carleigh, 93
media
  censorship of, 54–55
  Iraqi, 112–13
Michael, Bryane, 160
Middle East
  anti-American sentiment in, 84–85
  economic effects of Iraq war in, 162
  history of, 167–68
  peace talks in, 65–66
  ramifications in, of democratic Iraq, 70–72
  U.S. military dominance in, 52–53
  see also Arab world

Nakash, Yitzhak, 145
Nation (magazine), 171
National Association of Iraqi Human Rights, 102
NATO (North Atlantic Treaty Organization), 164
Natsios, Andrew, 161
Nordhaus, William, 163
North Korea, 85
nuclear weapons, 32–34, 36–37, 47

O'Dell, Matthew, 95
off our backs (journal), 137
oil
  demand for, 11–12
  desire for, dominates U.S. policy, 75–77
  discovery of, in Iraq, 11
  embargoes, of 1970s, 76
  importance of, in Iraq, 51–52
  industry
    France's and Iraq's, 169
    Iraq's place in global, 11–13, 162
    reconstruction of Iraq's, 13–14, 131–32
  as motive for Iraq war, 13, 89–90
  U.S. demand for, 12–13, 75–77
Organization of Military Industrialization (OMI), 28
Origins of Totalitarianism, The (Arendt), 124
O'Sullivan, John, 57

Pakistan, 41
Panama, 150
Paul, James, 12
Persian Gulf
  importance of, 75–77
  U.S. military should withdraw from, 73–74, 81
  see also Middle East
Petraeus, David, 54–55
Pfaff, William, 171–72
Pickard, Iain, 131
police force, Iraqi, 109–10, 113–14
Pollack, Kenneth M., 146
Ponticelli, Charlotte, 116